HISTORY ON
THE GROUND

HISTORY ON THE GROUND

MAURICE BERESFORD

SUTTON PUBLISHING

First published in 1957 by Lutterworth Press

First published by Alan Sutton Publishing in 1984

This revised edition published in 1998 by Sutton Publishing Limited
Phoenix Mill · Thrupp · Stroud · Gloucestershire

A catalogue record for this book is available from the British Library

ISBN 0 7509 1884 5

*Cover illustration: part of an original by Alan Sorel (1954), based on the 1586 plan of
the former village of Whatborough, Leicestershire.*

™ ALAN SUTTON™ and SUTTON™ are the
trade marks of Sutton Publishing Limited

Printed in Great Britain by
WBC Limited, Bridgend, Mid-Glamorgan.

This worke then is composed of *Geographie* (which is a description of the knowne Earth and the parts thereof) and Historie, which is (*Oculus Mundi*) the eye of the World. These two goe inseparably together, and as it were hand in hand . . . and are like two Sisters intirely loving each other, and cannot without pittie be divided.

Preface *to the first English edition of Mercator's* Atlas (*1636*), *by Henry Hexham, translator.*

Contents

	PAGE
List of Illustrations	9
Author's Preface 1957	13
Author's Preface 1984	14
Author's Preface 1998	15
Acknowledgements	16
List of Abbreviations and Short Titles	17

CHAP.

1. INTRODUCTION	19
2. A JOURNEY ALONG BOUNDARIES	23
3. A JOURNEY TO ELIZABETHAN VILLAGES	63
4. A JOURNEY AMONG DESERTED VILLAGES	93
5. A JOURNEY TO NEW TOWNS	125
6. A JOURNEY TO ELIZABETHAN MARKET-PLACES	151
7. A JOURNEY THROUGH PARKS	185
APPENDIX: THE MATERIAL FOR THE SIX JOURNEYS	237
INDEX	250

List of Illustrations

(Between pages 128–129)

Plates

1. Old Byland: part of Saxton's plan, drawn in 1598.

2. Maids Moreton in 1596: the N.W. portion of Langdon's plan.

3. Maids Moreton in 1596: the village centre.

4. Maids Moreton: a cottage on the west of the main street; *and* a view down *Balles Crosse Waye*.

5. Salford: the village in Langdon's plan of 1596.

6. Salford: part of the open-fields in 1596.

7. Midley: ruined church *and* Wormleighton: Tudor house of the enclosing squire.

8. Wormleighton: sheep graze over the village site; *and* Fawsley: two tombs of the Knightley family.

9. Whatborough: part of Thomas Clerke's plan of 1586.

10. Looking from Halstead parish boundary eastward to the site of the deserted village of Whatborough.

11. Wharram Percy: the ruined church *and* a fifteenth-century peasant house.

12. Hedon: the grass-grown Market-place and St. Augustine's church.

13. Higham Ferrers: John Norden's plan of 1591.

14. Toddington: part of Ralph Agas' plan, drawn in 1581.

15. Holdenby in 1580 before the Park was made.

16. Holdenby in 1587 after the Park was made.

17. Parks of Northamptonshire: Saxton's plan of 1576, with the parks ringed by little pales.

9

Figures   *Page*

1. Parish boundaries in the fenland of Hunts., now reclaimed.
                                                                            33

2. Parish boundaries in Warws. and Northants., west
   of the Roman Watling Street.
                                                                            40

3. Braunston and its bounds.   41

4. Old Byland, its parish bounds and neighbours.   54

5. Maids Moreton in 1596, redrawn from the All Souls
   plan.
                                                                            71

6. Salford in 1596, with its depopulated neighbour, Hulcote.   89

7. Tusmore Park, and the site of the village destroyed
   by the Black Death.
                                                                            98

8. Dean and its two depopulated hamlets, Upper and
   Lower Chalford.
                                                                           104

9. Wormleighton: the Ordnance Survey plan.   106

10. Fawsley: the wall-monument of the Knightleys.   112

11. The depopulated township of Snorscomb.   114

12. The depopulated village of Whatborough and its neigh-
    bours.
                                                                           116

13. The New Towns of the Humber with the old town and
    port of Beverley.
                                                                           132

14. The New Town of Hedon laid out in the fields of
    Preston.
                                                                           140

15. Higham Ferrers, its Park, neighbours and local road
    system.
                                                                           161

16. Higham Ferrers in 1789.   166

17. Toddington in 1581.   181

18. Fountains Park, the home park of the Abbey.   196

19. Milton Abbas in 1776.   200

20. Milton Abbas: the park to-day.   202

21. Elford: the park pale from a plan drawn in 1508.   204

22. Wilstrop: the medieval village and the Tudor park both
    now submerged into farmland.
                                                                           206

23. Holdenby: key to the plans of 1580 and 1587.   215

Figures   *Page*

24. Higham Ferrers Park, in relation to the thirteenth-
    century Forests of Rockingham, Salcey and Whittle-
    wood.   217

25. Sheriff Hutton: the Jacobean house in the fourteenth-
    century castle-park.   220

26. Sheriff Hutton: the modern Ordnance Survey plan.   221

27. Wootton Underwood village, drawn from the plan of
    1649.   226

28. Sutton Coldfield, showing the modern bounds of the
    Park.   234

Author's Preface 1957

THE aims and limitations of this book will be found set out in the first chapter. It owes its existence to the suggestion of the publishers that some of the field-work which I have carried out in some specialist studies might commend itself in a less technical setting. Since the book tries to rest on a sound foundation of documents and maps my first thanks must be to the archivists, librarians and estate-owners who have given me access. The permission to reproduce some of the maps which I have studied is acknowledged below. The formal acknowledgment to the Ordnance Survey is inadequate for the debt which I owe—like all field-workers—to the successive generations of field-surveyors and cartographers who have given us the various editions of the Ordnance Survey maps and plans. In the last thirty years the work of their Archaeological Officers has gone far to on permanent record whatever remnants of the past the landscape still carries; and one who works only in a small field must salute the magnitude of their task.

Much of the incentive for me to carry out local investigations came originally from work undertaken in collaboration with Dr. J. K. St. Joseph, Curator in Air Photography in the University of Cambridge. Although none of his photographs are used in this book—which is specifically designed for the inquirer without wings—my study of the face of England has greatly profited by access to the collection of his own air photographs which he has assembled, and which is annually increasing.

No organized school of "on-with-the-boots" field-workers (happily) exists, but my own education in these matters cannot help bearing signs of the influence which the writings and conversation of H. C. Darby and W. G. Hoskins have had upon it. My freedom to visit archives and work in the field is largely due to the University of Leeds and to Professor Arthur Brown, the Head of the Department on whose research funds I have always been allowed generously to draw. John Hurst, an Assistant Inspector of Ancient Monuments, has done a great deal to introduce me to the archaeology of my subject and to some of the particular earthworks described in the succeeding pages.

Whenever I have travelled faster than my own legs would carry me it has usually been with the assistance of friends who do not share my chronic inability to drive a car. In journeys which make up this book I have been driven by my colleagues Philip Sheard, John Cox, Maurice Kirk and George Rainnie, and by my former students Clive Semple and Clifford Farrar. For two periods of intensive field-work with car, tent and cooking-gear I had the company of Dr. Keith Allison and for one that of Dennis Swann, both former students. The photography which is an essential part of recording field-work has for several years been carried out for me by Clifford Farrar. Back from the field, I have leaned heavily on the lady whose particular contribution while in the field is recorded in the dedication.

Author's Preface 1984

THIS edition of 1971 was intended to be a reprint with minor corrections, representing therefore the stage of the author's researches and the state of the historic English landscape in the years just before 1957. However, in the course of preparation the loss of some original blocks made it necessary to make certain substitutions and deletions involving minor changes in the text, and occasionally coming forward beyond 1957. (The new plates are nos. 6, 7, 10 and 11.)

Author's Preface 1998

The original text of the 1957 edition was reprinted in 1971 and again in 1984 with no alterations except the replacment of three plates (nos. 6, 7, 10 and 11) for which the original materials could not be found. No further alterations have been made for the present edition which continues to represent the stage of my researches and the state of selected parts of the historic English landscape nearly fifty years ago.

The names of teachers, colleagues and friends mentioned in the Preface of 1957 indicate that I was already not alone in seeking history on the ground; and since then there have been developments both in the fields treated in the chapters which follow and in others then undreamt of. Societies for Medieval and for Post-Medieval Archaeology and a multi-disciplinary Deserted Medieval Village Research Group were to be founded, together with their own journals. These were the decades when William Hoskins essayed the landscape history of his own county, Devonshire, and set off the great project of *Landscapes* county by county, taking their title from his own seminal *Making of the English Landscape*. Towards the end of his life that great work in educating the general public was crowned by his highly personal television series for the BBC.

All these developments make it impossible – even if it were desirable – to augment and amend what I wrote (between 1954 and 1956) as 'Six Studies in Maps and Landscapes' at the instigation of Margaret Stewart, then book editor of the Lutterworth Press and the brave champion of *The Lost Villages of England* (1954) against some of her colleagues.

In the title that I chose to embrace these disparate essays, both 'History' and 'Ground' were more than usually an author's declaration of intent. The epigraph (p. 6), taken from the first English edition of Mercator's *Atlas* of 1636, did indeed suggest that the essays would be following its seventeenth-century author into an association of History with Geography, a marriage on which I have always looked with favour. On the other hand the 'Ground' in 1957 was a declaration that, given time and patience, I intended soon to complete a contract already signed with the Cambridge University Press to view landscape histories very differently, calling in aid the air photographs taken by Kenneth St. Joseph for our *Medieval England: an Aerial Survey* (1958 and 1971). The present book was therefore a pendant to one book and a trailer to another. It was indeed a joy to be alive, and to be young was very heaven.

Acknowledgments

PERMISSION to reproduce plans and photographs is gratefully acknowledged. Mr. R. A. Skelton of the British Museum, Sir Edmund Craster, Librarian of All Souls College and Mr. P. I. King of the Northamptonshire Record Office kindly assisted in obtaining copies. The Rev. H. E. Ruddy of Braunston assisted in the field study of Chapter 2, and the manuscript was reduced from chaos to ordered typescript by Mrs. J. F. Brothwell.

Plates 2, 5, 8, 9a, 10, 12, 14, 16, 18, 21, 22 and Figure 10 are from photographs by Clifford Farrar; Plates 3, 4, 6, 7 and 11, with Figures 5 and 6 from All Souls College MSS. by permission of the Librarian; Plate 1 from P.R.O. MPB 32 by permission; Plate 9b from the manuscripts of Earl Spencer, Althorp Park, by permission; Plate 13 from the Bibliothèque Nationale, Paris, MSS. 706 Anglais, by permission; Plate 15 from B.M. Add. MSS. 38065, by permission; Plates 19 and 20 from Northamptonshire Record Office, Finch-Hatton MSS. 272 by permission of the Northants. Archives Committee.

Figures 1, 2, 3, 4, 7, 8, 9, 11, 12, 14 and 15 are based on the Ordnance Survey maps by permission of the Director-General; Figures 18, 20, 22, 26 and 28 reproduce parts of Ordnance Survey maps, also by permission; Figure 16 reproduces part of P.R.O. MR 205, by permission; Figure 17 is based on B.M. Add. MSS. 38065, by permission; Figure 19 reproduces part of a plan at the Royal Institute of British Architects, by permission of the Librarian; Figure 21 reproduces parts of Birm. Ref. MSS., Elford 49, by permission of the Librarian; Figure 24 is based on a map in *Trans. Royal Hist. Soc.*, iv (4th ser.) 1921; Figure 25 reproduces part of B.M. Harleian MSS. 6288; Figure 27 is based on part of the manuscript plan at the Aylesbury Museum.

Figures 1, 2, 3, 4, 5, 6, 7, 8, 11, 12, 14, 15, 17, 23 and 24 executed by Mr. D. A. Fawcett; Figure 13 by Mr. G. Bryant. Index by Mrs. A. Mason.

The quotation from "Little Gidding" (T. S. Eliot, *Four Quartets*, Faber & Faber Ltd.) is made by permission of the Publishers.

The endpapers are from B.M. Add. MSS. 32467.

List of Abbreviations

AND SHORT TITLES OF WORKS FREQUENTLY CITED IN THE
FOOTNOTES

Other works have full references at each appearance, op. cit.
being reserved for adjacent references.

*The names of English counties are usually abbreviated in
footnotes.* Archaeological, Historical, Journal, Natural History,
Review, Transactions *and* Society *are abbreviated in the titles
of periodicals, as here.*

Add. MSS.	Additional Manuscripts, B.M.
Ag. Hist. Rev.	*Agricultural History Review*
Beresford	Maurice Beresford, *The Lost Villages of England* (1954)
Birm. Ref.	Birmingham Reference Library Manuscripts
Blundell	J. H. Blundell, *Toddington* (1925)
B.M.	British Museum
Bridges	J. Bridges, *A History of Northamptonshire* (1791)
Cal. Chart.	*Calendar of Charter Rolls*
Cal. Close	*Calendar of Close Rolls*
Cal. Inq. Misc.	*Calendar of Inquisitions, Miscellaneous*
Cal. I.P.M.	*Calendar of Inquisitions Post Mortem*
Cal. Pat.	*Calendar of Patent Rolls*
C	C followed by a number indicates a class of Chancery record at the P.R.O.
Darby	H. C. Darby, *The Domesday Geography of Eastern England* (1952)
Darby and Terrett	H. C. Darby and I. M. Terrett, *The Domesday Geography of Midland England* (1954)
DL	DL followed by a number indicates a class of Duchy of Lancaster record at the P.R.O.
Dugdale	Sir William Dugdale, *The Antiquities of Warwickshire* (ed. of 1730)
E	E followed by a number indicates a class of Exchequer record at the P.R.O.
Ec. Hist. Rev.	*Economic History Review*
Geog. Journ.	*The Geographical Journal*
G.R.	G.R. followed by six figures indicates a grid reference from the Ordnance Survey maps.
Grundy	G. B. Grundy, *Saxon Charters of Gloucestershire*, 2 vols. (1935-36)
Hartshorne	E. S. Hartshorne, *Memorials of Holdenby* (1868)
Hist. MSS. Comm.	Royal Commission on Historical Manuscripts, *Reports*
HO	HO followed by a number indicates a class of Home Office record at the P.R.O.
Hutchins	J. Hutchins, *A History of Dorset* (ed. 1861-70)
Leadam	I. S. Leadam, *The Domesday of Inclosures*, 2 vols. (1897)

Leland	John Leland, Itinerary (ed. L. Toulmin Smith) 5 vols. (1906-8)
Martin	C. T. Martin, *Catalogue of the . . . Muniments of All Souls College Oxford* (1877)
Mowat	R. B. Mowat, *Sixteen Old Maps . . . of Oxfordshire* (1888)
MP⎱ *MR*⎰	MP and MR followed by a letter and number indicate maps at the P.R.O.
O.S.	Ordnance Survey
P.N.	*P.N.* followed by a county name indicates a volume of the English Place-name Society's publications
P.R.O.	Public Record Office, London
Rot. Hund.	*Rotuli Hundredorum* ("The Hundred Rolls") 2 vols. (1812-18)
SP	SP followed by a number indicates a class of the State Papers at the P.R.O.
St. Ch.	St. Ch. followed by a number indicates a class of the Star Chamber records at the P.R.O.
T.N. MSS.	Temple Newsam MSS., Leeds City Library, Archives Dept.
V.C.H.	*V.C.H.* followed by a county name indicates a volume of the *Victoria History of the Counties of England*

Chapter One

INTRODUCTION

THE journeys described in this book began in libraries and ended in the open air. The traveller, armed with maps, was sometimes seeking what a document suggested he might find, and sometimes coming back to books and documents in order to explain or confirm what he noticed in the landscape. One fellow-traveller in the history of landscapes has publicly declared that by exploring the English countryside on foot he makes at least one major historical discovery a week. The journeys described in these pages cannot claim to have extended the frontiers of knowledge at this revolutionary rate, but every English historian with an interest in field-work is dealing with an inexhaustible source of evidence, more than enough for one man's lifetime.

Field studies such as those in this book have always a mixed character. There is exploration which confirms what documents and books have already suggested; and there is exploration which examines maps and landscapes when documents themselves are lacking, seeking always to call in one technique to supplement the other. With documents, books and travel the historian is thrice armed in his perpetual war against oblivion, and the intellectual journey is always triangular: from field to archives, from archives to libraries and from libraries to the field.

The "field" and the "landscapes" of out-of-doors investigation are not only those of the countryside. The landscape of towns needs the observant and inquiring eye as much as the landscape of earthworks and hedges. A topographical interest is as relevant to urban history as to rural history. Nor are the fields and landscapes which are worthy of historical attention exhausted by the six studies in this book. The present selection of topics omits whole periods of English history. The prehistoric and the Roman enter only as accidental and incidental influences on succeeding landscapes. The industrialization of England in the last two centuries has modified even those rural landscapes which are far from chimneys, but none of the six field studies in this book has for its central theme an historical subject as recent as the industrial revolution.

The theme which unifies the six studies is the bringing of documentary evidence to bear on particular villages, particular fields and particular towns. Among the documents which are used it will be seen that manuscript maps and plans play a large part. By examining the work of these sixteenth- and seventeenth-century cartographers we are admitted not only to the landscape of the Tudors and Stuarts portrayed on the parchment but to the far older landscape which had not then been completely effaced. From the limited number of such plans surviving we can recognize the historical structure of certain landscapes and then apply our knowledge to the much greater number of towns and villages for which no such early plans survive, and where the landscape itself—in default of other manuscript evidence—will have to be scanned as a document.

The journeys among the open fields and the deserted villages in Chapters 3 and 4 proceed in this way, beginning with Elizabethan maps and ending in the countryside itself. The journey to Elizabethan market-places in Chapter 6 also begins with manuscript plans which are among the earliest ever made of English towns. The second chapter deals with boundaries which were settled many centuries before the first English maps, and here the modern landscape as recorded in the Ordnance Survey plans must afford the principal evidence, although at the end of the chapter we are able to follow the Elizabethan cartographer, Christopher Saxton, along the bounds of a Yorkshire parish for which his manuscript plan has survived. The medieval town-planning which prompted the journeys of Chapter 5 has also left its mark in modern topographical features which can be studied on the ground and in the Ordnance Survey plans; while in Chapter 7 evidence assembled from documents, manuscript maps and printed books is linked with the parks from all periods which are to be found in the English landscape.

Illustrations are a poor substitute for taking the reader and showing him first the old maps and then the modern landscape, but they must suffice. Several of the plans are relevant to more than one chapter: Higham Ferrers, for example, has something to tell us about fields, boundaries, market-towns and parks. Cross references are given in such cases, for the narrative in the text is often closely geared to a particular illustration or figure.

All but one of the seventeen manuscript plans are, it is believed, published here for the first time, and acknowledgment to their owners or custodians is made on page 15.

The photographs are a selection of those taken for record purposes by Clifford Farrar. The choice has inevitably been limited by the weathers and seasons in which the journeys were made. The conditions which they record may also have changed since our visits, for the English landscape of town and country is not a museum. Men will not scruple to grub up a hedge, bulldoze earthworks, lay out aerodromes, build reservoirs and put the landscape to a dozen other uses which alter its shape and remove old landmarks. But it has been always so: landscapes have come and gone in accordance with the ebb or flow of changing economies and fashion. The tide will not halt for the convenience of antiquaries; and economic historians, who earn their bread and butter by chronicling the ebb and flow of seas, are not in a strong position to cast themselves for the role of Canute. If change moves fast across the English countryside its historians must keep pace, and the journeys which follow represent only a few of the rewards which offer themselves to those who take to their feet.

The traditions in which the author has been reared frown on the first person singular: what matters is what the author has to say and not what he is wearing at the time or how his liver feels. By and large, I assent to the tradition, and cheerfully write "the author" and "we" to subdue the interfering ego. Occasionally, however, the following pages will slip into autobiography. After all, the choice of places to visit on these journeys was highly personal, and what was observed on them was also bound to depend on who did the observing. It has been necessary from time to time in the description of the journeys to explain in what season, in what mood and in what company a particular inquiry was carried out. Other seasons, other moods and other company might well produce a different report even from the same observer.

The choice of six subjects has been guided by the wish to make my own journeys the starting point for other people's. I have more than once been placed in the position of being curious about the history of a place or district of England without any previous knowledge of the terrain. I was faced by this mixture of curiosity and ignorance when I moved from the Midlands to Yorkshire in April, 1948, and anyone who first begins to acquire an interest in the history of his own locality will be in the same position. These chapters describe some topics which I have personally found worth investigation.

Some of my field-work over the last ten years has already been incorporated in my *Lost Villages of England* and in the work which Dr. J. K. St. Joseph and I have done for the second volume of the *Cambridge Air Surveys*. I have tried in this book to repeat myself as little as possible, and to apply a technique learned in one investigation to the study of fresh material. My professional colleagues will inevitably recognize among these essays some themes from specialised researches, but academic research has its own channels by which results are reported, and this book is not intended to be one.

In one sense, it is an ordinary travel book designed to those who like reading about other people's journeys, and it will take them by proxy into parts of an England which I suspect they do not know, but which I hope they will like to know better. The book is also designed to lead other readers out from the armchair to think about repeating some of my journeys for themselves. In different seasons of different years there is no danger that my journeys will be exactly matched and duplicated.

There was a final category of readers in mind when the book was planned. These readers would be more interested in why and how my journeys were made than in the particular places and findings, for they are men and women who are curious about their own neighbourhood and want to learn more of what documents, maps and field-work can tell then. They may also extend their curiosity to other parts of England where business or pleasure may take them. They may wish to carry out similar investigations to mine, and for them the final pages of the book are designed. The six main chapters describe journeys very much as they were taken—on foot, by bus or by car. The description of the journeys is interwoven with historical comment and quotations from documents, but the narrative is not interrupted by long accounts of the source-material which prompted each journey and suggested that it might be worth while looking over a particular hedge or down a particular street. Yet this source-material may be what some readers will want to assist them in their own local inquiries, and the distinct character of the final pages will, it is hoped, meet their needs while clearing the ground in the other chapters, which are self-contained, each telling a story in its own right.

2

A JOURNEY ALONG BOUNDARIES

BRAUNSTON (NORTHAMPTONSHIRE)
HIGHAM FERRERS (NORTHAMPTONSHIRE)
OLD BYLAND (YORKSHIRE, N.R.)

> *The Lords Records and the Tennants informations, are the pillars of a survey.*
> JOHN NORDEN, *Surveiors Dialogue* (1607)

Chapter Two

A JOURNEY ALONG BOUNDARIES

I

A THOUSAND years stand between the first settlement of English villages and the first successful attempts to portray them in accurate plans. In the interval, the appearance of the countryside could only be recorded in words, sometimes written on parchment, sometimes committed to memory and handed down orally from generation to generation. It is on sources of this kind that we must depend if we wish to confirm the antiquity of some medieval feature noticed in the course of a country journey, but documents have had many enemies, of which mice, damp and salvage campaigns have been the most successful, and survival is always a matter of chance. Where documents do survive and contain topographical matter it is important that any opportunities which they offer for comparison with the modern landscape should be seized, for only by becoming familiar with the earthworks, crop-marks and buildings which documentary evidences prove to be medieval can an explorer pass on with confidence to the much larger number of physical remains for which there is no documentary elucidation. This is the justification for the seemingly minute antiquarianism of a beginner in field-work; only then is it possible to proceed from the small area of the known to the larger area of the unknown, and to the visible remains of the past with which the English countryside is so well endowed.[1]

In the later chapters of this book it will be possible to compare Elizabethan town- and village-plans with the modern appearance of the same places and to learn the alphabet of topographical history in the normal way. But there are features on the English landscape which are older than any map, and in some cases older than any

---

[1] The best anthology of English earthworks is still A. H. Allcroft, *Earthwork of England* (1908). For a recent general survey, W. G. Hoskins, *Making of the English Landscape* (1955).

document. Among these are the boundaries of parishes and town-ships. It was only in the sixteenth century that the art of the surveyor encompassed large-scale plans with the parish boundaries accurately measured,[2] but earlier generations had been forced to adopt more crude methods of recording. In the Psalter of Kirkstead Abbey there is a primitive plan of the boundaries between cow-pastures in the Lincolnshire Fens. The plan was entered in the Psalter about 1300 but may have been first drawn about 1150. The bounds of Sherwood Forest were shown on a crude plan drawn about 1376. In the cartu-lary of the Northamptonshire Priory of Fineshead, written c. 1300, the scribe attempted to show the ownership of meadowland by a sketch which is half diagram, half plan. A monk of Chertsey Abbey made a plan of its demesnes (c. 1432). The bounds of the Isle of Thanet are shown on a plan made about 1414. The technique of these plans is of the roughest, and the plan of Elford made in 1508 (fig. 20), is very little better. The contrast with the plans made by the Eliza-bethan surveyors (e.g. Plates 3, 4, 6, 7) is striking.[3]

Yet, long before the description of fens, forests and villages in crude pictures, men had puzzled out how best to record the position of boundaries and give them certainty. Written record begins with the Anglo-Saxon boundary charters of the seventh century. These documents recorded the outer bounds of estates when they changed hands by gift, sale or lease. In many cases, an estate included all the territory of a village and had the bounds of the modern parish or township; when it was less than a whole village its perimeter will coincide with only part of the present circuit.

The use of an old boundary charter to settle a dispute is referred to in a document itself as early as 896. The mention in it of a pro-cession headed by a priest also suggests that something akin to the Rogationtide perambulation of the bounds (p. 28, below) was already in progress. This charter refers to some woodland at Woodchester, a village in the western Cotswolds near Stroud. In 741 a king of the South Angles had given the monks of Worcester a block of wood-land here, and in 896 the bishop complained that the land had been

[2] E. Lynam, *British Maps and Mapmakers* (1944); "English maps and Map-makers of the Sixteenth Century", *Geog. Journ.*, cxvi (1950), 7-28; F. G. Emmison, ed., *Catalogue of Maps in the Essex Record Office* (1947).

[3] The plans mentioned are listed and illustrated in D. J. Price, "Medieval Land Surveying", *Geog. Journ.*, cxxxi (1955), 1-10; with the exception of the Fineshead plan which is Lambeth Palace MSS., Arches Ff. 291, fo. 58d.

filched from them. The supreme council of the kingdom, the *witan*, met at Gloucester and settled the problem by taking out the old charter of 741 and comparing it with the ground.[4] The claimant was ordered

> to ride with the priest of the people of [Wood] Chester . . . along all the boundaries as he read them from the old books [i.e. charters].

Only a small number of places have documents as early as this, yet firm boundaries were successfully established and their position handed down orally from generation to generation. This word-of-mouth tradition was reinforced by frequent perambulations of the bounds and (later in the Middle Ages) by enrolment in the records of the manor courts. In the course of this chapter we shall move from the unknown Anglo-Saxon villagers who first determined the bounds of the Northamptonshire village of Braunston to the surveyor, Christopher Saxton, making his way around the windy bounds of a North Riding parish in 1598. The journey includes a short visit to Higham Ferrers in Northamptonshire (the subject of Chapter 6) to consider its manorial survey of 1591 which stands midway between the verbal traditions and the surveyors' maps.

The boundaries of parishes and townships are among the oldest features marked on any modern Ordnance map. Only the Roman and prehistoric antiquities are older. No medieval building is as old. In English towns, the last two hundred years have seen many transformations of old boundaries when new churches have been built for growing industrial populations, but the rural parish boundaries have suffered very little change. Where there have been any minor administrative changes, they usually date from the last century, when anomalies of local government boundaries were tidied up, but over that period the successive ten-yearly Census volumes have always recorded such changes. In cases of doubt, the plans of the first edition of the six-inch Ordnance Survey and the numerous Tithe and Enclosure Awards of the period between 1730 and 1850 can be consulted. The dots which signify a parish boundary on the first edition of the O.S. map often mark a line unaltered for a thousand years, perambulated at Rogationtide by generation after generation of parishioners.

The Ordnance Survey plan occupies a curious place in the history

---

[4] Grundy, ii, 276-77.

of parish boundaries. It provides a reliable record of their position, but the very accuracy and permanence of the map record has brought the older methods of recording and remembering the bounds into neglect. If so few processions now beat out the bounds at Rogationtide it is because the Ordnance Survey has done their job for them. It is also true that in the last century the parish has been replaced as the effective unit of local government by rural districts, urban districts and county councils. It has become much less important to know where one parish ends and another begins. There was a time when a whole range of duties and payments hinged very much on which side of the boundary one lived.

The time most appropriate for examining a parish boundary would be Rogationtide, the Monday, Tuesday and Wednesday before Ascension Day. The custom of processions on these days seems to have originated in Auvergne about 470, following the disastrous eruption of a volcano, and, as the word *rogation* (= petitioning) indicates, the processions were intended as expressions of guilt and as requests for divine mercy. By the time that the English church took up the ceremonies (*c.* 750) they had changed their emphasis. They were now designed not to avert a particular disaster but to ask a blessing on the coming agricultural year. Since Ascension Day moves with Easter, Rogationtide fell anywhere between April 7 and June 2. At this season, with lambing over, the villagers' interest lay in preserving their young crops from wind, drought and flood; the Rogation ceremonies may, therefore, have taken over one aspect of the pagan fertility rites, leaving others for Plough Monday and May Day.

Between 750 and 1550 the processions acquired on additional purpose, that of beating the bounds.[5] It is easy to see how the change took place: a procession which went the circuit of the fields in order to bless them was easily transformed into one whose main purpose was to examine the boundaries of the fields. In the reformed church of Elizabethan England the order of service prescribed was one which combined both features. It is interesting to see that the prohibition of religious processions in the royal injunctions of 1547 and 1559 deliberately exempted the Rogation ceremonies. All other

---

[5] A short account of Rogation ceremonies will be found in *Catholic Encyclopaedia*, xiii (1913), 110; for a typical prosecution for not perambulating see P.R.O. E159/9 Eliz., Trinity term *Recorda*, m. 151.

processions were Romish, superstitious and idolatrous, but the beating of the bounds was too useful to be allowed to lapse. As the Queen ordered in 1559,

> the clergy shall once in a year at the time accustomed walk about their parishes with the Curate and other substantial men of the parish . . . and at their return to the church make their common prayer.

A reminder of the Auvergne volcano was the recital of the Litany and of Psalms 103 and 104.

> He hath not dealt with us after our sins: nor rewarded us according to our wickedness,

says Psalm 103, but the next Psalm is much more reminiscent of geography and boundaries. Psalm 104 is not only long enough to make a useful marching chant, it is also most geographical and economic in its imagery. It praises God through the beasts of the field drinking; the fowls of the air; the grass for the cattle; wine for the thirsty; trees for timber; goats; conies; sea-going ships and sea-going animals. Speaking of the rivers, the Psalmist says

> thou hast set them their bounds that they shall not pass,

but the less literate of the Elizabethan villagers must have thought how well this fitted the work in hand, the marking out of the bounds between neighbour and neighbour: and on the long processions by hedge-banks and river-side many of the younger villagers may have wondered whether the psalmist had their village procession in mind when he wrote

> they go up as high as the hills and down to the valleys beneath.

Elizabeth I's injunction of 1559 assumed that the procession would begin from the parish church and return there for final prayers. Very few churches stood alongside the boundary of their parishes, so that the procession would have to make its way across country before beginning the circuit. Occasionally the name of a field or lane preserves the memory: thus, one of the grass tracks among the arable fields of Higham Ferrers (p. 51 below) was called Procession Way. This track is not at the edge of the parish of Higham and it must have been the route taken by the procession on its way out to the bounds.

The clockwise circuit of the bounds involved a walk of anything from three to ten miles, depending on the size and shape of a parish, and in the large parishes of the uplands this distance was often exceeded. We have seen that three days were allocated for the ceremonies and all this time would be needed in a large parish. Quite apart from the distance to be covered, there were halts to inspect boundary points and to resolve any disputes. It was usual to recite a passage from scripture at the major turning points and the name Gospel Oak shows where the processions halted. Nor could it have been always easy going: as anyone who tries to follow a parish boundary to-day soon finds, there are few footpaths exactly along the perimeter of a parish. It is true that the thornhedge, barbed-wire and ditches of modern fields have brought new obstacles to anyone beating bounds, but there is no sign of a boundary footpath even on the surviving Elizabethan village plans. The procession would have had to make its way along the edge of ploughed and sown land, along the marshy edge of rivers and through woodland scrub. Only when it came to common grassland and the fallow field could the procession quicken its pace.

The sacrifice of so much time and energy suggests that there were hard, practical reasons for the processions. Had the fertility of the crops been the only concern, their well-being might have been assured by less uncomfortable journeys along well-trodden paths and lanes. The Rogation procession was both a statement of the past rights of a village and the means by which these rights should be preserved in the future. The social purpose, as opposed to the religious purpose, was the education of the young in this important set of facts. If there is a touch of sympathetic magic in beating bounds to make the solid earth remember its lawful owners, there was also a crude educational psychology in beating the adolescent boys to make them remember their fathers' lawful property. Here and there, folk ceremonies admitted other variations to the same end. At one place in the Lincolnshire fenland two teams had a tug-of-war across the ditch which divided their two parishes: the winners remembered the place of their victory and the losers the place of their drenching. In a village on the border of Huntingdonshire and Cambridgeshire vicars were still held upside down in a hole even in the decorous nineteenth century.

The procession, reading and singing were more than a picturesque

30

ceremony: the establishment of an accurate boundary was important both for the church and the villagers. Boundaries only become important in social life when more than one claimant is envisaged. So long as there were no claims to a stretch of heath, moorland, sand-dune or marsh, it was literally no-man's-land, and for that reason was any-man's-land. When there was only one squatter or one village community making use of a piece of newly-cleared forest-land the question of bounds was still academic. Villages only became concerned with bounds when rival claimants appeared. It is easy to imagine an early stage in the Anglo-Saxon settlement when small villages had been established at intervals on easily-won soil: there would still be an immense reservoir of uncleared land available for any newcomers in the spaces between one village and the next, and, so long as they kept their distance, additional settlers could safely be tolerated. More houses and more fields could be established without taking away anything which the first-established villages prized.[6]

At a later stage, to which it is still impossible to give a firm date, villages of the first and second generation were becoming thicker on the ground, and clashes of interest began to arise. One might think that the clash would have come when a village wished to make fields out of forest which its neighbours regarded as "theirs", but the way in which Anglo-Saxon bounds are drawn suggest that bounds were disputed, fought over and settled long before the debateable lands were actually reached by rival ploughs. The march of clearance, moving out from the village centres into the forests, was a slow and difficult labour, and in many parts of England could not have reached the present boundaries even by Domesday Book (1086), when some indication of the area under the plough and the number of plough-teams maintained is given.

Yet by 1086, as Professor H. C. Darby's county maps have strikingly shown, the vast majority of villages in the English plains were already established,[7] and for a number of villages there are documents which describe parish boundaries of the ninth century. These bounds must, therefore, have been settled at a time when the dividing line passed over ground which the villagers had not yet

[6] For this "second round" settlement in Devon see W. G. Hoskins, *Devon* (1954), 69-75.

[7] H. C. Darby, *Domesday Geography of Eastern England* (1952); H. C. Darby and I. B. Terrett, *Domesday Geography of Midland England* (1954).

begun to think of as ploughland. This is not to say that the ground had no economic value. The plough needed plough-beasts, and plough-beasts had to be fed. Sheep, goats and swine also made demands on non-arable land. The grass-eating animals gave a high value to meadowland and rough grazing; swine and goats were more accommodating; they fended for themselves in the forest. Thus a village acquired an economic interest in maintaining unchallenged use of forest and grass which were distant from the ploughed fields, and the first challenges probably came not from ploughmen or wood-cutters but from swineherds and shepherds at a time long before the debateable grounds were taken in for tillage.

A convenient way of examining the parish bounds of a county is to use the Index Diagrams which the Ordnance Survey publish as a key to their six-inch and twenty-five-inch plans. These diagrams show the bounds of civil parishes in bold outline, whereas the one-inch map (using the conventions of grey lines or dots) subordinates the bounds to other details. On these diagrams the parish with an unusual shape or size is easy to pick out: the large-scale maps of the particular parish will, of course, then be needed for study.

The index diagrams sometimes show parishes which have an unusually long, curving sweep in their bounds. One such will be seen in fig. 15, p. 161 where the curve proves to mark the pale of a medieval park. Another such curve follows the perimeter of Devizes park in Wiltshire. At Devizes the park cannot be older than the new Norman castle and town which were planted in the open countryside of Bishops Cannings parish, and the Anglo-Saxon boundaries would here have had to be adjusted. There are already many references to earlier palisaded enclosures (*haga*) in the Anglo-Saxon charters of the ninth century in other parts of England. Minting (Lincs.) is another parish with a park pale clearly fossilised in its western boundary.

In some parts of England, such as the villages of the Lincoln Heights, geographers and historians have long noticed a fearful symmetry in parish boundaries which run parallel to each other for many miles, giving each village a piece of heathland on the hill-top, a piece of arable below on the hill-side, and a piece of meadow in the lowest part of the parish where the boundaries follow the riverside.[8]

[8] E.g. G. I. Smith, *The Land of Britain, Part 76 (Lincolnshire)* (1942), 479 and 502.

It is difficult to resist the assumption that these villages were settled at about the same time and that each village subsequently reclaimed the land above and below it at about the same pace as its neighbours.

Some villages which lie on the edge of the Huntingdonshire fens are shown in fig. 1, and it will be seen that they have long fingers stretching into the fens. For many generations the fenland would only have been useful for fish, fowl and reeds, but when it came to be reclaimed the villages were able to assert their rights to that part which lay at the edge of their old fields, and the parish boundaries kept in step with each other. The intrusion of Holme into Glatton is an interesting exception; but there was no Holme in Domesday

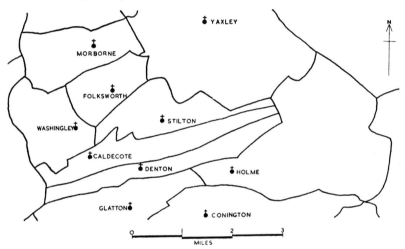

Fig. 1. Parish boundaries in the Fenland of Hunts., now reclaimed. Six parishes shared the fen. The new village of Holme (*c.* 1200) stands between Glatton and its fen.

Book, and the village was a late off-shoot of Glatton on a low neck of land jutting out into the fen.[9]

The bounds of Higham Ferrers, seen in fig. 15, p. 161, have a noticeable break in the local symmetry where Chelveston intrudes between Higham and Raunds. The explanation probably lies in Chelveston's need to have access to the ford over the Nene and to the Nene-side meadows. It will be noticed that the bridge on the London-Leicester main road, which has replaced the ford since at least 1227,

[9] *V.C.H. Hunts.*, iii, 184; survey of Holme (1579): P.R.O. DL/43/4/1; 1279: *Rot. Hund.*, ii, 651.

actually lies in this narrow strip of Chelveston parish. The accommodation of parish boundaries to already-existing rights of grazing is well shown also in the parishes of the Weald and the Essex marshes which have distant detached portions. Not having woodland or marsh near by, the villages had acquired the habit of going a distance to it, establishing a right of drift (i.e. driving) for their herds over the intervening lands of other villages. When parish boundaries came to be fixed, these rights were well-enough established for the bounds to have to make concessions to them.

There are other parish-boundary patterns which suggest old-established rights: boundaries sometimes have the shape of a star, converging on a central point which may once have been common to all the surrounding parishes. It is sometimes a pool, sometimes an important road junction, and sometimes a surviving block of common-land in an area of clearances: in each case the bounds suggest that all the neighbours had conceded each other's right of access for an important purpose, so strong as not to be denied. Fig. 2, p. 40, shows seven parishes converging at one point on Dunsmore Heath, near Rugby.

Another such curious projection of one parish into another will be seen in fig. 4, p. 54, on the north-west of Old Byland where the bounds of Murton township have a narrow 400-yards-long projection into Dale Town and Boltby. The piece is still called *Lord's Tongue;* similar projections elsewhere in England are sometimes called *Nick,* as if the biting teeth rather than the projecting tongue were pictured; and some are called *Ness,* that is "nose", another application of anatomy to geography.

Some of the medieval diocesan boundaries also act as pointers to the early settlement of peoples. Thus, Warwickshire was cut in two by the boundary between the see of Lichfield and the see of Worcester. Worcester was the cathedral city of the bishop who ministered to the Saxon people known as the Hwicce, who had probably worked their way along the Cotswold ridge-ways and across the Severn valley. Lichfield was the old centre of the Mercians, an Anglian people who had colonized the Midlands from the Trent basin. The two colonizing movements met in mid-Warwickshire. Centuries later, when tribal and political distinctions had been submerged, the medieval boundary between the bishoprics, winding its way across the Avon valley, shows the old frontier of peoples. Indeed, there is a

34

little field in Radway parish called *Martimow* which was known in the thirteenth century as *Merclemere* and in an Anglo-Saxon charter of the tenth century as *Mercna Mere*, the "mere" (boundary) of Mercia. It also seems as if the bishops' boundary had to adjust itself to an existing frontier fashioned in the ebb and flow of competing settlement, for the boundary does not follow the obvious natural frontier of the Avon, which one might choose if one were making a boundary by treaty. It moves from one side of the river to the other, to and fro, taking in this parish and leaving out that, clearly paying attention to affinities of blood which have long since disappeared.[10]

It is not always possible to know when the bounds of bishoprics and counties were fixed, and the date of parish boundaries is equally uncertain. There are sufficient examples of bounds which square with the limits given in ninth- and tenth-century charters to make it likely that the densely-settled parts of England had already been parcelled out by the time of the Norman Conquest. It is true that after 1066 and particularly in the twelfth century new churches continued to be endowed and new parishes cut out of the old. Some of these, but only a small minority, were to cater for newly-settled communities such as the lead-mining villages of Nidderdale or the fenland farmers of Lincolnshire.[11] With these new settlements there had to be new boundaries whose course often gave rise to disputes. The growth of population in towns necessitated additional urban churches and new parish boundaries, but the majority of new churches of the twelfth and thirteenth centuries were to serve old-established villages which had so far remained unprovided. The lack of provision may have resulted from a lord's tardiness in making an endowment or from the reluctance of an established incumbent to surrender any of his parishioners and income; sometimes the village in question had only just begun to grow beyond the hamlet size and develop an ambition for a church of its own.

While the late foundation of a church must suggest some inherent inferior status in a village (such as a late settlement from a mother village), the dependence cannot always be safely assumed. There must always have been an element of chance determining which

[10] *P.N. Warws.*, 272; *P.N. Worcs.*, xvi.

[11] Nidderdale, 1361: J. T. Fowler, ed., *Memorials of Ripon* (Surtees Society, lxxiv (1882), 203-5; fens of Lincolnshire: H. E. Hallam, *The New Lands of Elloe* (1954), 39-40.

villages first had lords willing to endow a church and villagers anxious to have their own priest; and the villages first to have churches need not necessarily have been those longest settled. Yet there is little evidence that the multiplication of churches in the twelfth century created widespread boundary problems, and the most likely explanation is that the "dependent" village already had well-defined boundaries for secular, economic purposes and that these were taken over by the new church.

So far, the parish boundary has only been spoken of as delimiting the territory of villages. The Church has appeared at Rogationtide to assist and to bless. This simplification must now be corrected, although I believe that the order of treatment corresponds to the order of events, and that villages must have had boundaries before they had parish churches. We can see a sign of these old secular divisions in the upland parishes which still contain more than one village, for there have always been well-defined boundaries between the several villages (or townships) which make up the one ecclesiastical parish, and many of these townships have their bounds (as "civil" parishes) marked on the Ordnance Survey plans. These churchless villages can still be found in the north and west of England. In the English plains they are fewer, and the map shows a church in almost every village.

Yet there must have been a stage in the colonization of the plains when they, too, had large parishes with many villages within them and when there were many villages without a church. The Anglo-Saxon villages were created by pagans, and Christianity did not penetrate everywhere immediately after the Conversion of 597. The provision of a church depended on someone making provision for the cost of building and the maintenance of a priest. Churches came slowly. In these early days a "*parish*" meant simply the territory within which a particular church ministered, and from which the church drew economic support. As churches multiplied in number the parishes grew smaller, until at last the majority of villages had their own church.

Parish boundaries were now of added importance: they marked out not only the villages' claims to the agricultural assets of the kingdom but also the units of church administration and taxation. The boundaries of the parish marked the limit of a parish priest's responsibilities and the limit of the land from which payment of tithes was due. These levies of one sheaf in ten, one lamb in ten (and so on) were intended to maintain him. In the course of time other people and institutions acquired the rights to receive part of these payments, and this gave an even wider interest in parish boundaries. They became not only the cause of contention between neighbours disputing a piece of heathland but between rival claimants to the tithe on crops and animals.

The process of settlement may be suggested by going to a corner of Northamptonshire where the evidence of boundaries and place-names is supplemented by two tenth-century charters which confirm that at least seventeen parishes then had the bounds which they now have. The process can only be suggested, since the founding of these villages has not been explicitly recorded in documents. In the absence of these and of archaeological evidence, the dumb witness of the boundaries may sometimes hint at the truth.[12]

II

The village of Braunston stands on a long ridge above the river Leam. Across the river, to the west, is the now-disused church of the village of Wolfhampcote, the nearest of Braunston's neighbours. The river was the natural frontier between them, its waterside meadows affording hay and grazing for the plough-beasts. It was a frontier in an even more important respect, for Wolfhampcote lay over in the next county. It is not known exactly when the bounds of Warwickshire and Northamptonshire were settled, for when the latter was formed to administer the occupation-area of a single Danish army, late in the ninth century, the frontier seems to have been the Watling Street, which runs three miles east of Braunston. Soon afterwards, however, a sweep of country west of the old Roman road was incorporated in the county and the Leam became part of the county boundary.[13]

In making the circuit of Braunston parish the rogation processions touched on five Northamptonshire parishes in addition to Willoughby in Warwickshire and Wolfhampcote across the river. It is probable that all seven villages were in existence well before 956, the date of the charter. The remarkably even spacing of the villages in

[12] This group of charters is summarized in *P.N. Northants.*, 10-15; 26-8; and 30.
[13] *Ibid.*, Introduction, xviii-xix.

Northamptonshire has already been remarked upon by an archae-
ologist, to whom it suggested some central direction when the first
choices of site were made.[14] Whether the result of direction or of
hard-won experience, the spacing of the villages which border on
Braunston *is* remarkably even. From the parish church of Braunston
to the churches of its neighbours it is 1·5, 2·5, 2·6, 2·6, 3·0 and 3·1
miles respectively. Willoughby, the nearest neighbour by a mile, may
have been a late arrival, for the county boundary of Warwickshire
leaves a natural course along the Leam and Rainsbrook to take in
Willoughby, as if to include an outpost established on the low ground
near the river. All the five neighbours who stand between 2·5 and 3·1
miles distance from Braunston are on the plateau of the Northamptonshire Heights where the soils would be drier and easier to work
than the wet clays of the Leam valley. Thus spaced, the area of the
parishes are bound to be rather similar.

	Acres
Braunston	3,930
Barby	2,535
Ashby	2,050
Welton	1,690
Staverton	2,240
Willoughby	2,290
Drayton[15]	2,045

When the original choices of site were made no one could have
known the agricultural potential of the two thousand acres or so
which encompassed each village, since most of them were still forest.
Nor could anyone have known to what size each village would
eventually grow and how many acres would then be needed: that
day lay perhaps seven or eight hundred years ahead. Of course, the
choices of site need not have been made in the same year or in the
same generation: the archaeological and place-name evidence
permits the chronology of settlement to be only crudely known, and
the neatly-spaced two-and-a-half-miles-apart villages may be the
result not of an original disposition of settlers by some master hand
but of a gradual peopling by successive invaders. Yet the problem
of the even spacing remains, but may it not be the slowly-achieved

[14] W. F. Grimes in *Aspects of Archaeology* (1951), 156.
[15] This is the area of the northern half of Daventry, in which Drayton is now
included.

result of toleration and intolerance? The "standard" distance would thus be that at which a village felt it could safely allow a fresh group of arrivals to settle. Any group which could manage to find a resting place out of hailing distance of others was safe and could begin to clear the land and make preparation for the first winter. And it seems that in this part of Northamptonshire two and a half miles was felt to be a safe distance.

When it became necessary to agree upon bounds with a neighbour, what features were taken as a convenient demarcation line? It was easy to set up a stone between village and village just as peasants set stones between their own holdings, but a stone could be moved, and there might well be many other similar stones occurring naturally. A pool, a stream, a hill-crest, a cliff-top or a valley bottom served very well; they were already moulded in the landscape and not liable to be moved overnight. A tree was often taken for a boundary-point, but of course only in open or cleared country.

The villagers were sometimes able to find convenient landmarks not moulded by Nature but as unmistakable as any of the foregoing. These were an inheritance from a previous age, the barrows, hill-forts, camps, roads, villas and earthworks which often seemed the works of giants. The bounds of the Worcestershire village of Daylesford set down in 781, were said to go

> thence to the hill *Susibre*, an old city, and after that by the old camp (or villa) *"ceastel"* to the nuns' barrows.

The "old city" is the earthwork now known as Chastleton Camp, whose modern name incorporates the "ceastel" of the Anglo-Saxon.[16] The bounds of Badby (near Fawsley, fig. 2), meet Staverton and Catesby at the crest of Arbury Hill, the parish boundary following the outer ditch of a prehistoric hill-fort. The bounds of Byland (p. 54) paid respect to a barrow, prehistoric ditches and a ridgeway. Near Braunston the Roman Watling Street served as part of the bounds of several Northamptonshire, Leicestershire and Warwickshire parishes (fig. 2). The southern bounds of Everdon (fig. 11, p. 114) were set along a track which may have been pre-Saxon, now a deeply worn lane. It was the "Great Street" and the "Salt Street" in the charter of 944, presumably the way along which the salt from the Worcestershire pits came eastwards.[17] Three miles south of Braunston, on

[16] Grundy, i, 102-3.   [17] *P.N. Northants.*, 12.

the boundary of Staverton and Charwelton, is a hill whose name suggests that there had been frequent disputes about the exact course of the bounds. It is Studborough Hill, a name made up of two Anglo-Saxon words, *strut* (= strife) and *beorg* (= hill).

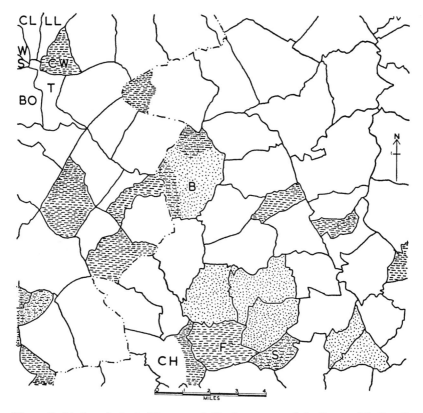

Fig. 2. Parish boundaries in Warws. and Northants, west of the Roman Watling St. (bottom right to centre top). Note the seven parishes meeting at a point on Dunsmore (top left). B: Braunston; Ch: Charwelton; F: Fawsley; S: Snorscomb.
  Dotted areas indicate parishes with Anglo-Saxon boundary charters; broken lines indicate parishes whose villages have decayed.

There were smaller man-made features which seemed to have sufficient permanence to fit them for a boundary-mark. Among these were sheep-cotes, ponds and folds. The boundaries of Braunston were set down in writing in 956 when king Eadwig granted lands to

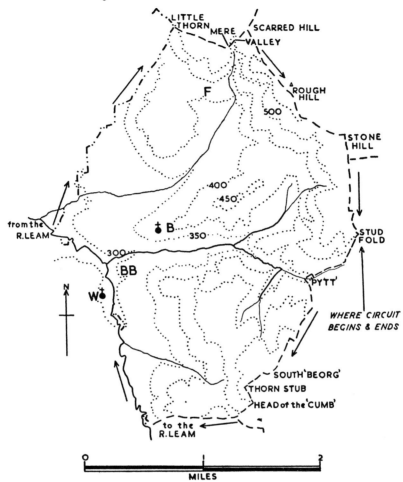

Fig. 3. Braunston (B) and its bounds, with the features mentioned in the Anglo-Saxon boundary charter of 956. BB, F and W indicate the sites of the depopulated settlements of Braunstonberry, Falcliff and Wolfhampcote.

his *thegn*, Edwig, and the circuit began at a "stud-fold", an enclosure for horses.[18]

An examination of the bounds of Braunston may help to indicate some of the problems and information which are likely to be

[18] Summary: *ibid.*, 14; original in W. de G. Birch, *Cartularium Saxonicum* (1885-93), No. 978.

encountered when a Saxon charter is taken out into the open air and compared with the appearance of the ground to-day.

The bounds of Braunston make a circuit of just over nine miles. It might be thought that a description of nine miles of countryside would need many thousands of words and the description of very many landmarks, but in fact it was possible to set out the bounds quite concisely. The compilers of the charter took certain landmarks as fixed points. They chose to begin at the eastern end of the parish where Braunston touches on Welton. Here there was a man-made feature of which there is now no sign, a stud-fold (*stodfald*), probably a rough enclosure of timber and stone. Moving southwards, the next feature to be taken as a turning point was a *pytt*, the valley where the Grand Junction Canal now enters its tunnel. The bounds then climbed again to a hill (*beorg*), the ridge on which the Coventry-Daventry road now runs. Here the boundary neither climbs nor falls, so that the next point could not be described as either hill or valley; it was a thorn-stub (*thorn-stybb*), the body of some unusual tree which had survived the clearances. From here the bounds passed to the head of a valley (*cumb*) which the 500-foot contour marks out on the one-inch Ordnance sheet. From here it descended uninterruptedly to the river Leam, which it then followed northwards for the next two miles. After leaving the river it crossed open country for two more miles, making a number of small, right-angled turns and returns. These individual turns were not described in the charter: the bounds run simply from the river to the little thorn, probably the north-west corner of the parish where Willoughby and Barby meet. The frequent turns and the absence of detail suggest that this land was already under cultivation, and the dividing lines at the field-edge so clear to the eye that it seemed unnecessary to set them down in writing.

From the thorn-tree at the end of these ploughed lands the boundary ran straight to the "middle of the mere", the small pool in Braunston Cleves Wood; along a stream and up the valley to the "scarred hill", that is along the stream which runs from the mere; and to the crest of the hill where the lane from Barby to Walton now runs. This road follows the boundary for more than a mile, and may be the successor of an old track over the hill which provided a succession of clearings and a convenient demarcation line. The charter described the hills here as "scarred" and "rough": the only two points on the course of the boundary were the top of the "rough hill" and a "stone-hill" where the boundary leaves the road and swings back to the *stodfald* at the starting point, having made the nine-mile circuit. 130 years after these bounds were set down in the charter the Domesday Survey offers another assessment of this village community. In 1086 the inquiry was concerned not with the bounds but with the value of agricultural land contained within them. There were ten plough-teams at work in the fields and 22 families were recorded.[19] In the last census of Queen Victoria's reign (1891) there were 280 families.

In the rainy summer of 1954 a group of us made the circuit of these Braunston bounds again, following in the footsteps of the Rogation processions and of that journey which must have been occasioned in 956 when the charter had to be drawn up. The Rector, the Rev. H. E. Ruddy, no longer beats the bounds here, but he secured the good-will of those farmers over whose land we should have to pass and went further by finding us a farmer who would allow us to pitch camp on his land for the two or three days which the study of Braunston and Badby demanded. A legalist might argue that the undoubted ancient use of the bounds has established a right of-way, but the disuse in recent times would probably be held to negative that right, should any zealous field-worker decide to become involved in a test-case. We preferred to acknowledge that we would be trespassing, and asked for permission.

The thorns and mud make it unlikely that the farmers will ever be afflicted again. We had performed a ritual and had bled for it. We had hoped to see the stud-fold, but ploughing had levelled the ground. The thorn-stub had also gone, but the valleys and hills remained. The river Leam has been less steadfast: the natural movement of the bed of a meandering stream has produced several discrepancies between the traditional boundary and the actual river bank. Northamptonshire is not always on the east side of the stream now. It slices off tiny, curving shreds of meadow on the west (or Warwickshire) side of the water. There are other county boundaries where the old course of a river is etched out as a curling land-fast series of dots and lines on the Ordnance Map: the North and West Ridings of Yorkshire are curiously interlaced in this manner to the south-east of West Tanfield where the Ure has changed its course.

[19] *V.C.H. Northants.*, i, 308, 340 and 371.

The discovery which pleased us most was one which only field-work could have yielded, the contour interval of the six-inch O.S. map being too large to show it. We found that the successive points mentioned in the Saxon charter were each just in sight of the next. This was particularly marked along the hill-top road on the north-east boundary. The line of the road is straight for more than a mile, but the ground rises and falls in small switchbacks, giving only a limited range of vision. But the points chosen to be described in 956 were all such that a man standing at one might see another man at the next. For a moment we saw the landscape as the men of Braunston had seen it a thousand years earlier.

There are other, more frequently-encountered, boundary features which throw light on conditions at the unknown moments in the Dark Ages when bounds were finally settled. If one particular part of a parish had not yet been under the plough, the bounds there could only have been set out roughly. A landscape of oaks and under-growth, bracken or scrub was not one where niceties of feet and inches mattered: a line from this bold landmark to that, from this valley-bottom to that outcrop of rock, was sufficient. The boundaries in this type of ground will have long, straight segments or very slow curves.

In contrast—as in the north-west of Braunston—are bounds which make a large number of small right-angled turns and returns within a short distance. What could already have been so firmly marked on the ground that the two disputing villages had to accept them and incorporate them within their design? surely, the edges of fields already ploughed, the *furlongs* of open fields similar to those which still survived at the time of the Elizabethan maps to be described in the next chapter. If one part of a parish boundary is jagged and another smooth, it may hint to us which way the clearances had first moved outwards from the village centre.

It would, in fact, be exceptional for a village to push its fields outwards in all directions at the same speed: the best and most easily cleared soils were followed, as a prospector follows a vein of silver or lead. The characteristic pattern of an open-field map, blocks of strips gathered into Furlongs, is evidence of this piecemeal progress, for the furlongs have very different sizes. Some are large and regular in shape, with neighbours of similar proportions and strips running in the same direction, thus suggesting that there was no

44

obstacle to steady clearance along this route. Other Furlongs are small and crabbed, having awkward corners, non-parallel sides; their strips change direction from one Furlong to the next, suggesting here that only small pieces of land were cleared at a time. On the edge of a parish these small clearances will probably be the final act in the conquest of the forest, the removal of the last trees as pressure of population pushed the fields to the margin. Nearer a village, such irregular Furlongs suggest difficulties and hesitancy. It would be interesting to take soil samples over a parish whose Furlong pattern is preserved in open-field maps and see whether there is any connection between the smooth run of furlongs across one part of the map and the qualities of easily-worked soil, allowing for the absence of artificial drainage and fertilizers in the old village.

III

The argument has moved too hurriedly, too eagerly invoking map evidence that is more than six hundred years later than the Braunston boundary charter. In these six hundred years the principal means of describing the countryside remained the written word, and when topographical information was committed to parchment there was usually a lawyer not far away. There is not a great deal of landscape painting in medieval literature: although something can be learned from the formalized illustrations of a manuscript. But if the modern historian is to use documents to people the medieval landscape with peasants, houses, fields, cottages, streets, roads, castles, monasteries and towns he must spend a good deal of his time among manuscripts which are concerned with legal and economic matters rather than poetry, romance or theology; and he will need to supplement the evidence of these documents by personal inquiry among the surviving buildings and earthworks of the medieval countryside.

Domesday Book, for example, is in some senses a geographical survey, and Professor Darby and his collaborators are demonstrating brilliantly how much of its detail can be turned into maps which reconstruct something of the landscape of 1086. But for the topography of an individual village Domesday Book proves disappointing: it lists the economic assets of a community without placing them in position. It is rather as if we were given half a dozen chess-pieces without any clue as to which square each one shall stand in. It is possible to see that White has a nice array of pawns with a knight and two bishops intact, and that Black has a queen and a rook, but the relative strength of the adversaries remains a mystery unless we know how far the pawns have advanced and how well protected the queen is.

Similarly, the abundant *extents* (or valuations) of medieval manors listed the assets which gave the lord of a manor his income, but there was no need for those who compiled an *extent* to say exactly where the assets lay within the parish. The statute of 1275 set out an imposing list of questions to be asked, and many of the extents drawn up on the death of royal tenants are full of detail: yet the questions they answer are economic rather than geographical.[20]

> There is in the manor a manor house, a dovecote, an orchard, a windmill, a kiln, a wood, some pasture, so much arable, so many peasants and so many acres of cultivated land. . . .

and there the description ends. It does not locate these figures and features. Rentals are equally tantalizing, for a house or holding is usually described only by its owner's name. A charter or deed which conveyed parcels of land from one person to another was forced to be more explicit about location, but here again it is not always possible to relate the details to any modern feature. If a block of pasture is said to abut on a churchyard or the castle ditch, and a block of arable strips to adjoin a windmill or the king's highway, then it may be possible to begin to place the pieces in the jigsaw. If the arable fields have directional names—North, South, Upper, Lower, Wood, Meadow—their approximate position may be hazarded. Sometimes modern field names can be linked to a field name in medieval rentals or deeds, but a village will need to have an unusual bulky survival of rentals and deeds before anything like a reconstruction of the village topography could be made from them.

Progress from a description in words to the pictorial descriptions of maps was dependent both on technical progress in surveying, and on the use of symbols. A map is a cunning abstraction which cannot afford the detail of a landscape painting. Unless it is on an immense scale it has to be economical in the words with which it labels its pictures. An interesting attempt to set down a whole parish on parchment is published for the first time in fig. 21, p. 204, and it will be

[20] *Statutes of the Realm*, i, 242.

seen that the labels occupy so much space that there is little room for anything else. This example is dated 1508. It is a great step forward from such a crude and crowded diagram to a plan such as that of Great Gidding[21] drawn in 1541, or the large-scale estate plans such as those made for All Souls College at the end of the century (Plates 3, 4, 6, 7 and 11).

The improvement in the surveyor's art in the sixteenth century was partly a matter of new instruments but also of increased demand and increased experience. The most active demand came from the proposals to re-assign the scattered strips of the open fields.[22] Small parcels of land were affected in every corner of a parish. Descriptions of boundaries were not enough; there had to be descriptions which could locate each of the scattered strips, often numbering four or five thousand. The area, the name of the occupying villager and the rent paid were also necessary information. The document which arose from this increased interest in the position and ownership of individual strips was the *terrier*, named from Latin *terra*, "land". A terrier was superior to a rental, for it was both economic and geographic. It placed the particular strip in the context of its furlong and field. When the open-field landscape is visited in the journeys of the next chapter it will be seen how—in turn—the surveyor's plan improved upon the verbosity of the terrier.

But it would give a false emphasis to suggest that the interests of Tudor landowners and surveyors were always centred upon boundaries within the open fields. All the great Elizabethan cartographers made estate plans in districts where the open fields—if there had ever been any—had long disappeared (e.g. Ralph Agas' Tangham sheep-walk[23] (c. 1576); Blagrave's Feckenham Forest;[24] the All Souls plans of Romney Marsh). The development of coal- and iron-mines in Elizabethan England also revived interest in the boundaries of the commons under which mineral rights were sought, and several early maps were commissioned in the course of such disputes.[25] The

[21] *V.C.H. Hunts.*, iii, 48.
[22] E. G. R. Taylor, "The Surveyor", *Ec. Hist. Rev.*, xvii (1947), 121-33; H. C. Darby, "The Agrarian Contribution to Surveying", *Geog. Journ.*, lxxxii (1933), 529-35.
[23] B. M. Egerton MSS. 2789B.
[24] Cited in E. G. R. Taylor, *art. cit.*, 133 fn.
[25] Benwell (1637): P.R.O. E178/5567; Cowpen (1598): P.R.O. E134/41 Eliz. Easter No. 19; these maps are reproduced in J. U. Nef, *Rise of the British Coal Industry* (1932), 305 and 307.

boundaries of the common pastures and the boundaries between township and township were being questioned for another reason: the same appetite for more pasture that was leading some Tudor landlords to convert their arable to grass was inducing others to overstock the old commons or to appropriate them to their now exclusive use. As one surveyor asked rhetorically,

> is not every Mannor a little common wealth, whereof the Tenants are the members, the Land the body, and the Lord the head?

It was as reasonable for a lord to wish to have an estate plan of this little commonwealth as for the Queen to encourage atlases and coastal plans of her kingdom.

Custom differed from village to village, and there was no ready-made, rule-of-thumb test that a lawyer could apply. It was necessary to inquire of Custom through its ancient oracles, the memories of the old men. They would be expected to declare on oath whether a particular piece of pasture lay within the commons, and whether the lord's right to turn beasts upon it had traditionally been subject to any limit. These were proper matters to be heard at a court of survey, a solemn statement by a sworn jury of villagers. In the earlier years of the sixteenth century the facts were elicited and recorded by a steward who put questions to the jury, examined evidences and from these compiled a survey of tenures.[26] In the later sixteenth century the courts of survey were often directed by professional surveyors, but the source of knowledge was still the ancient memories.

> The Lords Records and the Tennants informations, are the pillars of a survey

wrote John Norden in his *Surveiors Dialogue* (1607), a handbook[27] for the profession, which sought to instruct by means of a series of dialogues between a surveyor and typical characters encountered in the countryside: a sceptical landlord, a curious steward, a suspicious tenant and an industrious student.

The crude plan of Elford (Fig. 21, p. 204), drawn a century earlier than Norden's handbook, was occasioned by one of these disputes

[26] See Introd. to *Surveys of the Manors of . . . (the) Earl of Pembroke, 1631-2*, ed. E. Kerridge (Wilts. Arch. and Nat. Hist. Soc. Record Branch, ix) (1953).

[27] John Norden, *Surveiors Dialogue* (1618), 22; other quotations from Norden are from this edition.

over a piece of meadowland lying on the border between two manors. Attached to the plan is the formal agreement[28] of June, 1508 whereby the twenty-seven parties agreed to put an end to the contention by an arbitration, appealing to ancient memory and custom:

> as muche as it is meritorious, nedefull and one of the grettyst actes of charitie to sett and cause unitie and peace to be and contenewe where long tyme hath ben discord, debate and variance, and specially amonge men of honour, worship and grette power.

One of the claimants was of great local honour and great power, being the Bishop of Lichfield, but the verdict of the jury went against him, Willeford Meadow being declared

> tyme out of mynde of man (as we have herde our Anncestors and olde neybours say and report) parcell of the said Lordship of Elford.

It was sometimes necessary to determine how the land of a particular manor was scattered within a parish, for there were many villages which contained within their fields the lands of more than one manor. All Souls College, for example, as Plate 4 shows, was endowed with only one of the three manors in Maids Moreton parish. When a village was divided in this way it was of extreme importance to know which strips in the open fields went with which manor. When several adjacent villages acknowledged the same lord it was equally necessary to re-affirm the old boundaries, for different manors were governed by different customs of tenure, and these differences might be all-important in any conflict of will between lord and tenants. The abbey of Evesham owned the two adjacent manors of Badby and Newnham, near Braunston, and on their border was an area of common fields which must have been reclaimed from the waste by the two villages in co-operation, for the strips of the two manors were intermingled here. In 1526 the abbey divided this part of the manor among the tenantry, but the complex geography was too much for any division into individual parcels,[29] and even at the beginning of the present century the Ordnance Survey maps had abandoned any hope of weaving a parish boundary between Badby and Newnham, assigning a block of land as still "common to both parishes".

[28] Birm. Ref., Elford MSS. 55; another draft of the plan is *ibid.*, 49.
[29] G. Baker, *Northamptonshire* (1822), i, 253; *P.N. Northants.*, 11-13.

When a sixteenth-century surveyor came to record the bounds of a village (and other tenurial matters which do not concern us here), he usually had the assistance of a specially-summoned "court of survey", made up of local inhabitants of substance and experience. Since the usages of the past were an important issue, the old men of the village were essential witnesses. It was from old men, as we shall see in Chapter 7, that John Norden learned there had once been a village at East Lilling, and from old men that the surveyor Thomas Clerke learned of the foundations which showed where the town of Whatborough had once stood. There were, however, limits where age passed into senility. A witness in the Whatborough hearing, said to be one hundred and twenty years old, was described by another[30] as

> wavering, unconsistent and so unadvised, either by reason of age or lack of conscience.

Norden's handbook deals principally with the duties of a court of survey called for these purposes. It should begin, he wrote, with a description of the bounds.

> You shall duely and diligently set downe all the circuit buttes bounds and limits of the same . . . the best experienced tenants accompany [the Surveyor] for information and some of the youth that they may learn to know the bounds in time to come.

His readers were then referred to the authority of Proverbs 22:28

> Remove not the ancient landmark which thy fathers have set.

In Chapter 6 we shall be accompanying this same John Norden on a visit to the Northamptonshire market town of Higham Ferrers, whose parish contained a borough and a manor intermingled. In 1591 Norden came as a young assistant at a court of survey summoned by the Queen, a landlord wishing to know better her tenants and their tenures. Yet the record of that court begins not with a list of tenants but with a "bounder", that is a perambulation described in words, exactly in the manner of the old Saxon charters of Braunston, Badby and Newnham 600 years earlier. It begins:[31]

[30] All Souls, Whatborough MSS., No. 145, f. 77.
[31] P.R.O. DL42/117, f. 174.

| The bondaries of the said Burrow and mannor | That the bondarie and circuite of the said Burrow and mannor is thought moost fitt to begynn on the west parte thereof at a crosse called Mill Hole furlong which devideth this mannor and the mannor of Russenden [Rushden], and from the said crosse eastwarde to a place called dead woman's grave. . . . |

We are already among landmarks that had become fixed in the memories of the townspeople: a hole by the riverside where there had once been a mill; a cross erected to record the bounds of Rushden; a suicide's grave in open country, unhallowed no-man's-land. The whole circuit is too long to print here in full, but the landmarks can be set out as a list. From the suicide's grave the villagers passed along a *balk*, that is an unploughed lane at the edge of the arable fields; passing another cross they followed a road, leaving it to pass along more balks and headlands until they reached another cross, and from it to another grave, this time a man's. From a group of pits where stone or clay had been dug they followed a brook as far as some willows,

> and so contynnuinge the brooke according to the auncient water courst unto Annell Forde, therehence following the same brooke as it leadeth to the Queens river which divideth this mannor and Chelveston.

They followed the river Nene as far as a bridge, crossed a meadow to a pool, and then made for a "mere", or boundary-stone. From it they went to a ditch leading to some more willows, and then to a succession of mere-stones leading back to the old course of the river and so along the ends of the leys to the cross where the circuit had begun.

At Higham Ferrers the old and the new methods of surveying meet, for it was here (as we shall see in Chapter 6) that John Norden stayed to make one of his early town plans which, even in the rough sketch of the surviving manuscript (Plate 13), far surpasses the rough picture-plan of Elford (Fig. 21, p. 204). In its turn Norden's plan of Higham is surpassed by the estate-plans executed by his contemporaries for All Souls College and by his own later work for the Duchy of Cornwall. It is interesting to see that both Christopher Saxton and John Norden began with small-scale plans in which a whole county was reduced to less than one square foot, and only later turned to plans on the much larger scale necessary if the smaller property boundaries of the fields were to be shown. For topographical purposes even the rough town-plan is superior to a medieval town rental, and the rural estate-plans described in Chapter 3 are superior to a terrier. Even for the less-intricate task of defining a parish boundary, the plan had advantages over the old-fashioned "bounder".

IV

The final part of this chapter will move to Old Byland, a village in the south-west corner of the North Yorkshire moors, where Christopher Saxton was employed in 1598. Saxton's *Atlas* of county plans had been completed in 1579, and during the next twenty years he was at work on estate plans. In the north, plans of Manchester, Luddenden, the Isle of Axholme, Dewsbury and Notton are known from this period.[32] These large-scale plans demanded detailed measurements and the use of instruments; they were designed to show small landscape features. The small-scale county maps had needed only rivers and coastline with the silhouettes of church and a few houses to mark the villages; a few trees served for a wood or a park. But Saxton's plan of Old Byland[33] had to descend to the detail of sheep-cotes, single boundary stones, tumuli, earth banks and road-gates. We are back to the details which concerned Rogation processions and Saxon boundary charters.

In the northern uplands the arable fields of a village had rarely managed to spread so far as to reach the parish boundary on every side. In most cases the soil was poor or the slopes so steep that a plough would have been impossible to handle. It was on the open moorland that parish boundaries would meet. At Byland in 1598 the plan shows small fields and leys adjoining the open fields, but no more than half the parish could have been under the plough, even

[32] The first four plans mentioned are described by Sir George Fordham, *Geog. Journ.*, lxxxi (1928), 50; a copy of the Notton plan, together with original notes in Saxton's hand are among the Wentworth Woolley MSS., Brotherton Library, Leeds.

[33] P.R.O. MPB 32, formerly part of E178/2779; the formal progress of the suit is recorded in E123/24, ff. 167 and 283; a fragment of evidence has found its way to Hist. Mss. Comm., *Various Collections*, ii (1903), 109; the survey of 1539 is E315/397, f. 81.

allowing for the plots cultivated by the shepherds. George Hutton's evidence looked back to the days when his father had worked as the abbot of Byland's hind, with a flock of 500 sheep and twelve young oxen. As part of his wages he had been allowed to keep 100 sheep of his own, winter and summer, as well as six cows and their calves (until one year old). Elsewhere in the parish the abbot had 300 sheep, and in the next parish 1,700.

The moorland landscape was not an expanse of smooth Cotswold grassland. There was scattered timber, a reasonable quantity of which could be taken by every villager for house-building, plough-repair, fencing and fuel. One portion of the commons, actually the debatable ground of "Wetherlayers", was said by one witness to grow only thorns and crab-trees. Elsewhere the villages had the right to cut turves. The abbot's hind was allowed to have any corn he could raise on "three little fields", presumably a small allotment of land near the sheep-cote.

When the moorland above a village was vast and the flocks small, there was no need for too precise definition of boundaries. Indeed, there are still some areas marked on the Ordnance Survey maps as possessing no boundaries. Land is common to two or three adjacent parishes (e.g. Allendale and West Allen (Cumb.); Stanhope and Wolsingham (Co. Durham); Hawksker, Stainsacre and Fylingdales (Yorks. N.R.). Here the old toleration has been undisturbed by scarcity of pastures and quarrels over stints. Here shepherds and their flocks have grazed without rancour. But at Old Byland in 1598 the craving for pasture disturbed the flocks and set the lawyers hunting among documents. Shepherds came to blows, and boundary stones were set up one day and pulled down the next night.

The roots of the dissension lay deeper than a mere disagreement between competing neighbours, such as might have been met with anywhere in England at the time. Disagreement was fomented by the departure of an old landlord and the arrival of two newcomers. In 1538 the estates of the abbot of Byland had been confiscated by the king, and when the estate in Old Byland passed to two different grantees all was set for a clash of wills, the more angry for being also a clash of evidence.[34] Before 1538 villagers might—and did—differ on the question of where the township boundaries ran, but so long as both Old Byland and its neighbour, Murton, were held by the

[34] *V.C.H. Yorks., N.R.*, ii, 3 *sqq.*

same lord the matter was in abeyance; it might serve to set the old men arguing on an idle evening or the young men wrestling at the sheep-shearing feast: but herdsmen did not come to blows and attornies did not finger their briefs.

In 1598 the rivals at law were Sir Edward Wotton and Sir William Bellassis. Sir Edward owned the greater part of Old Byland, having

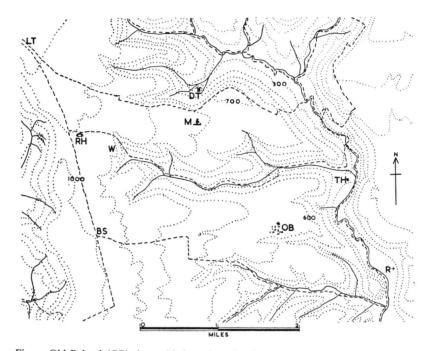

Fig. 4. Old Byland (OB), its parish bounds and neighbours. TH: Tile House, the first site of Byland village; R: Rievaulx Abbey; DT and M, the depopulated settlements of Dale Town and Murton; W: Wetherlayers, disputed ground of 1598; BS: boundary stone; LT: Lord's Tongue; RH: Round Hill (cf. Plates 1-2).

inherited it from his father-in-law, the original grantee of Henry VIII. The neighbouring parish of Murton was owned by Sir William, and the contention would not have arisen had not Sir William also owned an estate within Old Byland parish called Wethercotes, which had served the abbot in his day as a home farm. In 1538 this property had not gone with the rest of Old Byland but had been bought by Sir William's father. (See fig. 4.)

Sir Edward claimed that Bellassis had taken over a piece of ground called *Wetherlayers* (there were variant spellings) to form a bridge between his two estates. This ground, claimed Sir Edward, had always been part of Old Byland manor and enjoyed as common by his tenants. This ground, claimed Sir William, was part of Murton manor and never grazed by Byland men. The law-suit began by Sir Edward putting in a statement of his case in the form known as an English Bill; Sir William made a counter-statement. These two documents were considered by the barons of the Court of Exchequer, which probably accepted jurisdiction because the land in question had formed part of the monastic estates acquired by the Crown and administered by the Court of Augmentations until that Court was absorbed by the Exchequer in 1554.

London was more than two hundred miles from Old Byland, a long journey for witnesses. The Elizabethan judges were willing to accept sworn depositions taken before a Commission sitting in the provinces. Several thousand membranes of these depositions survive in the Public Record Office, and to one bundle of such questions and answers was attached the Saxton plan. Several other bundles of depositions in the Elizabethan Exchequer are accompanied by plans which assisted the judges in following the complications of local geography when they were reading the depositions and meeting an array of minor place-names. It will be recalled that both John Norden and Christopher Saxton executed work for the Duchy of Lancaster; and the Duchy Court—where cases involving Duchy tenants were heard—has, if anything, more early plans than the Exchequer; perhaps because a close concern with revenue from the estates had brought the Duchy officials to early recognition of the utility of surveys and surveyors.

These plans were not evidence put in by one party to favour his case but a record of common ground, a legal metaphor particularly appropriate in disputes of the Old Byland type. When the Court of Exchequer made an order in July, 1598 for

a perfect plott of the places and grounds mentioned in the pleadings

it was to be

at the equall chardge of both the said parties

and on the map itself the local Commissioners attested that

55

Christopher Saxton as well by the consent and apointment of the Commissioners and of the Solicitors of the parties plaintyff and defendant did make this Platt and was sworne that the same was truelie made to the best of his Skill.

In the title of the map,

A plat of the parishe of Old Bylande

Saxton noted that it was "per sacramentum"—on oath—and explained how he had tried to bring out the three main matters at issue:

All the Inclosed groundes are colored red; the commons are colored with yelowe; the Defendants bounder betwixt Oldbyland and Morton is drawn with a grene lyne; and the confines left white. Made by Christopher Saxton. Anno Domini 1598.

The whole plan, on the scale of 8 inches to a mile, measures 16 inches by 36 inches and is too large to reproduce here. Only a small portion is shown in Plate 1, but it is the section of the parish where the boundary dispute was hottest.

On the east, the bounds of Old Byland could not be disputed; the river Rye flowed through the Ryedale meadows and divided Byland from Rievaulx. On most of the northern and southern boundary there were tributary streams also running in deep dales, *Cairedale* and *Nettledale*. A third dale, *Pipedale*, led up from Ryedale to the plateau on which were situated the village, the arable fields and most of the pastures. Here, Saxton had no longer to crowd his dale sides with little trees; he could reach for the bolder and more sweeping colours of red and yellow for the enclosed ground and the common pastures; on the open stretches of the arable fields which surrounded the village itself he had ample room to write in the names of the three Fields: *East, West* and *Landende*.

Saxton's plan was created by the marriage of field-measurement and the evidence of witnesses. From instrumental measurement and personal observation it got its woods, streams, common fields and pastures, but the Commissioners had gathered evidence from the oldest inhabitants. Saxton must have been present at its taking or have been given access to it, for his map is more than a collection of conventional signs and stylized drawings. When drawings and colours were inadequate to express the contending allegations he had to take refuge in prose:

56

The high Leies which the Plaintyff claimeth to be parcell of the Demanes

The place where they washe shepe

The new feilde somtyme in tillage as the Plaintyff saith and now lying common

The wetherliars so called by the plaintyff, and Morton wetherlaines and morton thornes by the defendant

The supposed bounder by the defendant being the edge of the browe.

The Commissioners and the witnesses had assembled at Byland Abbey on August 24, 1598. It is useful to pause and see who they were and what they had to say, for the method by which topographical information was laid before the Court was soon to be outmoded by the work of those who followed in Saxton's profession. The evidence was elicited by putting two sets of questions to each witness. One set was prepared for the plaintiff and one for the defendant, and each sought to elicit facts which would support his case. The answers were written down by a clerk, read over to witnesses and attested by them. After the Commissioners had added their certificate and signatures the bundle of parchments was sent off to London.

The evidence of nine witnesses has survived, and since the first questions put in the interrogatory were to establish credentials, we know who they were and where they came from. The first noticeable feature is the age of the witnesses. Four were over seventy and two others were over sixty. The youngest was forty-five. It was through such men that the old traditions could be recovered. When old-established customs were in dispute, who better to declare the old traditions than Christopher Kilvington (seventy-seven) a husbandman from Boltby, the village whose pastures stretched up the side of the scarp to greet Byland along its western flank? or Robert Storey (seventy-six) of Nunnington, whose memory went back to 1536, two years before the suppression of the abbey by the shell of which the witnesses were gathered?

The father of George Hutton was born at Wethercotes and had been the abbot's herdsman there for fifty years. Young George, now seventy-one and a yeoman from Helmsley, had helped in the work. The youngest witness, John Metcalfe (forty-five) had lived for twenty-one years at Great Murton, the Bellassis manor, so that his comparative youth was balanced by his specialized knowledge. John Belwood, a husbandman of seventy-one, had come from Hunsingore, twenty-five miles away: he was born in Boltby, and had become the miller of Byland in 1538. He was later appointed bailiff of the manor, and in 1564 was given the tenancy of a farm there which in 1598 his son held as tenant of Sir Edward Wotton. Christopher Garbut, a labourer who lived in a cottage above Sutton Bank, retailed stories his grandfather had told him; in Queen Mary's time (1552-58) he had himself driven cattle over the Byland pastures; he was now a labourer living at Whitestone Cliff (where the Ordnance Map marks Garbutt Farm, presumably named after other members of his family). The witness who had come farthest was John Blanchard of York, a freeman silkweaver of London; he had been away making his fortune too long to be able to have personal knowledge of Byland, but from 1554 to 1568 his father had been bailiff of the manor.

What of their evidence? No summary can do justice to the patriarchal prose of the depositions. They had no student dissipations to recall in the fashion of Justice Shallow and Justice Slender in a Gloucestershire orchard, but their prose is of the same vintage and prolixity. The dispute turned so largely on boundaries that the evidence deals mainly with the location of particular fields, the position of dykes and ditches, the customary rights of common and the position of boundary stones. The important details were translated into Saxton's plan. In the course of the evidence the witnesses often turned aside to mention some incident in the past which had stayed in their memory and helped them to remember the answer to a question; these asides have been drawn upon for the quotations and incidental description.

On the matters at issue, the evidence favoured the plaintiff, and helps also to explain how the defendant had conceived a counter-claim of pasture for his sheep in the eastern half of Old Byland although his manor of Wethercotes lay in the west: in the time of the abbot, whose flocks grazed both east and west, there had been limited common rights which cut across the Dyke dividing the manors. On the east of the dyke the tenants of the western manor had common and on the west the tenants of the eastern manor had reciprocal rights. The rights were limited to windrake, that is passage to a drinking place, and the witnesses were positive that flocks and herds had never been shepherded over the Dyke, which was appropriately named Lamb's Dyke. In the picturesque phrase of the witness George Hutton, they had never been "staff-herded".

In the north and west of the parish the witnesses agreed that there had been no boundary dispute before the sale of the monastic estate. John Belwood

> knoweth the place where one stone now standeth which is called Murton stone, and he knew the grounde before there was any stone set there; that one Thomas Seysworth was the first that did cause that stone to be set there, which is about 48 yeres ago [i.e. *c.* 1558].

This stone will be seen on Saxton's map in Plate 1. It lay about half-way along the row of stones on this western boundary. Had the defendant's claim to Wetherlayers been sound, it would have been the first stone in Murton.

Belwood's evidence describes how a perambulation of the parish had tried to counter these claims.

> Mr. Mennell being Steward of Old Bylande (who was afterward serjeant at the lawe) went the bounders with the tennants when Bartholomew Storye was Bailiff of Bylande, and found faulte with the setting of that stone and pulled it downe; and it was afterwards sett up; and then one Pybus pulled it downe; and then it was long tyme down and set up again, and after that [Belwood] pulled it downe when he was Bailiff to Sir William Pickering, but since it was set up again.

Belwood then described the whole circuit of the parish bounds in detail,

> as he hath often been with the tennants of Old Bylande

and the deposition takes on the character of the Higham bounder and the Braunston boundary charter.

It was the line of bounder stones which proved fatal to the defendant's case. Saxton records these on the map without any qualifying "suppose". The stones formed a straight line (where the parish boundary still runs) parallel to the steep edge of the Hambleton Hills. The stones began at a "rownde hill" on Hesker Dyke where Old Byland meets Murton. Dyke, Hill and Bounder-stones were all man-made features. The Dyke (Hesketh Dyke of the O.S. plan) is a long barrow, shown in Plate 2; while the Stones marked the bounds of the parish across the open moorland where there were no convenient prehistoric earthworks to utilize. There were no natural features in the way of valleys and crags in this sector, which is an almost level plateau along which the old ridge-road from York to Yarm ran. The nine stones were planted at intervals along the 2,400 yards of the western boundary of Old Byland. Some of them might be moved by night, but not all, and they must have been difficult for Bellassis to explain away. The verdict of the Court is not, in fact, known, and it may never have been given. I guess that the defendant retreated in the face of the evidence: the Decree Book of the Court records the arrival of the depositions and map in London on June 25, 1599, but no judgment is entered in the succeeding pages. I cannot think that the defendant entertained a high opinion of surveyors and maps.

I visited Old Byland in May, 1951 and in September, 1955. At my first visit, on foot, I came southwards from Murton, the seat of the defendant, Sir William Bellassis. Murton is an empty township, high and windswept. There is no village, but a large group of farm-buildings and cottages. A witness in 1598 described how Bellassis had pulled down a second farm at Cold Murton. The nickname Cold appears again at Cold Kirby, Old Byland's southern neighbour, which occupies as exposed a position as Murton. Less than half a mile north of Murton was Dale Town, a hamlet which had been completely destroyed by its Tudor landlords when they turned its fields from arable to sheep pasture.[35] (Fig. 4, p. 54.)

In 1598 there were eighteen houses in the village of Old Byland, and it is no larger to-day. It nestles in a deeper, warmer valley than Murton and Kirby, and the village was out of sight as I came down the track which enters Saxton's map in the centre of the northern boundary at Cockwathyate (Cock-ford-gate), dropping steeply from the "gate" and winding down into Carrdale. A little to the east of the ford in 1598 was

the place where they washe shepe

and, lower down, *Cairedale mill*, and also a fulling mill, *Walkemill-howse*, with a cleared space on the hillside above it, *Tenterbanke*, where the cloth was stretched.

[35] M. W. Beresford, "The Lost Villages of Yorks.", *Yorks. Arch. Journ.* xxxviii (1954), 297.

From the mills the dale broadens and joins the main valley of the Rye. Very near the junction, *Tylehowse* is shown on Saxton's map, and the broken ground near the present farmhouse has had a curious history. The original village of Byland was here; that is, the village where Domesday Book recorded in 1086 three ploughteams, seven families, a priest and a wooden church.[36] When the abbey of Byland was founded in 1143 the Cistercians were given a large block of land, and following their usual quest for solitude they moved the village away from the valley when they began to build the monastery. They chose a site near the head of Pipedale at a place already known as *Stutekelde*. This is probably the "keld" or spring which Saxton shows a little to the south of the village as "Kell Trough", a store-basin gathering the water as it comes from the hillside. The new village was given the old name of Byland. The Norman work in the village church must date from this period, although the inscribed Saxon sundial may have been brought up from the old site. The neat plan of the village around a central green is probably the result of this re-planting of the community. This is not the end of the story of migrations, for the abbey was to move in its turn. Rievaulx abbey was founded only two miles further down Ryedale, and in 1147 the friction between the two houses made the monks of Byland seek another site, five miles to the south, where the abbey ruins now stand. The move made a New Byland, and gave the prefix "Old" to the moorland village; historically, it is merely "Older", for "Oldest" Byland stood in the Ryedale meadows.[37]

From Tile House it is possible to scramble up again to the higher ground where Twelve Penny Flatt and the other open fields appear on Saxton's plan. From the stone-walled fields which have replaced them there is a good view towards the cluster of houses which make up Old Byland village and to the moorland pastures beyond. In 1955 I found that the track which led through the West Field to the pastures had become a grass lane unfit for cars; I had to take a circuitous route unknown to Saxton, the modern metalled road through Cold Kirby to the edge of the Hambleton Hills, and then back northwards along what Saxton called

Hammelton rase being the high way betwixt York and Yarum.

[36] *V.C.H. Yorks.*, ii, 186, 257 and 314.
[37] Sir William Dugdale, *Monasticon Anglicanum* (ed. of 1846), v, 343 and 351.

Here the modern road has been confined within stone walls, and has only a narrow verge. Medieval and Tudor traffic took a less confined course, seeking not only firm, dry passage but also a track not churned up and rutted by previous travellers. Many of these twisting tracks can be seen intermingled in the rough grassland to the west of the modern road.

The road leaves Old Byland parish at its north-west corner where *Hesker Dyke* crossed the *Yarum waye*. The prehistoric ditch and banks of Hesketh Dyke are well preserved on the east of the road. They are grass- and heather-covered, and the southern bank now bears a field-wall upon it. *The rownde hill* of Saxton's plan is the barrow to which the O.S. gives the name of Silver Hill, embodying the common local tradition that precious metals can be dug out of these burial mounds. The barrow is shown in Plate 2; no boundary stone could be found standing, but since the stone wall of the field crosses the mound it is possible that the stone has been incorporated in it.

I was not able to photograph the Bellassis Farm at Wethercote, but the name is retained by some buildings a little to the north. The most interesting survival, and an unexpected one, lay in the grass verge of the modern road. I was watching the side of the road in order not to miss the point where a long wall brings the parish boundary in from the east. My eye was caught by a gleam of grey in the grass at this point. When the grass was pulled away it revealed a "bounder-stone", at the site of Saxton's "first bounder-stone". It stood out 18 inches from the soil and was deeply embedded. It had no ancient inscription, but it served a modern purpose of which Christopher Saxton would have approved. On it, the field-surveyors of the Ordnance Survey have carved their broad arrow and the horizontal line which make up the "bench-mark", the indication of a measured altitude and a fixed point in space. In my left hand I held a photostat copy of the four parchment sheets

made by Christopher Saxton anno domini 1598 per sacramentum

and in my right hand Sheet SE58 of the 1:25,000 plan

printed and published by the Director General of the Ordnance Survey, Chessington, Surrey, 1954.

The lichened stone was a bridge across three hundred and fifty-six years.

3

A JOURNEY TO ELIZABETHAN VILLAGES

MAIDS MORETON, BUCKS.
SALFORD, BEDS.

Certes, I would gladly set down all . . . the villages in England and Wales . . . but as yet I cannot come by them in such order as I would.

WILLIAM HARRISON, *The Description of Britaine* (1577), book ii, chapter vii.

Chapter Three

A JOURNEY TO ELIZABETHAN VILLAGES

I

THE previous chapter has shown how the new *plot*, or large-scale plan, began to supplant the verbal description of boundaries. During the medieval centuries it was at the boundaries of a village territory that disputes were likely to arise, and if memory and a simple written *bounder* were sufficient to record those boundaries, it is not surprising that there were so few attempts to picture houses and fields in the same period: for there were few occasions when any major revision of the village features were projected. Houses decayed, and were rebuilt within the same crofts; streets ran where streets had always run; the church and the churchyard were stolidly placed as if to face eternity; the windmill saw no reason to change its position so long as winds still blew from the same quarter; the watermills were unlikely to move until streams failed them; and if—most fickle of all the buildings—the manor house sought a new position suited to changing tastes, then its position was of little interest to anyone except its owner.

Yet it was in villages and fields rather than along boundaries that the surveyors learned to master their art. We have seen that medieval documents rarely attempted a full description of every piece of land in a parish; and the thousands of small, scattered parcels of land shown in any Elizabethan open-field map emphasize the complexity of the task when words were the only tools. The same complexity also demanded considerable skill in measurement and instrumentation from those who were learning the new craft of Tudor map-making, and the acquisition of skills and the development of instruments took time. Even so, the big steps forward took place almost within a generation. One may see the revolution beginning in the map of Great Gidding[1] made in 1541: this plan encompassed the

---

[1] Reproduced, *V.C.H. Hunts.*, iii, 48.

houses and gardens of the village with commendable accuracy but it did not aspire to show every strip within the open fields. In the fifteen-eighties the plans made for the Warden of All Souls College show the cartographers undeterred by the sight of the open fields, and every strip has its occupant's name written on it; in the case of the College's own properties the area of the strip is often given. There are *terriers* of Maids Moreton in 1534 and 1592 among the College muniments, but with the maps all the details of position, size and ownership which had previously needed the verbosity of a long roll or bundle of parchments were now concisely stated, and the whole disposition of the estates lay before their owners' eyes.

In the sixteenth century the lords of manors were no longer passive spectators of the economic scene, and there were many incentives to make a thorough revision of the uses to which an estate had traditionally been put. The great inflation made landlords anxious to revise old contracts and step up rents; the good market for grain and meat in the towns made them anxious to reorganize their estates, to lower costs and to increase output; in southern England timber was at a premium; in the north the development of coal and iron made landlords look with increased interest at land which might carry mineral rights with it; while in the first half of the century the cloth industry's growing demand for wool had helped to swing thousands of acres over from corn to grass.

There are very few estate plans which are early enough to coincide with the great sheep-enclosures, but the Elizabethan plans mirror all the other projects which have been mentioned. Some were commissioned by landlords anxious to develop their estates and some by landlords who were nervous of their tenants' claims; some were the result of litigation and some were designed to avoid it: but, whatever the motive, the plan had to descend to the smallest parcels of land, the smallest differences of tenure and the most accurate record of occupancy. No established feature was immune. The stability described in a previous paragraph was challenged. Old-established village houses were allowed to decay or were pulled down; streets and gardens became part of the pastures; windmills were pulled down when grass replaced corn in the fields; the watermill could be harnessed to serve a clothier as a fulling-mill or a gig-mill; the manor house could move away into a grassy parkland; even the church was not immune. When the Nottinghamshire historian, Thoroton, rode

66

the county in the 1670s he saw the church of Thorpe-le-Glebe turned into a shepherd's cottage and an ale-house, and Shakespeare's Pericles spoke of the grazier who had swallowed the village—

church, steeple, bells and all.

Not all landlords had the will or the legal security which were necessary to engineer a complete removal of a village; for every one depopulator there were dozens of landlords whose ambition stretched no further than a consolidation of scattered holdings and a more economical use of his land. Yet, whatever his intentions, a landlord would find the disposition of his open-field lands of most immediate interest, and some of the finest Elizabethan plans were concerned with open-field villages.

In the period 1570-1620 the surveyors were producing not only estate plans for private commissions but also county and town plans for publication. We shall be examining some of the latter in Chapter 6. The surveyors were also propagandists and advertisers, concerned to assuage popular fears and make the world aware of the benefits which came by employing them. In the fashion of the day their atlases and county surveys were prefaced by self-justifications in which some general principles were appealed to. A few surveyors went further and published handbooks for the instruction of others and for the persuasion of potential patrons. One of these was William Folkingham, surveyor for the diocese of Lincoln; his *Feudigraphia* was published in 1610. Its title page has the persuasiveness of a modern book-jacket.

> Very pertinent to be perused of all whom the Right Revenewe Estimation, Farming, Occupation, Manurance, Subduing, Preparing and Imploying of Arable, Meadow and Pasture, and all other plots doe concern . . . and for Purchasers Exchangers or Sellers of Land and for every other Interesse in the Profits or Practice derived from their compleate survey. . . .

and in the Preface, written at his Lincolnshire home, Folkingham boldly sets out the virtues of map-making:

> The Beame and Chaine balke no Truthes nor blaunch Un-truths; the Empirick or the Methodist which is the better Phisician? Take away Number, Weight, Measure you exile Iustice and reduce and haile-up from Hell the olde and odious Chaos of Confusion.

On the title page of another handbook of the period, Aaron Rathborne's *Surveyor*, published in 1616, the social value of the surveyor's craft is raised even higher. An engraving shows a surveyor treading on two other men, one of them ass-headed and the other crowned with a coxcomb.

In the pages which follow we shall visit two Midland villages, Maids Moreton (Bucks.) and Salford (Beds.) taking with us the large-scale plans made by Thomas Langdon in 1596 for All Souls College, Oxford, the proprietor of these two manors. Warden Hovenden, a careful steward of the College properties, had been early convinced of the value of employing a man with a beam and chain, the "methodist" who could set down the "number, weight and measure" of the College estates. As a result the College possesses four portfolios of unsurpassed Elizabethan estate plans.[2]

In our visits to Maids Moreton and Salford the aim will be to take the Elizabethan plans as a point of departure in two directions. In one direction these plans point backwards to the days when the characteristic pattern of open fields was being created by successive generations of villagers. In the other direction they look forward to the village and fields of the present day as the observant traveller sees them and the camera records.

In each case, the journeys are to fields in the South Midlands. Now, if the only result of studying these two plans and these two villages was a deeper understanding of one Bedfordshire and one Buckinghamshire village, its appeal would be severely limited. The purpose of studying these rare surviving plans is to equip the reader for other journeys into villages and fields where no early open-field map was made or where none has survived. Unhappily the majority of villages fall in this category, and although open-field maps continue to come to light in public and private archives there is no reason to think that the number will ever be greatly augmented.

In the plan-less villages it is likely that some vestiges of the medieval field landscape will have survived, just as they have survived at Salford and Maids Moreton. Comparisons between the modern fields and the maps will enable features to be recognized, and their recognition in such well-authenticated surroundings may

---

[2] Hovenden Maps: All Souls College Library; separate roll-maps of Padbury (Bucks.) and Whatborough (Leics.).

help their recognition where there are no maps or equivalent documents to elucidate the history of a village and its fields.

Equally clearly, Salford is not Bedfordshire, Maids Moreton is not Buckinghamshire, and these two counties are not the whole Midlands. Nor are the Midlands all England. In other parts of these two counties, and in other parts of the country, the open fields took different forms in response to local conditions. In some parts of the country, local conditions of soil, vegetation and climate seem to have militated against the establishment of this type of agriculture in any form; even in villages of the open-field type there will always be small local variations from the general pattern shown at Salford and Maids Moreton; in other parts of England the process which, in these two villages, created open fields, stopped short of completion. This halfway house situation will not be dealt with in this book. The purpose of the two journeys which follow is to examine a typical open-field landscape, but the account of the evolution of the open-field landscape may serve as a basis for those who wish to study further the many local variants.

In the previous chapter a general picture was given of villages and fields which were multiplying in number in the centuries after the Anglo-Saxon invasions. The countryside was becoming more crowded, with more houses, more men, more ploughs, more stock and fewer trees. The life of the medieval villager has often been described in words; to see it in pictures one must turn to the illustrations in medieval manuscripts, to the chance details of sculpture or to the landscapes of Continental painters where the medieval fields survived longer than in England. With only a few minor alterations one can see it surviving in Europe still: the German villages near the source of the Danube and the Austrian villages between Vienna and Salzburg have preserved most of the features of medieval villages and fields.

In England, the large-scale plans of the late sixteenth century came in time to record this same landscape, some of them on the very eve of its transformation to the familiar modern landscape of hedged fields. The Tudor plans have this double interest: they look back to an agriculture that had been a thousand years in the making; and they carry obvious signs that the traditional forms were already being challenged.

In their backward look, these sixteenth-century plans are good guides to the open-field landscape of earlier centuries simply because the period between 1350 and 1550 had brought so little change to those particular aspects of open-field farming with which maps are concerned, that is, its geography. The economics and social structure of the village had changed radically in these two hundred years: but in the villages which have maps like those of Salford and Maids Moreton the surveyors were confronted with a field pattern which was virtually unchanged from that of 1350. Thus, the map makers were often the agents of change and the recorders of what was about to be changed. In aiding the revolution they have preserved for us a picture of the *ancien régime*.

II

There is no record of when settlers first made a permanent village at Moreton. No Anglo-Saxon boundary charters are known, but the village was probably at least two or three hundred years old when it was recorded in Domesday Book (1086). Its name simply means "the settlement (*tun*) at the *mor*", and *mor* has the sense of "swampy ground" or "fen". Obviously there would have been no village in the swamp: it was a piece of near-by wet land which gave the settlers and their neighbours a way of distinguishing their village from the next. The village itself is on high and dry ground looking down over the upper valley of the Ouse, whose meadows form the eastern part of the parish, and over an unnamed small tributary which forms the northern boundary of the parish. Either of these could have provided the swampy ground in the days before drainage.

In this part of Buckinghamshire the villages are a little more than a mile apart, giving parishes with areas of from 1,000 to 1,500 acres. Those families who had settled by "the swamp" eventually annexed to themselves some 1,360 acres. On the east of them was the community which had settled at Foxcote (*the fox-infested cottages*); on the north were those who had their centre at Akeley (*Aca's clearing*) and on the south the *hamm* (or village) of Bucc's people had settled on a narrow hill surrounded on three sides by the Ouse. In the late tenth century this village of Buckingham was enlarged and fortified as a borough, the capital of the county.[3]

On the west of Moreton the country became less attractive to the

[3] *P.N. Bucks.*, 40, 45 and 60.

Anglian settlers. The broad belt of green on the modern map indicates the remains of Whittlewood Forest, a belt of rough country where the county based on Buckingham met the county based on Northampton. Not all the woods in Stowe Park are the descendants

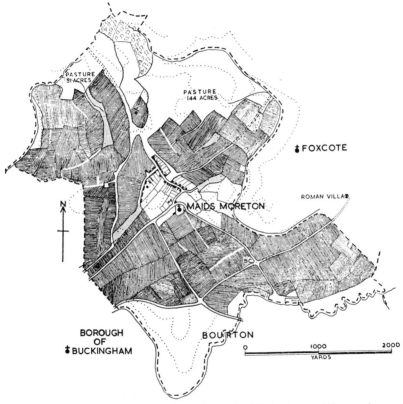

Fig. 5. Maids Moreton in 1596, redrawn from the All Souls plan. The meadow and pasture are left white and the slades shaded grey. BC: *Balles Crosse*; contours (dots) at 25-foot intervals.
N.B. The fine lines indicate the open-field Furlongs; the direction and size of the strips could not be shown accurately on this scale: but see Plates 3-4.

of medieval forest, but even in 1596, when Warden Hovenden commissioned the map of Moreton,[4] there was a block of woodland in the north-west corner of the parish nearest to Stowe (Plate 3).

[4] Hovenden Maps: portfolio i, Nos. 3-7; other documents cited are listed in Martin.

71

Some part of this survives. Near to it on the map was a patch of ground where the surveyor, Thomas Langdon, wrote

iiij ac[res], wherein the tennante hath the Firres and bushes,

and on the other side of the wood was a large stretch of pasture, 144 acres in area, ominously named *The Fursan*. This was rough ground which easily went back to furze. It was pasture probably because the ploughmen would have none of it. In 1596 it was the *Heardes Pasture*, and 51 acres of *Almeade Leaes* on the south side of the wood had also passed into the care of the herdsmen.

If we add *A gorsye Close* of 5 acres, a total of just over 200 acres (or about one-sixth of the parish) was under wood or grass in 1596. The ten strips marked in *Almeade Leaes* suggest that the plough had once been in this rough quarter of Moreton, probably in the hungrier days of the early thirteenth century. But the Anglian settlers who had first come to settle here had not come in order to cut timber and run swine in the woods; nor to find grass for herds to watch their flocks. The Angles and the Saxons, like the Scandinavian invaders after them, were hungry for plough-land to feed their families. Their achievement was to make plough-land out of the forest, and the thousand acres of Moreton fields in the plan of 1596 bear witness to what successive generations and races of settlers had been able to make of it.

In 1086 the record of Domesday Book shows that the parish of Moreton was divided among three manorial lords, with five, four and two ploughs respectively.[5] This tripartite ownership did not affect the agricultural life of the village; the land of the three manors was intermingled in the fields. It also explains why there are blank areas on the map of 1596. In 1442 the College had been given only one of the three manors, that known as *Grenehamme's*, the name of the owner in 1432; where adjacent plots of land belonged to these other two manors the cartographer of 1596 left his map blank. Thus most of the right-hand (or east) side of the main street in Plate 4 is blank, although there are several Elizabethan buildings still to be seen. One other consequence of the tripartite division was that there were three manor houses. The "scite" of the house belonging to the manor which the College acquired is shown on Langdon's plan on

[5] *V.C.H. Bucks.*, i, 219, 250 and 275.

the right of the church. The other two were along the village street, where the map is blank.

The map shows twenty-four houses but the empty spaces make it impossible to know how many houses there were in Elizabethan Moreton. In 1086 there were twenty families, and the eleven recorded plough-teams may well have been tilling already more than 1,000 acres; and the whole parish, it will be remembered, is only 1,365 acres in area. The meadowland down by the river was reckoned to provide enough fodder for eight plough-teams in 1086, and also down by the river at that time—as in 1596—was the village mill.

Nearly all the remaining area of the Moreton plans shows a pattern which is quite different from the little trees of the map-maker's woodland or the tinted open spaces of his pasture-ground. The pattern is made up of some 4,000 small units, for which the modern word is *strips*. The word used in the College terriers of 1534 and 1592 is simply *acre*, and it is the double meaning of this word which makes it preferable to call the pieces of land *strips*. The word "acre" to an Elizabethan meant a unit of area, roughly the modern 4,840 square yards; but it also meant simply one of these strips. This double meaning gives trouble to-day, for it naturally leads people to assume that a strip, such as one sees on the Moreton map or reads about in medieval documents, was one acre in area. In fact, strips varied a good deal in size, as a glance at Plates 3 and 4 will immediately show, and the average area was nowhere near an acre: only about one-third of an acre. It is possible to take the scale of perches (each of $16\frac{1}{2}$ feet) which Thomas Langdon provided on each sheet of his map and measure the strips to see whether this is true. Fortunately the surveyor saved both us and the College time by writing in the area of some of the strips. Thus, in the blocks of strips nearest to the wood the areas are given as

1 rood 17 perches	(i.e. $\frac{57}{160}$ or ·356 acres)
1 rood 20 perches	(·375 acres)
1 rood 22 perches	(·38 acres)
1 rood 3 perches	(·27 acres)
1 rood 23 perches	(·39 acres)
1 rood 20 perches	(·375 acres)
1 rood 35 perches	(·47 acres)

73

The acre-which-was-not-an-acre sounds very peculiar to modern ears. Yet words meaning both a measurement and a thing are still in use to-day and create no trouble. How many readers have feet which are a foot? In fact, Elizabethans also used other words for a strip: *land* occurs frequently, and another word, to which we shall soon return, is *ridge* or *rigg*. In the Latin of medieval documents the word is *selion*.

The second thing the eye notices, even in the most casual glance at an open-field map such as Moreton's, is that the strips do not everywhere run in the same direction; they seem to be gathered in bundles. In each bundle the strips may not all be quite the same length but they do share the same direction. My friend Dr. W. R. Mead has hit on the phrase "the grain of the strips" to describe the direction in which they run.[6] So, in Plate 3, the grain is usually from the top of the map to the bottom; but near the wood it is different. In Plate 4, away from the woods, the grains are varied, while at Salford (Plate 7) they also vary in different parts of the map.

A bundle of strips sharing the same grain was described in Langdon's day by a word which also rings ambiguously in our own day. The map shows that each had a name, *such-and-such-Furlong*. Here again it is a Furlong-which-is-not-necessarily-a-furlong, but fortunately the average length of a Furlong does often come out at near 220 yards: the map, of course, shows some shorter and some longer than this. A little arithmetic will reveal that the strips which were about one-third of an acre in area and 220 yards long must have been just over 7 yards wide. (7 yards × 220 yards = 1,540 square yards or about one-third of 4,840 square yards, the acre.)

The Furlongs were all named, and many of these names are unchanged from the earliest surviving records. It was necessary to use their name in describing a strip which was being sold or let out; the village steward would use them in his record of how much grain had been sown each autumn and spring; the parson used them in setting down on paper the number and location of the strips which made up his glebe estate. The Furlong names are sometimes so corrupted and twisted by use that, when they first appear in writing, they seem meaningless and need the attention of a philologist. Many others are like village names, in that they embody either a personal name of

[6] W. R. Mead, "Ridge and Furrow in Bucks.", *Geog. Journ.*, cxx (1954), 34-42; see also *ibid.*, cxxi (1955), 125-26.

some long-dead worthy or the name of some distinguishing physical feature.

Altogether there are thirty-four Furlong names on Langdon's map. The majority are recognizable and meaningful at sight.

Stone hill	Marl pit
Wind mill	Brooke
Waterslade	Meade

There are some named after the road or field-track which passed by:

Causeway	Wood way	Portway
Ridgeway	Hollow-way	

and one riverside Furlong was called Buckford, presumably from the ford of the same *Bucc* who had given his name to Buckingham itself. There were several pairs of Furlongs distinguished by their length.

Long Flaxlands	Short Flaxlands
Long Chadwell	Short Chadwell

and several named after trees which must once have been cleared from them or which stood at their edge

Oakentree
Elder

and the name of another, *Copped More*, carried the memory of copped or pollarded trees at the marsh edge. The *Flaxlands* were remembered by their crop and were so called in a deed of 1236 when *Rielond* and *Linlond* also occur; a name known in 1236 but not appearing on the 1596 map is *le Wingherd* from the old English word *wingeard*, a vineyard. Was Buckinghamshire sunny enough for grapes? the south-facing slopes of Moreton are pleasantly sited: only 300 yards away in Foxcote, on the stream which parts the two villages, is the site of a Roman villa which we may be sure had an eye for a sunny spot.

Langdon's map has one other set of names written over it besides the Furlong-names and the names on the strips: in bold letters four *Fieldes* are named—*Chattel, Rodwell, Hollowaye* and *Meade*. Field has been spelt with a capital "F" here because it, too, is liable to be ambiguous, joining *acre* and *furlong* in a trinity of confusion. To-day "field" is used for a hedged, fenced or walled portion of land of any size, and in a single modern parish there are dozens of fields. In a

75

medieval and Elizabethan parish there were rarely more than four, sometimes only two, and this would give each an area of as much as 300 or 400 acres. The Field was not, as to-day, a unit of ownership; we have seen that the unit of ownership was the strip. In the Middle Ages the Field was the unit of fallowing. A proportion of the arable area was rested each year to keep the land in good heart. If the strict order of fallow was maintained, the two-Field village would have half its arable land resting each year, the three-Field village one-third and the four-Field village (like Moreton) one-quarter. However it is likely that the strict order was more flexible in practice than the necessary generalizations of text-books pretend.

All four of the Fields at Moreton were named—like some Furlongs —after physical features which the villagers had noticed in them: for how long the four Fields had had these names is not known, but two of them occur in a document of 1241. Chattel (or Chaddle) is from the old English words *ceald wielle*, "cold spring"; Rodwell is *read wielle*, "red spring"; the Hollow-way is the deeply incised field road, now only a grass track; the *Meade* is the meadowland by the Ouse. Thus there is plenty of water in the Field-names as well as in the village name of "Moreton".

Two other features of the 1596 map distinguish it from any modern map. One is the rarity of hedges: the little miniature bushes which make up the cartographer's hedge appear only near the village houses (Plate 4) and along the edge of the wood and the parish boundary (Plate 3), although some type of fencing probably divided the Fields from each other and from the meadows. It is this absence of hedges which gave the Fields their wide vistas and the modern name of Open Fields.

The second feature which marks the All Souls map off from the modern Ordnance Survey maps is the widely scattered ownership of the strips. Even the College, the largest proprietor, found other people's strips intermingled with its own in virtually every Furlong. When it acquired the manor in 1442 the abbot of Oseney also owned land here, and his strips were scattered; and although the abbey lands had passed to laymen at the Dissolution in 1538 their memory was still preserved in 1596: three of the strips in Woode Waye Furlong near the wood in Plate 3 have *Abbott of Oseney* written on them, even though there had been no abbot for fifty-eight years. But countrymen had long memories, as we have seen in Chapter 2, and

76

it would have seemed no more unnatural to keep calling these the abbot's strips than to keep calling Buckingham after the long-dead Bucca. The modern name of Maids Moreton also illustrates the same habit: two ladies of the Peyvre family rebuilt the church, and the nickname "Maidenes" begins to appear in late fifteenth-century documents of the Bishop of Lincoln to distinguish this Moreton from the other Buckinghamshire village of the same name.

III

How did Moreton find itself with Fields cast in the pattern which Langford's map has preserved for us? how did they become so grained? so open? so scattered in ownership? so fragmented?—and not only Moreton, but thousands of other English villages whose Fields were once open? The answer seems to lie in the Dark Ages of English history, with few documents to help and only the evidence of later forms to suggest explanations.

An explanation can be framed in one sentence: this landscape was created by the piecemeal clearing of forest land by villagers whose principal need was for arable crops and whose social organization had accustomed them to do many operations of the farming year alongside each other. This sentence can now be expanded with particular reference to what the map tells us of Moreton.

We can assume that the first settlers made their permanent homes somewhere near where the 1596 map shows (Plate 4) the church and the field *sometymes the site of the manor*. At the time when the Anglian settlers came there were probably trees and scrub on all sides, broken only by the waterside marshes. Corn-land could only be won by clearing away the trees and scrub. The fields around the Foxcote Roman villa must once have been cleared in the same way, but by the time that Moreton was founded the villa was in ruins and probably hidden in the forest which had returned to cover its fields.

The return of scrub and trees to cleared land was a threat at any period: the 1596 map shows the furze encroaching at the north. This threat, and the magnitude of the task of clearing made it necessary for the first villagers to pool their resources of tools and manpower; indeed, they had probably brought from the Continent a tradition imposed on them by similar conditions in their previous home. Manpower was extremely scarce in the earliest days of Moreton:

77

even by 1086 there were only twenty families. Equally scarce were ploughs and plough-beasts. The plough was an expensive tool, with its iron parts; and the plough-beasts were expensive animals, with appetites which competed with hungry villagers, since the same fields had to feed everyone, man and beast.

With manpower and animals scarce it was necessary to act together. All hands went to the plough, just as all hands had assembled to cut oaks, grub up roots and burn the scrub. The wealthier families contributed an ox each to the yoke. What more natural than to share the product of this labour, the first harvest of the first cleared patch? and what better way to sharing the responsibility of ploughing and keeping it clear than to allocate it among those who had created it out of nothing? The division into strips seems to have begun here: this is the origin of a pattern which was eventually to appear irksome to would-be enclosers, but which seemed the natural, efficient and just way of behaviour to many centuries of villagers.

If the strip represents an allotment of land at the first clearing, then the Furlongs in which the strips are grouped must represent the successive stages in clearing away forest for fields. We do not know which of the many Furlongs near the houses of Moreton village was the first to be cleared, and, indeed, the growth of the village may have covered it with houses: but it does make sense of the pattern of Furlongs covering Langdon's map if we see each as once having been a fresh conquest. In this way the different "grains" also become reasonable. The shape you chose to give a new clearing and the direction in which you first plough it must obviously depend on such things as natural obstacles, the slope, the drainage and the space left by previous operations of the same kind in earlier generations. It was not possible to make every Furlong the same size, the same shape or of the same "grain", but as the village population expanded and there was a further incentive to produce food, so the Furlongs spread across the parish until they eventually reached the boundary on all sides.

We do not know exactly when this happened, but it was probably not until the end of the thirteenth century that the ploughs reached the parish boundaries in every direction. This progression must have had its years of standstill and even its years of retreat, but, on balance, movement was outward until the less rewarding days of the mid-fourteenth century brought a check. Even so, some small areas of

Moreton never came under the plough. Even when men were hungriest for corn they had to provide some fodder for the animals, particularly the oxen. Something could be made of grazing the stubble after harvest, and the fallow field would yield a poor crop of grass and weed, but for hay the riverside meadows were used. The hay crop was shared out by balloting for pieces of meadow set out according to tradition; we know from the survey of the glebe in 1607 that the village then had the meadow customs set down in writing:

as it is allotted by the Medow book,

says the terrier made for the archdeacon's visitation.[7] The steep banks of the stream on the north of the parish were ploughed almost to its edge, and each strip-holder had a small piece of meadow at the end of his strip. On the south of the Fields were the flat meadows of the Ouse with the riverside *meades*. Grass was sought even in nooks and crannies: the *slades*, or stream-sides, run like arteries through the crowded strips of the Furlongs in the western part of the parish. *Almeade slade* can be seen in Plate 3 leading between the Furlongs to *Almeade Leaes*, a block of 51 acres of common pasture, which like the *Fursan* (144 acres) seems to have become permanent grassland by 1596. In the hungrier days of the thirteenth century these two areas may have been ploughed.

Before all the forest and heath had succumbed to the plough they, too, could have been utilized to feed stock: the heaths for rough grazing and the woods for swine, but with the destruction of timber and the reclamation of heaths the animals could only use what could be spared of the commons, together with the little crofts, the fenced, garden-like enclosures behind each of the peasant houses. The map, Plate 4, shows that by 1596 the village houses had extended north-east from the church and then north-west along a main street. This street had houses on both sides, but those which were not College property were ignored by the surveyor and left blank: none of the village houses in the modern street is wholly Elizabethan in structure, but several of them stand on the same spot where Langdon shows a little cottage. After the Warden and Fellows of All Souls acquired the manor in 1422 there was no resident lord to need a house, and by 1596 the manor house had already fallen into disuse, only its "site"

[7] Bodleian Library, Oxford: MSS. Oxon. Arch. Deaconry Papers, Bucks., c. 242.

being shown in a hedged field of 15 acres across the lane from the church.

We drove to Maids Moreton in April, 1955 from Kettering, coming into the parish from the north-east along the A422, already a cross-country road in 1596, *the waye from Buckingham to Stonye Stratforde*. We halted at the sign-post for Maids Moreton on the site of *Balles Cross*, and looked towards the church along *Balles Crosse Waye* which divided *Meade Fielde* from *Hollowaye Fielde*. This *waye* also leads from the village to the riverside meadows and to the watermill, *Burnes* (sometimes *Burnte*) *Mylne* in 1596. Much traffic has worn it below the general level of the fields on the crest of the hill and it might well have been called a hollow-way (Plate 5), but the *hollow waye* which gave its name to the second Field was that which ran down to the Stratford road and the meadows a little nearer Buckingham: it probably led to *Buckford*, the crossing of the Ouse. This hollow way was not accessible for a car and had to be sought in a field. It seems to have passed out of use now that villagers do not have to reach their strips in the Furlongs on either side of it.

Thwarted here, we decided to go round through Buckingham and attack the village from the west. Like the *hollow waye*, the *waye from Buckinghame to Moreton* shown in 1596 has fallen into disuse: a main road, the A413, runs a little to the north of it and only skirts the end of the village. Diversions of this kind are very common in the countryside even before the age of double-carriageway by-passes and may often be dated to the period when country roads were improved for the use of through horse-drawn traffic by the various local turnpike trusts (here, the Buckingham-Towcester Trust).

I had noticed that the old direct road to the village did not appear on any modern map and I hoped that some signs of its former course might remain—perhaps as a second hollow way. I was unprepared for the sight of a brand-new, green "footpath to Buckingham" sign pointing exactly where the track led in 1596. This was not all: the sign pointed straight into the garden and across the lawn of a new house, right past the french windows. We hesitated to invade privacy even in the cause of historical research and tried to find a way round: all other ways were securely barbed. The house proved to be empty, so we followed the *waye to Buckingham* across the lawn, tactfully deviated for the flower beds, and reached a fence over which a grass field could be seen.

Later in the afternoon we met the owners of the house who explained that when they bought the land they were unaware of the claim that a right of way passed over it; their closure of the route had been challenged and the lawyers were at work trying to settle the matter. I felt that the villagers who trod out the original way and the successive generations who had perambulated the bounds might have been pleased that Quarter Sessions were still attentive to the old rights, but I also sympathized with the house-owner. I do not know whether this particular case is yet settled, but I might perhaps reassure householders who fear that Elizabethan maps might resurrect a public way through the privet. In most villages the formal enclosure of the open fields by authority of a Georgian or Victorian Act of Parliament provided for the survival of only a limited number of footpaths which were duly described in the official Award. The recent Footpaths Surveys made by the county councils have brought many of these awards out of the county archives for scrutiny.

The enclosure of the open fields of Maids Moreton took place in 1801 after its Enclosure Bill had passed through Parliament. The Award of the officials who carried out the enclosure[8] shows that the four open Fields had remained very much as they are shown in 1596. In this, the village was exceptionally conservative. It is usual to find that a good deal of piecemeal exchange of strips had gone on long before an enclosure Act, the purpose of the exchanges being a solid block of land, under a single ownership, which could then pass out of the open-field routine with everyone's agreement, compensating those who lost the right to graze its stubble. The 1596 plan shows that the College and other proprietors had gone some way to annul the original scatter of ownership, but none of the consolidated blocks which the College possessed out in the Fields seem to have been hedged, although the small hedged "closes" near the village houses may have been taken out of the Fields in this way at some earlier date.

One way of seeing the enclosure of Maids Moreton's strips is to turn up the Enclosure Award at the county Record Office and read its careful, legal recital of the proprietors' new holdings. The enclosure commissioners had redrawn the map. The result of the enclosure of 1801 may also be seen in the fields themselves. The straight-hedged fields which abut on the main roads to-day are the creation

[8] W. E. Tate, *Handlist of Bucks. Enclosure Awards* (1946), 35.

of the enclosure commissioners; the old tracks through the Furlongs were consigned to oblivion when the new hedged fields could be reached from the road or from the farm-roads; the open fields ceased to be open commons in the fallow year; the new fields assigned to the proprietors were in exchange for their scattered strips, and all other rights to graze others' fields or for others to graze theirs were extinguished.

It was sometimes more economical for a farmer to live in the centre of his compact block of land and not, as for centuries, in the village itself. In 1596 there were no farmhouses other than those in the village. To-day Chackmore Farm, Wellmore, Moreton House and College Farm stand out in the fields. College Farm is in the centre of the land awarded to the College in 1801 in lieu of the manorial strips. It is conveniently set at *Balles Crosse* alongside the Stratford road where we had first halted to see Maids Moreton church across the fields. (Fig. 5, p. 71.)

Later in the day, after our encounter with the rights-of-way controversy and a visit to the church, we went to see *Burnes Mylne* standing pleasantly by the Ouse and the disused canal. The water-wheel has been removed, but some of the stonework of the millhouse stands as Thomas Langdon drew it in 1596, and water still rushes through the mill-race. We could not find the site of the windmill which gave its name to *Windmilne hill Furlong*, for the fields in the north-west of the parish have been extensively ploughed, and the earth-mound of the mill must have been levelled when the villagers found somewhere else to grind their grain: it must lie near the little summit marked by the Ordnance Survey trigonometrical point. Yet in its day the windmill was as much a product of the great forest-clearing of the thirteenth century as were the latest furlongs at the parish edge; for windmills spread across England in that century to supplement the old-established water-mills and to help grind the increasing quantity of grain which the newly-acquired fields were yielding.

Our final quest was for another relic of the open fields of Moreton, the peasant's strips. The old map showed us where each of these lay and how the grain of the Furlongs ran. Did the surface of the fie d show any remains of these? or were the hollow-ways which had led among them the only survivors?

What had William Folkingham, the surveyor whose Preface was

quoted earlier, to say about the appearance of the strips in the fields which he surveyed? Living on Lincoln Edge he was familiar with the open fields of the clay plain and the open fields of the limestone uplands. Arable land, he wrote,[9] is ploughed in "selions", and he defines a selion as "raised land between two furrows". The "selion" (or strip) could be either flat or ridged. The flat, unridged strip was

> necessarily required on light and leane land, to the end that it may the better retaine any inforced vertue, against the washing away by showers.

The strips were ploughed into ridges where there were

> fat, strong and fertile grounds that be tough, stiffe, binding cold and wet, lest the fatness should suffocate the seed;

he also advocated a grass balk between the strips in heavy soils

> in such soyles it were frugall providence to spare from the plow a grasse-balke of some competent breadth.

Narrower ridges (or Stitches) were recommended for

> cold and stiffe ground inclining to barrennesse . . . and these Stitches are common in Norfolke and Suffolke even in their light grounds, and in Harfordshire where the Tilths are rich.

Of these three categories, Maids Moreton needed broad ridges. The strips shown on the 1596 map were ploughed into high ridges, leaving a boundary furrow between each strip, and leaving the strip as Folkingham had defined it:

terra elata inter duos fulcos

—raised land between the two furrows.

I have written elsewhere about my conviction that the ridge-and-furrow which one sees in the Midland pastures is simply the fossilized strip pattern of the old open fields.[10] In comparing visible ridge and furrow with old open-field plans I have tried to show that the ridges

---

[9] The quotations are from William Folkingham, *Feudigraphia* (1610), 48.

[10] For the argument (and some dissent) see M. W. Beresford "Ridge and Furrow and the Open Fields", *Ec. Hist. Rev.*, i (n.s.) (1948), 34-45; E. Kerridge, "Ridge and Furrow and Agrarian History", *ibid.*, iv (1951), 14-36 and "A Reconsideration of Former Husbandry Practices", *Ag. Hist. Rev.*, iii (1955), 26-40; also W. R. Mead, *art. cit.*, *supra*; agreed note by W. R. Mead and M. W. Beresford, *Geog. Journ.*, cxxi (1955), 125-26. See also pp. 118-19, *infra*.

—both in position and in "grain"—mirror the strips and Furlongs of the sixteenth- and seventeenth-century village plans. These comparisons can also be made, although with more difficulty, when the ridges have since been ploughed out, for air photographs reveal the curving line of the old furrows as crop-marks or soil-marks.

Naturally, an open-field map as old as Maids Moreton's, and on the scale of 1:2376 (1 inch = 66 yards), was a valuable opportunity to make yet another comparison, since there are sceptics—both in and out of my profession—who will have none of this nonsense, believing that ridge and furrow is a modern creation, younger than the hedged fields.

Two conditions are necessary for the comparison of open-field maps with the ground: there must be the type of soil where the ploughing of land within the long, narrow strips in the medieval centuries was likely to build up and retain the ridge-formation. The light soils of sand and chalk were easily blown and washed level and they can never have had the firm ridges of the heavy clays, although some air photographs do show crop-marks of the characteristic reversed-S strips in them.[11] But the chances of seeing very much from the ground in these lighter soils is small; and these soils are also very likely to have been heavily worked by the plough in the last two hundred years within the hedged boundaries. But in heavier soils a good deal of land went down to grass at enclosure and has stayed grass, retaining the form of the strips from the years before enclosure; and even when these hedged fields have been ploughed, the soil has retained a pattern of strips which can often be seen to run through the hedge—that comparative newcomer—and to change "grain" in mid-field at the point where two pre-enclosure Furlongs met. Dr. W. R. Mead has examined the air photographic cover of Buckinghamshire, and the distribution map which he published in 1955 shows how the chalk in the southern half of the county is rarely imprinted with ridges, while the central and northern villages have a high proportion of their fields showing the characteristic pattern of narrow strips and furlong blocks.[12]

At Maids Moreton the obliteration has been fairly thorough, at least as far as the observer on the ground is concerned, and I have not seen any air photographs. Ridges appear with clarity in only six

[11] S. R. Eyre, "The Curving Plough Strip", *Ag. Hist. Rev.*, iii (1955), 80-94.
[12] W. R. Mead, *art. cit.*

fields, four of which are under grass. The best example, and one which can easily be checked against the 1596 map, lies on the west of the Northampton main road on Overn Hill, now brought within the borough of Buckingham. At this point the road follows a field-way (unnamed in 1596) a little to the north of the *Cawswaye* which ran direct to the village from the county town. Here the strips of *Cawswaye Furlong* can be seen on the west of the road, running down to a small valley or slade where the 1596 map shows no strips but only the tinting of the meadow or "*Slade*". At this point the ridge and furrow ceases: only to begin again on the opposite slope in *Porteway Furlong* where the map begins to mark strips again.

The strangest survival I have left until last, for it makes a curious tailpiece to a comparison of old and new within a village. I have described how we found a garden across which *the waye to Buckingham* was alleged to have passed and how antiquity was harassing the owner of the garden. I have not mentioned another feature of his garden: the grass had an unusually corrugated surface for a civilized lawn, although I have seen cricket-pitches, football-grounds and golf-courses which suffered from the same malady of siting: for the lawn was set where the north-east part of *Cawswaye Furlong* had been. The strips of this Furlong are shown in 1596 with their grain at right-angles to *Buckingham waye*, the very direction in which the undulations in this lawn were running.

"I don't seem to be able to do anything with a roller," said the gardener. I did not feel I could offer him much comfort. The ridges had been a long time building up, and one hundred and fifty years of disuse had had little effect. It was really a matter for a bulldozer rather than a garden roller. I drew out my photograph of the All Souls map again and showed what caused the rise and fall in the lawn. The map had already depressed the house-owner by showing him how old was the right of way, and it now showed him the age of the switchbacks in his lawn. I left with the thought that he might well feel that the open-field Furlongs and roads were waging a vindictive war on him.

The plan of Maids Moreton shows the College to have been a conservative landlord. The manor which they owned did not com-prise every acre of the parish, as the blanks on the map show, but within it the old order of medieval farming was only slightly modi-fied. There is no sign that the College was one of those landlords

85

who had worked hard to gather the demesne strips into large compact holdings, a frequent halfway house to piece-meal enclosure. Here and there, a group of adjacent strips bears the College's name [e.g., at the top of Plate 4,] but such groups are never larger than 2 or 3 acres. The manor was leased to a "farmer", John Harris; the manor house had fallen down; the lords of the manor seem to have been satisfied to be absentee rent-receivers, and there was no serious re-organization of the open fields of Maids Moreton until the Parliamentary enclosure in 1801.

IV

For maps which show a greater degree of change we must move on from Maids Moreton. There can be few more startling evidences of change than another All Souls estate plan, the map of Whatborough, Leics., drawn in 1586, with its mournful centrepiece (Plate 11).

the place where the towne of Whateboroughe stoode.

The fate of Whatborough, a victim of sheep-enclosures, is described in the next chapter. A less extreme example of a landlord throwing together his holdings is seen in another plan[13] made by Thomas Langdon, that of Whitehill (Oxon.) made for Corpus Christi College in 1605. Here, there were four open fields, and the whole township was still covered with blocks of strips: at first glance the landscape is as medieval as at Maids Moreton. Yet when the names on the strips are examined a curious monotony appears: there are only two names in the whole map! The other occupants must have been bought out at an earlier date, leaving only these two giants poised with equal power. So balanced, they were either unwilling (or unable) to agree on a final re-adjustment which would have given them compact holdings and enabled them to hedge their fields, so that the township remained open until the early nineteenth century. The single great field in the north-west of the parish to-day represents the portion which one proprietor was given at enclosure. It has lost its strips but stretches to the horizon in the manner of an open-field landscape.

A third plan[14] by Thomas Langdon shows Upper Heyford (Oxon.) in 1606. Here, there had been a more partial consolidation: in some

[13] Reproduced in Mowat.   [14] Also reproduced in Mowat.

86

sections of the map whole Furlongs have strips with the name "Merry" alternating with strips bearing the name "Bruce", but there are also Furlongs with the full measure of intermixed tenants that appeared at Maids Moreton. More extensive consolidation of strips is shown in a fourth plan made by Thomas Langdon, that of Salford in west Bedfordshire, where All Souls College had become lords of the manor in 1438, four years earlier than their acquisition of Maids Moreton. Langdon's plan of Salford was executed in January, 1596, and is on the same scale (1 inch = 66 yards) as his plan of Maids Moreton. The final pages of this chapter take us to Salford, where a comparison of the Elizabethan map and the modern landscape brings out one or two further characteristics of an open-field village at the end of the sixteenth century.

The visit to Salford can be a short one, for many of the features in Thomas Langdon's plan are similar to those encountered at Maids Moreton. Fig. 6 shows that the village lay in the south-east corner of the parish, almost on the bounds. In the north of the parish was Salford wood, the successor of the woodland which the Domesday Survey in 1086 had reckoned to be sufficient to maintain 150 swine. The modern wood occupies exactly the same area as in 1596. It may be seen as the last survivor of the uncleared forest which faced the Anglo-Saxon settlers who first made their homes here and named their village after the "ford by the willows" (*sealh* = willow). These settlers probably came from the east, for when the county boundaries were drawn, this area was assigned to Bedfordshire although in fact it lies on the west side of the watershed between the Bedfordshire Ouse and the Buckinghamshire Ouze: the parish of Salford makes a beak-like projection of Bedfordshire into Buckinghamshire, as if some *fait accompli* of tribal affinity were too strong for the simpler logic of a watershed as the county boundary.

By the time of Domesday Book the plough had made substantial conquests here: five ploughs were maintained, one for the lord and four for the villagers, indicating perhaps 600 of the parish's 900 acres already under arable. A rental of 1453 shows that the College, as lord of the manor, had in Salford

arable	pasture	meadow	wood
215 a.	20 a.	22 a.	26 a.

and in the map of 1596 the College estate was

87

arable	pasture	meadow	wood
160 a.	112 a.	24 a.	25 a.

The contraction in arable at the expense of grass will be noticed. The conversion was mild compared with the depopulated Whatborough (p. 118), but it had brought with it a small contraction in the number of villagers. In 1553 there were twenty-three families, and in 1596, fifteen; in both years there were also tenants in the Manor House and vicars in the Vicarage. In Domesday Book seventeen families had been counted.[15]

The college interest in Salford did not end with the rent it received from the tenant of the manorial home farm, although this was substantial. When the lease was renewed in 1586 the manor buildings comprised a house, dove-cotes, barns, stables, orchards, gardens and fishpools. These can be seen in the plan of 1596 when Mrs. Langford, widow of John Langford, once Chancellor of Worcester, was the College tenant. At the beginning of the century the manor house had been rebuilt, and the lease of 1504 shows how the responsibility had been divided. The tenant, Thomas Pedder, (whose descendants occupied a small twelve-acre holding in 1596) promised

> to buyld and arrere up ther a newe Hall and a parlor with loftes above . . . and chymneys.

The college provided the "grete tymber" and the "tyle" and an allowance of £6 13s. 4d. in cash.[16]

The College's other interest in Salford came from the rents of the 550 acres occupied by the thirteen tenants whose cottages appear on the village plan and whose names are written on the scattered strips, on the meadow and on the small number of enclosed fields. These tenant holdings were the descendants of the villein holdings of the middle ages, and there were also two freeholders in the village, but one of these, says a note on Langdon's plan, had been bought out by the College between the making of the survey and the drawing of the plan.

There were three other buildings shown on Langdon's plan which were in one sense or another for public use: north of the Manor

[15] *V.C.H. Beds.*, i, 238 and 246; maps: All Souls Library, Hovenden Maps, portfolio i, Nos. 23-27. Other documents cited are listed in Martin.
[16] 1504: All Souls, "Salford Leases No. 2"; 1586: *ibid.*, No. 23.

House stood the parish church; south-west of the village, along the little mill-race, stood the corn-mill; and in the middle of the northernmost row of village houses stood the "town howse" presumably used for village meetings; a very similar building stood at the north of Toddington green when Ralph Agas drew his plan in 1581 (Plate 15).

The extent of the open fields of Salford can be seen in fig. 6, and

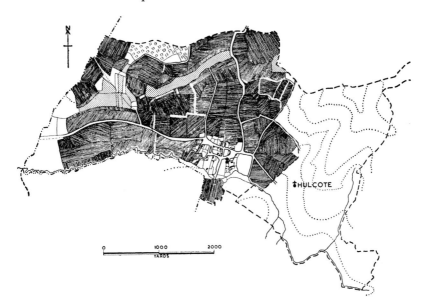

Fig. 6. Salford in 1596 with its depopulated neighbour, Hulcote. Pasture in Salford is left white and meadows shaded grey. Fine lines indicate open-field Furlongs; the direction and size of the strips could not be shown accurately on this scale: but see Plates 6-7. Contours (dots) at 25-foot intervals.

something of the complexity of intermingled strips in Plate 7. Apart from the open fields there was a central belt of meadowland along the sides of a small stream. In 1596 this meadow was assigned to the villagers in a fashion which went back to Anglo-Saxon days. Its 46 acres were broken up into "doles", that is portions, and each spring the doles were allocated among the villagers by drawing lots. When the enclosure of the open fields in 1808 was followed by the building of a new farm-house in the newly-hedged fields west of the village, the farm was called Whitsundoles (Plate 8). The season of lot-drawing was Whitsun, the animals being then turned off the winter grazing and the grass allowed to grow until the hay-harvest. In 1596 the ration of animals which a villager was allowed to keep on the commons—that is, the fallow strips and the winter grass—was ten sheep and three kine.[17] The woods were also shared by the villagers.

Only one other new farm was built away from the village centre after the Parliamentary enclosure of 1808; this was Holcotmoors Farm which stands where in 1596 Thomas Langdon's plan shows the strips of *Over Duncrosse Furlong*: the remainder of the newly-hedged fields continued to be farmed from the houses in the village.

The Salford plans bear signs that they were used in the College Office long after Thomas Langdon and Warden Hovenden were dead. It will be seen from Plates 6 and 7 that a later and heavier hand has written a fresh set of names across the house-crofts and across some of the fields. From the rentals in the College muniments and from a note on the back of the plans themselves these additions can be assigned to the year 1769.

The boldest-written name is *Sir Villers* and it usually occurs where the Elizabethan plan has "Mrs. Langforde", the tenant of the Manor House. Even in 1596 this demesne estate was remarkably compact, consisting of whole Furlongs near the Manor and in the eastern field; in 1769 it was further consolidated and increased by another exchange of lands. The final enclosure of the open-field strips was not achieved until 1808, but in 1769 there seems to have been a small enclosure by agreement involving Hulcote Field where lands of Salford and Hulcote lay intermingled. A piece of land was assigned to Sir Villers in lieu of

the single lands in Holcot Fields before the Inclosure,

and the opportunity was taken to replace the system of Lot Meadows in Salford by dividing the whole meadow among the villagers in permanent parcels. Thus it will be seen in Plate 7 that the name *Sir Villers* and the area 6 acres 1 rood 24 perches is written over the eastern part of the old *Deane Meadowe* and the names of *Henny* (sic) *Odell, Sarah Woodard*, and *R. Page* on other portions to the left. The Odells and Woodards of 1769 must have been the descendants of the

---

[17] The system of lot meadows is described in the cartouche of Hovenden Maps, i, 24.

Richard Odell and Robert Woodeward whose names appear on the strips of Middle Field in 1596. In Plate 7 Sir Villers' name has also been written over a near-by block of eleven strips in the west of *Water forowes* which were still in divided ownership in 1596, although well on the way to consolidation since Mrs. Langford held nine of them.[18]

The bringing together of scattered strips into compact holdings was a frequent precursor of total enclosure, but it will be noticed that there are no signs that the consolidated block of strips had been hedged. The only advantage achieved—but a considerable one— was that of economy in working the land in one parcel. The rights of common while the land lay fallow seems to have remained to the other villagers until the Act of Parliament in 1808 whereby the open fields of Salford were totally enclosed with hedges and the rights of common extinguished. This was the period, as we have seen, when the two new farm-houses were built out in the fields.

Until 1808 all the houses of the village lay together, as they appear in the map of 1596 (Plate 6). The shape of the village is irregular, but the wandering loops of streets of which it is composed suggest an interesting development in its plan. In 1596 two Greens were shown, one at the *weste ende* where the *Lowe Waye* leaves the village for *Brooke Fielde* and the meadows, and the other immediately to the north of the church and Manor House at the east end of the village. The arrangement of houses in between these two greens strongly suggests that there was once a single open space running from one end of the village to the other. To re-create this space we shall have to wipe away the houses which lie on the irregular islands of ground between which the narrow lanes and passages make their loops. If these houses are taken away, where were the villagers living? There is still a substantial frontage left along the north and west sides of the green. In 1596 there were vacant spaces enough along these fronts to take half a dozen houses.

If this simple plan was the first stage, and piecemeal encroachment upon the green a second stage, there is further change to record since Langdon's plan was drawn. Gardens have widened and streets have narrowed, so that even *Weste end greene* has now disappeared. And where there were four "islands" of houses in 1596, there are now only two. The road down to *Milne Lees Partinge Grasse* has disappeared

[18] Details from the endorsements of Hovenden Maps, i, 23; areas of holdings: *ibid.*, i, 26, cartouche.

under an orchard. It is a long time since any one went that way to draw lots for his share at the "parting of the swarde", as Langdon called it.

Although there are empty spaces where Langdon shows cottages and some cottages in positions where Langdon shows none, there are some which survive in the position he indicated. One such is seen in Plate 8, a T-shaped building with a small cottage joined on to a larger, the exact shape shown by Langdon when he drew *Widow Letten the freehold tenement and close*, 1 rood 35 perches in area, belonging to the widow of John Letten, husbandman. The smaller thatched cottage has only had minor alterations since 1596 (e.g. the tall brick chimney), but the longer house at the end of it has had substantial alterations. These Bedfordshire villages are near enough to the brick-kilns to have been much transformed architecturally in the last century.

The dove-cote in the manor *Coneygree* (or rabbit warren) has gone; and only earth-banks mark the site of the ornamental garden south of the church; the Manor House itself has been reconstructed since Mrs. Langford occupied it, but the ornamental pond still has its ducks; and there are willows still by the ford, as there were when the village was named; and as there were when Thomas Langdon drew a panel at the foot of his map, ornamented it with a grotesque of pillars, animals, flowers and figures, and then wrote within it on carefully ruled lines[19]

> The description of the manor of Salforde in the countye of Bedford beinge parcell of the possessions of the warden and college of the sowles of all faithfull people deceased of Oxon., drawne & made in the moneth of Ianuary in the yeare of our lord one thowsand five hundred fower score and fifteene (*sic*), and in the yeare of the raigne of our most gratious souveraigne Elizabeth by the grace of god of England Fraunce & Ireland Queen defender of the faith &c the xxxviii th. Roberte Houeden Doctor in divinity then being warden.

[19] The wording of the cartouche varies slightly on the five sub-sheets of the plan.

4

A JOURNEY AMONG DESERTED VILLAGES

TUSMORE, OXON.

TILGARSLEY, OXON.

CHALFORD, OXON.

WORMLEIGHTON, WARWS.

FAWSLEY, NORTHANTS.

SNORSCOMB, NORTHANTS.

WHATBOROUGH, LEICS.

I have taken all possible pains in my country excursions for these four or five years to be certain of what I alledge.

OLIVER GOLDSMITH, dedicatory Preface to *The Deserted Village* (1770)

Chapter Four

A JOURNEY AMONG DESERTED VILLAGES

I

IN the previous chapter it was shown how the landowners' eagerness
for large-scale plans of their properties provided a powerful
incentive for surveyors to sharpen their skills and multiply their
numbers. It also appeared that many of a landowner's anxieties
arose either from his fear that others might lay claim to a particular
piece of land or from his desire to make claim on a piece of land
hitherto possessed by someone else. The survey and map might equally
well be weapons of defence or attack. In the Elizabethan villages
surveyed for Warden Hovenden of All Souls the projected changes
went no further than a continued re-shuffle of open-field strips, as the
College and the other freeholders sought compact blocks of strips
and to cancel out that scattering of strips throughout the open fields
which medieval colonization had created.

But one of the maps drawn for the College at this time concerned
a property in which much more radical changes had taken place,
even so far as to eradicate the village and to transform the appearance of its fields: the open-field strips are replaced on the map by
large hedged pastures, and instead of streets, houses, crofts and
gardens, the surveyor drew his pen around a central area on his map
and simply wrote

the place where the towne of Whateboroughe stoode.

In this chapter a journey will be made across the Midlands from
Tusmore in Oxfordshire to Whatborough in Leicestershire. The
rather circuitous route, beginning fifteen miles north of Oxford and
finishing twelve miles east of Leicester, is designed to take in a number of examples of other Whatboroughs, viewing the earthworks of
medieval villages which have perished. Some of these deserted
villages were destroyed by landlords who had no need for villagers
in a new economic order based on the grazing of sheep and cattle;

95

others had decayed slowly over several generations: but in either event the surviving earthworks which mark the village site carry the same stamp. Familiarity breeds comprehension, and the rather tangled mass of mounds and depressions at Whatborough is more meaningful if village earthworks have been first studied where they lie in greater clarity and order.

As with so many archaeological features, a succession of visits leaves behind it a more comprehensive picture. The details which show to advantage at one point are reinforced by other details which the passage of time has chanced to leave better displayed at another; one site has the advantage of an early map, and another has the advantage of a succession of explicit documents; here, folk-memory has preserved the tradition of a site, and there it is only the superior vantage point of an aerial photograph which reveals the pattern of the former village in the colour variations of a ripening August crop. But in order to amalgamate these pictures of deserted villages it is necessary first to assemble them.

The similarity of their physical form conceals the variety of causes which have brought houses and streets into decay, and a sequence of visits will enable these various causes to be separately illustrated.[1] To begin at Tusmore is to step into the misfortunes of the mid-fourteenth century when a succession of pestilences robbed the countryside of its manpower and the town tradesmen of their customers. The exact degree of mortality in each village is not certainly known; equally uncertain is the degree to which population had already been falling since the end of the thirteenth century. What is certain is that the Black Death of 1349 and the successive returns of the plague over the next twenty years created an economic situation which was in many respects the very opposite of that which had nourished the growth of villages and the extension of their fields.

The great expansion of cultivated land and population which culminated in the thirteenth century has already been viewed retrospectively through those Elizabethan village and field-plans which chart the great achievement of many generations' colonization and reclamation. The Elizabethan maps were seen in the previous chapter to be such a good guide to the thirteenth century simply because the fourteenth and fifteenth centuries had brought so few additions to

[1] See Beresford, caps. v-vi.

the number of villages in the English countryside and so few additions to the area of field-land. This stagnation or quiescence had as one of its causes a contraction of population in the course of the four-teenth century. Thus, in 1412 the abbot of Pipewell Abbey reported to the Pope that his tenants at the Northamptonshire village of Elkington had abandoned their arable fields, and that on account of the pestilences everyone had left the village except three or four servants of the abbey.[2]

This contraction of population changed the whole climate of rural life. Something has been said in the previous chapter of the centuries during which the number of fields and villages was increasing and in Chapters 5 and 6 a similar tale of innovation and expansion will be told in terms of town life. But the fields and villages to be visited in this chapter are tokens of very different circumstances: instead of an increase in numbers there is depopula-tion; instead of new fields there are places where arable cultivation is being abandoned; and Tusmore, halfway between Brackley and Bicester, is one of these.

II

The village was named after the pool, *Thur's mere*, which has now been transformed into the ornamental lake to the west of Tusmore House. The village was surveyed for Domesday Book in 1086, and a list of its landholders was compiled two centuries later in 1279 for Edward I. The *Hundred Rolls* of that year list nineteen manorial tenants and four freeholders, in addition to the lord of the manor. These twenty-four heads of households must be multiplied by some such factor as four or five to arrive at the total population, which had about 500 acres to maintain it.[3]

In 1355, six years after the first arrival of the Black Death in England, the village was empty. The Exchequer remitted the whole of the tax due, and two years later the lord of the manor was given permission to divert the road from Souldern to Cottisford which had previously run through Tusmore village, now "void of inhabitants". It looks as if he intended to make the best of a bad job and use the unpeopled acres as parkland, of which the modern Tusmore Park is

[2] *Calendar of Papal Registers*, vi (1904), 393; *V.C.H. Northants.*, ii, 119.
[3] *P.N. Oxon.*, 216; *V.C.H. Oxon*, i, 411; *Rot. Hund.*, ii, 825

a descendant. A footpath is marked on the Ordnance Map passing very near the site of the village which can clearly be seen to the north-west of the House on either side of the little stream which fed Thur's mere. The Census of 1851 shows how the parish remained empty of farm-houses for five hundred years. In Tusmore House

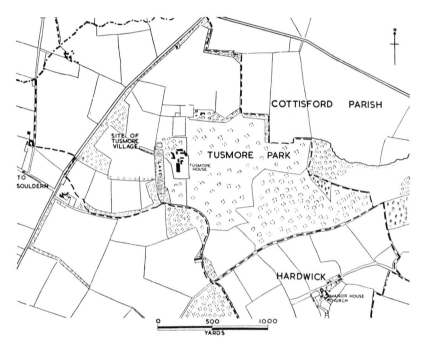

Fig. 7. Tusmore Park and the site of the village destroyed by the Black Death. In 1357 the road from Cottisford through Tusmore was diverted when the fields of Tusmore became a park.

there were seven members of the owner's family and eighteen servants; three houses sheltered the families of a gamekeeper, a groom and a labourer, while (outside the park) there were two farming families.[4]

Those whose taste for exploration has been whetted by an easy view of Tusmore may care to search for the site of another Oxfordshire

[4] 1355: P.R.O. E179/161/30; 1357: *Cal. Inq. Misc.*, iii, No. 258; 1428: *Feudal Aids*, iv (1906), 201; 1851: P.R.O. HO107/1729.

plague victim, Tilgarsley.[5] This hamlet lay within the large parish of Eynsham and must have been a substantial settlement. In 1279 there were fifty-two tenants recorded; and in 1334, when tax quotas were fixed for all English villages, it was assessed at the substantial sum of 95*s.* In 1359 the tax-collectors reported to the barons of the Exchequer that no one had been living here since 1350. The lord of the manor was the abbot of Eynsham and he had other empty tenements on his hands elsewhere in Oxfordshire. Documents show that by 1422 the abbey had abandoned the use of villein labour to work the fields of Tilgarsley and had let the former open fields out in large closes. It is likely that these were used for grazing by men of Eynsham, for there is no more mention of Tilgarsley village and the Exchequer gave up all hope of collecting the 95*s.*

The exact site has yet to be discovered. It had been suggested that a spot known as "Til's Grave" might commemorate the village, but I could see nothing suggestive on the surface of the fields there in August, 1955. An open-field map of Eynsham drawn in 1782 has been published, and it shows the north-west quarter of the parish already cut up into closes, and it would seem reasonable to look for Tilgarsley in this direction. The Place-Name Society's Oxfordshire volume locates it at Britannia Inn, probably on the authority of Sir Edmund Chambers who thought it had been at Barnard Gate (G.R.404106) on the border of Handborough. Amateur detectives are also warned that Eynsham Hall is now occupied by a Police Training College.

Landlords like the owners of Tusmore and Tilgarsley had been faced with a shortage of labour which made it impossible to exact the old terms of rent and services which the husbandmen had rendered. If land went down to grass it was because there were not the hands to man the plough; or more explicitly, that with less demand for corn and with the shrunken rural labour force commanding high wages it was not worth maintaining the plough in these particular villages. Many, if not most, English villages felt the bite of the plague. Why were there not many more Tilgarsleys and Tusmores?

The principal reason was that the plagues provided the opportunity for a general reshuffle. The vacant holdings were occupied

[5] 1279: *Rot. Hund.*, ii, 859; 1334: P.R.O. E179/161/12; later events summarized in H. E. Salter ed., *Eynsham Cartulary*, Oxford Hist. Soc., li (1908), 46-47; documents, 1359-83: *ibid.*, ii, 69-80; Sir Edmund Chambers, *Eynsham Under The Monks*, Oxon. Record Soc., xviii (1936), 102-6 with plan of 1782 at end.

by those who had been landless or by those who moved in from less attractive soils. If everyone moved down the queue one might expect to find somewhere the place where the tail of the queue had been standing before the plagues, when men were hungry even for poor quality land. This marginal land, from which there are signs of a retreat in the fifteenth century, lay scattered over England. It is most noticeable where ruined churches dot the landscape, their empty windows looking out on to parishes emptied of villagers. It was in the late fourteenth and early fifteenth centuries that petitions began to find their way to the Vatican asking that livings might be amalgamated and the obligation of the parish priests to hold services eased. The registers of the Bishop of Lincoln, with his great diocese extending down to Oxfordshire, contain a number of such decrees authorizing amalgamation.[6] Thus in 1397 the parishes of East and West Wykeham on the Lincolnshire Wolds were united to Ludford Magna; and in 1437 the rector of Dunsthorpe successfully petitioned for an amalgamation with Hameringham on account of

> the lack of parishioners, the fewness of peasants, their low wages, the bareness of the lands, the lack of cultivation and the pestilences and epidemics with which the Lord afflicts his people for their sins,

while in 1455 the church of Thorpe by Newark was disappropriated on account of

> the fewness and poverty of the inhabitants, as a result of which lands once fertile and arable are now sterile and fallen back to grass.

The ruined or completely destroyed churches of the Lincolnshire Wolds are only equalled in frequency by the picturesque ruins of the Norfolk Breckland whose dry and windswept sands proved equally unattractive once better land was to be had elsewhere.[7] It is probable, but not certain, that the ruined churches of Romney Marsh also date from this period of readjustment after the plagues.

III

Yet these excursions to Lincolnshire, Norfolk and Kent are diversions from the main journey which leads on from Tusmore to villages

[6] Wykeham: C. W. Foster, ed., *Lincolnshire Domesday* (Lincs. Record Soc., xix (1924), lxxi-ii; Dunsthorpe: *ibid.*, liv-v; Thorpe: Register of Archbishop Bothe, ff. 229-30, quoted in A. H. Thompson, *English Clergy* (1947), 112.

[7] K. J. Allison, "The Lost Villages of Norfolk", *Norfolk Archaeology*, xxxi (1955), 116-62.

whose death was not the direct or indirect result of the plagues but of the appetite of enclosing landlords in the late fifteenth century. If these landlords had merely stepped in to empty or underpopulated fields and put the land to profitable, productive use there would have been few complaints. Instead, there were many, the most celebrated of which are the complaints of the Tudor pamphleteers that sheep had become so fierce that they were now ravenously eating up men. Even in the early seventeenth century the surveyor John Norden, who was a protagonist of improving enclosure, nevertheless echoed the contemporary belief that enclosure accompanied by depopulation could not be for the good of the common weal, however much it added to private profit.[8]

> When the ox and sheep shall feed where good houses stood . . . who will not say it is the bane of a commonwealth, an apparent badge of Atheism and an argument of waspish ambition or wolvish emulation?

As it happened, these complaints were most vocal after the main flood of depopulation had been checked, but the memory was bitter. Agrarian rioting and public discussion of enclosure throughout the sixteenth and seventeenth centuries were haunted by the deserted village.

The evidence of government inquiries, such as that by Wolsey's Commissioners in 1517 and 1518, tells the same story as the pamphleteers; as Bishop Latimer's sermons; as Sir Thomas More's *Utopia;* and as Shakespeare's *Pericles* where the depopulating landlord is the great whale who has swallowed a whole parish, "church, steeple, bells and all." Even this evidence is not the complete story, for the first anti-depopulation act (one protecting the Isle of Wight) was not passed until 1488, and the various Tudor inquiries and prosecutions did not have power to look back beyond 1485.

These depopulated villages may briefly be called "sheep-depopulations", since the profits of sheep-farming were the principal incentive which made landlords consider a revolutionary change in land use. The sheep had been a necessary complement to arable farming for centuries, not only for his wool but for his dung, his skin and his meat. Nevertheless, all over the English plains the ordinary village had maintained the plough, and the plough was a maintainer of men. With the arable fields given over to a new crop, grass, the

[8] John Norden, *Surveiors Dialogue,* 224.

whole structure of the open-field village was in danger. A complete conversion of the whole acreage of a parish to grass put an end not only to the routines which had depended on ploughing, sowing and reaping but also to the need for most of the villagers. Compared with the sown acres, the sheep was a light taskmaster. It was no accident that the shepherd and his dog were taken in so many contemporary denunciations as the symbols of depopulation. (The phrase "deserted village" did not gain currency until Oliver Goldsmith's poem of 1770.) The small cost of the labour force was an additional incentive to a calculating landlord or lessee, but the principal incentive came from the profitability of the new crop, the fleeces of the shearing season.

Come boom, come slump, the long-term trend in the demand for wool was steadily rising. It came from English looms, principally in East Anglia and the clothing counties of the south-west. In the early stages of the development of this semi-rural industry the demand had been met by taking up English wools which had previously been exported for the use of weavers in northern Italy and the Low Countries, but in time this source of supply proved insufficient, and only an expansion of the home wool supply could satisfy the needs of the English clothmakers. Small progress might be made by increasing the number of sheep on the common pastures, but the biggest rewards were to be obtained by those who could increase their flocks not by dozens but by scores and hundreds, and for these numbers the existing commons were insufficient: only the conversion of arable to permanent grassland remained.

The agents of change were to be found all over the Midlands among landlords of all social levels and both lay and ecclesiastic. It is naturally the largest proprietors about whom we are best informed, for their actions brought them within the law, and large offences made prosecutions worthwhile. The family papers and the great houses of these many-manored landlords make it easier to read their progress in wealth, but the "waspish ambition" of which Norden wrote was emulated by many small proprietors and those who held land on long leases. The juries of 1517 and 1518 usually ended their reports of depopulation with the phrase "an evil example to those of like mind", and the numbers of provincial gentry involved made it difficult for governments to see their way to enforce what the moralists were urging, and difficult to get juries to convict.

The activities of the sheep-masters may be observed by a round of visits to five Midland parishes involving a journey of not more than fifty miles. Such a journey would, indeed, pass within a few miles of many other similar depopulations, but only the most striking have been chosen here. A gazetteer of known sites with fuller comment has already been published.

The round of visits may begin not far from Eynsham where the elusive Tilgarsley was being sought. Travelling north-west over the Cotswolds the valley of the Evenlode is reached near Charlbury, whence the Chipping Norton road (B4026) climbs to the watershed between the Evenlode and the little river Glyme. Two miles short of Chipping Norton there is a point marked on the map as Chalford Green where five lanes meet. Of Chalford there is no sign. There is a clear view from the Green across the valley of the Glyme to the main road (A34) on the far side. In the valley bottom there is a farm and cottages bearing the name of Old Chalford. The earthworks which mark the site of the two medieval villages of Upper and Lower Chalford lie down-stream, two fields away from the present farm and extremely well-preserved. A footpath is marked on the map leading from the neighbouring village of Lidstone along the left-hand side of the stream, past the two Chalfords and so up the valley to Chipping Norton.

The former streets and houses are represented by the mounds and depressions in the turf on the hillside. The covering of soil and turf is only slight, so that the shape of houses is easily discerned. Plate 9 shows the author's hand near the stones of a house-wall exposed alongside a rabbit hole.

In 1279 these houses sheltered the nineteen families which made up the "hamlets". The earliest large-scale map of the estate, made for Oriel College in 1743 by Stephen Jeffreys of Minchinhampton, was published in 1888 by R. B. Mowat. In contrast to the neighbouring village of Dean, also an Oriel property, Chalford then had no open fields, although medieval deeds printed in Mrs. Lobel's *History* show the characteristic dispersal of small strips of arable in Chalford's two (and later three) open fields.[9] By 1743 the township was divided into large closes, some of them with significant names. As now, a farm, a mill and an adjacent set of cottages were the only

[9] M. D. Lobel, *The History of Dean and Chalford,* Oxon. Record Soc., xvii (1935); plans of 1743 in Mowat, Nos. 9-14.

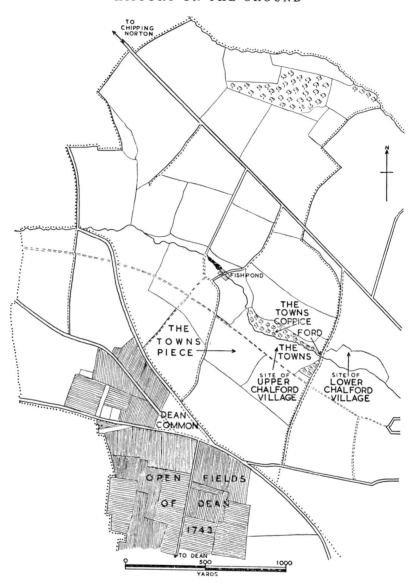

TO
CHIPPING
NORTON

N

FISHPOND

THE
TOWNS
COPPICE
FORD

THE
TOWNS
PIECE

THE
TOWNS

SITE OF
UPPER
CHALFORD
VILLAGE

SITE OF
LOWER
CHALFORD
VILLAGE

DEAN
COMMON

OPEN   FIELDS

OF   DEAN

1743

TO DEAN

0   500   1000
         YARDS

Fig. 8. Dean and its two depopulated hamlets, Upper and Lower Chalford. Field names are from the map of 1743 when Dean was still unenclosed.

104

buildings, but further down-stream, past the two-and-a-half acre mill pond, the map shows a close called "The Towns" with "The Towns Piece" and "The Towns Coppice" near by. It is in the fields called "The Towns" that the earthworks of streets and houses can now be seen. The word *town* is to be taken in its Elizabethan sense of "township" and not in any modern urban sense. (The surveyor of the depopulated Whatborough used the same word when he wrote on his map "the place where the towne of Whateboroughe stoode".)

Next to the mill pond was the close called "The Shearing Pen", used for the sheep whose ancestors had eaten up the village. The conversion to pasture probably took place between 1471 and 1485. The absentee landlords, Oriel College, acquired the estate in 1471, and if they had depopulated Chalford after 1485 it is likely that it would have been reported to Wolsey's Commission; the College's conversion of a small acreage in Dean and the eviction of four husbandmen in 1509 was reported to the Commissioners[10] in 1517.

The next deserted site to be visited lies on the northern edge of the Cotswolds, its church being set high on the scarp overlooking the Warwickshire plain to the north. The name of this village, Wormleighton, begins to appear on signposts six miles north of Banbury, and the lane from Fenny Compton to Byfield passes by the end of the village street. A name on a signpost? and a village street? yet a deserted village site? the contradiction can be resolved, for only the church of the medieval village remains. The modern village has grown up around a new Manor House on the hill, built at the time when the medieval village was deserted.

To reach the site of the medieval village it is necessary to turn down a narrow, sunken, hedged lane on the left of the village street near the church. The lane drops steeply down the hill-side and then swings back uphill to the village. It is necessary to leave it at its lowest point to enter the very large pasture field where the village once lay. A footpath crosses the site but the permission of Mr. Woodland of Home Farm will be needed to inspect the earthworks. The ground slopes away to the canal on the far side of the field and the gradient was utilized for a great chain of fishponds fed by springs high on the hill-side. The whole site, fishponds, houses, gardens and streets is now grazed by sheep, as Plate 10 shows. The containing banks of the ponds are prominent and well-preserved. On either side

---

[10] Leadam, 361.

of the ponds are the smaller depressions and mounds of houses, crofts and streets. At the end of the field furthest from the church and alongside the canal is the rectangular earthwork marking the moated manor house of medieval Wormleighton, the ditch now being dry. Above the village and just below the church, is a small pool, the sole survivor of the chain of fishponds, with a very large

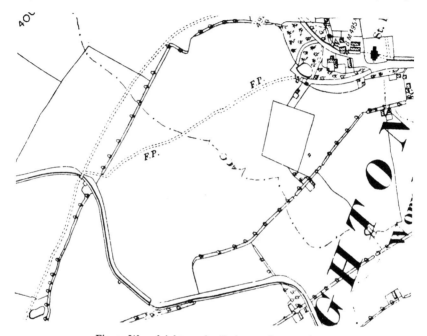

Fig. 9. Wormleighton; the Ordnance Survey plan.

rectangular field below it marking the site of the principal storage chamber from which the water once overspilled to feed the smaller chambers shown in Plate 9.

There are two early maps of the village among the muniments of Earl Spencer at Althorp, one of 1634 and one of 1724. Only the latter was suitable for photographic reproduction here (Plate 9). No significant changes had taken place since 1634 except the removal of the scattered park-like trees which had covered the field called "Old Town", the field of the fishponds shown in Plate 10. Chalford has already shown us that "Old Town" is a significant field name, but the removal of the houses from this fine piece of pasture is a more complicated story than that of Chalford.

The rise of the Spencer family from sheep-masters to the House of Lords is an example of the ease with which the fortunate and enterprising could climb the social ladder of the sixteenth century, and the acquisition of Wormleighton was an important step in the family's progress.

The first Baron Spencer, who died in 1627, had reason to be sensitive about his family origins. In May, 1621 the Earl of Arundel taunted him in a House of Lords debate:

> My ancestors have suffered, and it may be for doing the King and Country good service, and in such time as when, perhaps, the lord's ancestors that spake last kept sheep.

Arundel was called to the bar of the house, but refused to apologize except from his seat. For his defiance he was sent to the Tower, but subsequently he retracted. At one time the Spencer family consoled themselves by a claim to descend from the Norman Le Despencers, but their yeoman origin is well attested.[11]

They first came into prominence as the owners of property adjacent to Wormleighton on the north, the manor of Hodnell, which lies in the plain immediately to the north. Hodnell and its neighbours, Watergall, Chapel Ascote, Stoneton and the two Radbourns form a solid block of depopulated territory among which "wolvish emulation" was easily learned. This soil made—and still makes—excellent grassland, but the transfer from the traditional cereal crops to what may well have been an optimal crop of grass involved the removal of the husbandmen from all six villages.

The fate of Wormleighton was slightly different, as the map, fig. 9, p. 106, shows. In 1634 a village of a dozen houses was shown on the hilltop to the south of the church where the modern village of Wormleighton stands. At Radbourn, Hodnell and Chapel Ascote the churches are now only earthen banks, but that of Wormleighton still serves a village. Yet, as the name *Old Town* and the earthworks in that field show, seventeenth-century Wormleighton occupied a site different from that of the medieval village, only the church remaining in its old site to serve the new village. The prosecution of John

11 *V.C.H. Warws.*, v, 218-24; Dugdale, 515; for the Spencers: G. E. Cokayne, and G. H. White, *The Complete Peerage* (1953), xii (1), 153-61; the Arundel quarrel: P.R.O. SP12/121/15, 44 and 88.

Spencer in the court of Exchequer reveals what had happened, and why Wormleighton church did not follow Radbourn, Hodnell and Ascote into decay. Medieval Wormleighton[12] was much larger than either Chalford, Tilgarsley or Tusmore: in 1279, thirty villein households, three free tenants, four other tenants and three cottagers were recorded. In the taxation list of 1332 there were twenty-six households wealthy enough to fall in the taxable grade, and when the village tax-quotas were re-assessed in 1334 Wormleighton paid 72s., the local average being only 59s.

The succession of medieval lords of the manor ended with Sir Simon Mountfort who was attainted for treason in 1495. The forfeited estate was granted by Henry VII to his Cofferer, William Cope, at a rent of £13 6s. 8d. a year. Mountfort's rent had only been £8: the increase was made possible by the more profitable use to which Cope turned the estate. He bought out all the freeholders and in October, 1498, pulled down twelve houses and three cottages belonging to the tenantry, turning 240 acres from arable to grass. Twelve ploughs were thus displaced and sixty villagers lost their livelihood.[13] Their loss was the landowner's gain: property with an annual value of £40 in 1498 was valued in 1517 at £60, a considerable increment, even allowing for the small intervening rise in the general level of prices.

In September, 1506 Cope sold the estate for £2,000 to John Spencer of Hodnell. The purchase was to prove troublesome. On September 22, 1517, Wolsey's two Commissioners and a jury of sixteen Warwickshire gentry met at Allesley near Coventry to investigate complaints of depopulation under the Acts of 1489 and 1515 "against the pulling down of towns". The case of Wormleighton was presented to them, and the record sent off to the Lord Chancellor. In 1519 John Spencer appeared before the court of Chancery to show cause why he should not pay the fine specified in Wolsey's decree of July 12, 1518. Three petitions, two of which have been printed, were submitted during the hearing of the case, which dragged out over more than three years and was resurrected again in 1549. The map of 1634 corroborates these petitions.[14]

[12] 1279: P.R.O. E164/15; 1332: E179/192/5; 1334: E179/192/6.
[13] Six other houses may have been destroyed by Sir Edmund Raleigh acting as trustee for John Spencer's uncle (d. 1497), but Dugdale, the sole authority, may have misread the pleadings. No prosecution has been traced.
[14] Leadam, 403-4; 485-9; 648; 656-7; also P.R.O. E164/10/7.

The strong point of Spencer's case was that he had provided compensatory employment for some of the sixty persons whom Cope's enclosure had dispossessed. It is unlikely that Cope had enclosed all the common fields: 240 acres is only a small part of the 2,320 acres of the parish, and the Manor House, the rectory and six cottages remained. The six cottages were probably on the hill, and it was on the site of two of these that John Spencer began to build himself a new Manor House.

> He took down the same two messuages and upon the soil of the same builded a mansion place for himself to dwell in, with other houses necessary and convenient.

He had been previously living at Hodnell, but his nephew had come of age and wanted the Manor there for himself. The medieval Manor House of Wormleighton had been down by the fishponds where the canal now makes a right-angled turn. This moated manor, which had housed the Mountforts, was described by Spencer as "but a sorry thatched house."

John Spencer's new "mansion place" still has the embattled parapets for which he obtained the sovereign's formal permission in November, 1512, even the vestiges of fortification needing assent in an England not very far from the Wars of the Roses. Three original buttresses have survived and divide the front of the house into two. The building originally had two stories, each 15 feet high, as the remaining tall windows show; some windows have been removed or partially blocked and one has been converted to a doorway. The walls are of well-weathered early sixteenth-century bricks with yellow stone dressings. The parapet is also of brick, but there is a string-course of moulded stone running below it the length of the building.

In and about this new house John Spencer claimed that almost sixty people were set at work. He had probably rebuilt the four other cottages, and was able to claim that the total population was now within a score of that of a generation earlier, before the enclosures. He could not deny that some houses had been destroyed, and for these he threw himself on the mercy of the court, and when in 1522 he was ordered to turn grassland back to arable he again petitioned for reasonable time to act. The fields were stocked with cattle and sheep which it would be disastrous to sell "in the dead time of winter"; the hedges were twenty years old and a profitable source of timber in a district where there was little woodland; and might it not be, he asked, that a fresh inquiry would show

> due proof whether it be to a more commodity and common weal for the country there, that the said hedges to stand or to be throw down.

Finally he asked for the renovation of the parish church to be set to his credit.

> In building and maintaining of the Church [I] bought all "inornaments" as cross, books, cope, vestments, chalices and censers, for the church gear that was within the church at the time when husbandmen were there inhabited was not worth six pounds, for they had never service by note for they were so poor and lived so poorly that they had no books to sing service on in the church. And where they never had but one priest I have had, and intend to have, two or three.

His cousin Thomas who remained in the old family property at Hodnell died there in 1531 and wished to be buried alongside his father in the decayed parish church of the deserted village. Sir John Spencer was buried neither at Hodnell nor Wormleighton but at St. Mary's, Great Brington, the church nearest to his Northamptonshire estate of Althorp (another depopulated village). The magnificent series of Spencer tombs in this church have been repainted and can now be seen in their original splendour: they lie in the north Chapel added by John Spencer to the rebuilt chancel in 1514, six years after his purchase of the Althorp estate. The tomb of John (d. 1522) and his wife Isabella stands in the easternmost of the arches dividing the chapel from the chancel. On the ceiling of the canopy an angel holds the Spencer arms; Sir John's effigy lies on the tomb, and his wife wears an heraldic mantle with a rosary at her girdle. Nearby are the equally ornate tombs of his grandson, his great-grandson and his great-great-grandson, Sir Robert, the first Baron Spencer of the line.

The Spencers had intermarried with the Northamptonshire gentry. Sir William, son and heir of the first Sir John of Wormleighton, had married Susan Knightley of Fawsley, where the tombs and brasses of the Knightleys, another great enclosing family, can be seen in the parish church which stands alone above the lakes. The village has gone, and a short distance from the church door the decaying mansion of the Knightleys is partly occupied by a firm of timber merchants.

The church's setting in the deer park makes it perhaps the most scenic of all the Midland deserted villages for those who like their landscape tamed in the Capability Brown manner. A public road crosses the park past the House and church, which is normally kept locked, the key being obtainable from the Rector of Charwelton, a village on the road from Wormleighton to Fawsley. While at Charwelton the glutton for depopulated sites may call at Church Charwelton, 1000 yards south-east of the modern village, to see the isolated manor house and the church with its monumental brasses of more enclosing squires, the Andrewes. In a list of English wool-growers drawn up c. 1530-40 "mr Andrewes of Charwelton" was credited with twenty sacks of wool a year "of his own growing and gathering", the produce of perhaps 3,000 sheep. Sir William Spencer and "my lady his Mother" brought in about 9,000 fleeces, and Sir Richard Knightley some 4,500. Many of these fleeces must have come from sheep who had grazed the streets and fields of deserted villages.[15]

The villagers of Fawsley had had 1,550 acres of field land at their disposal when reclamation was at its height. The lords of the manor had obtained a market charter in 1223 and in the fourteenth-century tax-lists the village seems substantial. Ninety taxpayers over the age of sixteen paid their fourpenny poll tax in 1377. Exactly when the village became depopulated is not certain: probably just before 1485. There were certainly tenants at Fawsley in 1425, and also a lord of the manor intent on exacting the old ploughing services, for in May of that year certain bond tenants of Robert Knightley refused to perform the customary services and bound themselves by an oath to stand or fall together. In the end Knightley may have been in the position of the abbot of Eynsham who had to lighten the burden of services if he was to keep any labour force at all in the years of labour shortage. Fawsley thus stands on the bridge between two types of depopulation, the empty fields of a plague-stricken Tusmore and the fields of Wormleighton and Whatborough emptied of husbandmen by "wolvish emulation".[16]

The Knightley family name derived from a Staffordshire village

---

[15] P.R.O. SP1/238, ff. 264-88.
[16] A general account in Bridges, 64-71; 1335: P.R.O. C135/35/24; 1377: P.R.O. E179/155/23; 1425: P.R.O. C66/417, m. 18d.

whence came a Richard Knightley to purchase Fawsley in 1416. It was another Richard, who died in 1534, who probably depopulated the village. His white alabaster tomb is seen in Plate 10. On the south side of the base are the carved figures of his eight mourning children: among these was the Richard who married Jane Spencer of Wormleighton. On the floor, just behind the clasped hands of Sir Richard's wife, can be seen the raised monumental brass of Edmund Knightley (d. 1542), brother of Sir Richard and a leading Commissioner for the suppression of the monasteries.

Fig. 10. The Knightley wall monument at Fawsley.

The font in the background of this photograph is seen again on the left of Fig. 10, showing the elaborate wall monument to Sir Valentine Knightley, another of Sir Richard's eight children; to Sir Valentine's son, another Sir Richard; and to his grandson, a second Sir Valentine. In a panel in the bottom, right corner appears a text from the book of Proverbs which has an ironical application for these acquisitive squires:

The liberal Person shall have plenty, and he that watereth shall also have raine.

The church at Fawsley is not regularly used but is in good repair.[17] The Midlands have very few ruined churches of the fashion of Norfolk Breckland or the Lincolnshire Wolds. The characteristic creation of the enclosing squire was a park and a new manor house to match it, and despite the "badge of atheism" which this conduct seemed to Norden to wear, the squires needed the parish churches for themselves and their household and were in no mood to turn it into a ruin. The villagers' church took on the role of a private manor chapel, and the aisles (as at Fawsley) were filling with tombs like an elegant mausoleum. Only occasionally, as at Compton Verney, did an eighteenth-century squire, calling in Capability Brown or another fashionable landscape gardener of the day, think it necessary to remove the old parish church which stood Gothic and too near the windows of the great house and replace it by something more distant and in the classical style. Capability Brown was called to advise on Fawsley but left the church high above the lakes.

The Census papers for Fawsley in 1851 show the social composition of an emparked parish. On the night of the Census the Hall contained Sir Charles Knightley, aged seventy, with his wife, daughter, son-in-law and granddaughter. There were also two nephews, of whom one was Rector of Charwelton and the other, curate of Fawsley. In addition to the family there was one visitor and twenty-six servants. In a near-by house lived the estate-agent, a surveyor and his family, and in a cottage there was a shepherd. Outside the park was one farm of 350 acres.[18]

IV

Many other Midland villages which have lost their villagers never had parish churches, and thus have no building or ruin to call a traveller across from the main road, curious to see whether the isolated church has any characteristic village- and street-earthworks close by. The churchless Midland villages must make their absence felt by other means, most commonly by a sudden emptiness of the map.

[17] Church and tombs: Bridges, 64-71.   [18] P.R.O. HO107/1741.

There is one such group of half-empty parishes near the Warwick-shire-Northamptonshire border. The parishes each have one village intact; and the village has the parish church; but the area of the parish is large enough for two or more villages, and their former names will usually be carried by isolated farms. The one-inch map looks bare in these quarters: instead of a network of roads, red and yellow, it shows an inferior system of unmetalled lanes, unfenced roads across large pasture fields and footpaths that have long fallen into disuse; the signposts bear the warning that minor roads are about to cross old pastures and parklands: "Gated Road" they proclaim, and the passenger in the car empties his lap and prepares to dismount every 400 yards and admire the variety of "please shut the gate" notices.

Immediately outside the east gate of Fawsley Park there is the

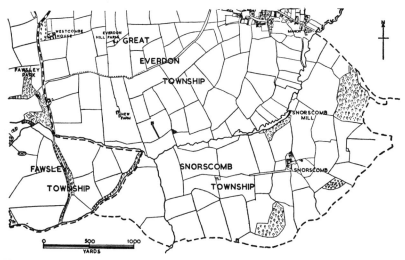

Fig. 11. The depopulated township of Snorscomb, a village destroyed in 1509 by the Knightleys of Fawsley (cf. Plate 10). The southern bounds appear in a charter of 944.

parish of Great Everdon, some 1,900 acres. Great Everdon is an attractively-set village, and Little Everdon is a small hamlet near the Hall; the southern part of the parish is empty. A lonely, unfenced and gated track leaves the Everdon-Farthingstone road near the mill and follows the south bank of the stream up a valley which steadily becomes more desolate. The map shows this road continuing for half a mile beyond Snorscomb Farm before dwindling into a footpath to Preston Capes, but in fact it ceases to be negotiable at the farmyard. Why should there be three continuous miles of low quality road? why should a valley look so desolate, although only a mile or two from sunny, intensively settled country? An examination of the fields behind Snorscomb Farm supplies the answer.

There is a great field of poor quality pasture pitted with hollows and laced with the banks of fishponds: this is the site of the small village for whose depopulation Sir Richard Knightley of Fawsley was summoned to answer in the Court of Exchequer in 1520. It was alleged that the nine houses of the village had been thrown down in February, 1509, fifty villagers evicted and 200 acres put to grass.[19]

The emptiness of Snorscomb is felt in an enclosed valley from which no extensive view of the rest of the world is possible, but the same feeling can be evoked by the continuous, empty, flat pastures at Radbourn, Hodnell, Ascote, Stoneton and Watergall. T. S. Eliot has described the same emptiness at the depopulated Huntingdonshire village of Little Gidding;

> Dust in the air suspended
> Marks the place where a story ended.
> Dust inbreathed was a house—
> The wall, the wainscot and the mouse . . .
>
> Water and fire succeed
> The town, the pasture and the weed . . .
>
> Water and fire shall rot
> The marred foundations we forgot,

and on the high ground to the east of Leicester, bordering on Rutland, the same intermittent desolation begins again.

Once served by a parody of Parliamentary trains, and now difficult of access by any public transport, the sites of Baggrave, Marefield, Owston, Newbold, Withcote and Whatborough provide another concentrated round of deserted villages. The height of the hills hereabouts is not great—Robin-a-Tiptoe Hill reaches up to touch 726 feet, and Whatborough Hill is 755 feet above sea level— but the streams have cut deep valleys, and there are rapid changes of gradient and view as the cyclist switchbacks northwards from the Youth Hostel at Loddington or the walker shoulders his pack at John

[19] Documents printed in translation in Beresford, 410-12.

of Gaunt station, just off a train as deserted as the villages he is about to visit. "Early Closing Day Thursday" said the British Railways time-table optimistically: but the shutters have been up for centuries.

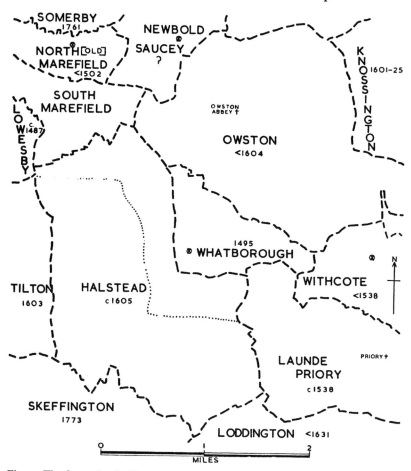

Fig. 12. The depopulated village of Whatborough and its neighbours, Withcote, Newbold Saucey and North (Old) Marefield, also depopulated. The dates in each parish are those of enclosure. The dotted line indicates a part of Whatborough thrown into the fields of Halstead in 1494 (cf. Plate 11).

Bleak in winter, the top of Whatborough Hill may have been sunny on the August 15th, 1586, when a strange party assembled there. There were twelve yeomen from surrounding villages, "substantial men" and "indifferent" to the cause at issue, a protracted dispute in the Court of Exchequer between the Warden of All Souls College, and Henry, Lord Cromwell. This Cromwell was the grandson of the Thomas Cromwell with whom Sir Edmund Knightley of Fawsley had worked as a Commissioner for the suppression of monasteries, one of which, Launde Priory, adjoined Whatborough Hill. In the usual way, the Barons of Exchequer had deputed Commissioners to come and take sworn evidence from local and knowledgeable inhabitants.

Assemblies of this kind, perambulating bounds and noting the landmarks, cross-questioning old men about the local customs of husbandry, tenure and common-rights could have been seen somewhere almost every week in Elizabethan England: the attested records of their depositions make formidable bundles in the Public Record Office. Accompanying the party to Whatborough Hill was Thomas Clerke of St. Martin's parish in Stamford, a surveyor and cartographer. Five weeks later he completed his map of Whatborough and the adjacent fields, surrounded it with a highly ornamental border, added a cartouche and an inset copy of the Exchequer warrant, and then presented it with two rougher copies to his patron, Robert Hovenden, the Warden of All Souls. Dr. Hovenden (1544-1614) was the author of a life of Archbishop Chichele (of Higham Ferrers, p. 176); and he put his historical researches to practical use. He sought out lapsed titles to land, discovered property which had strayed into the hands of the Crown, and finally recorded the landed endowments of his College for all time by commissioning a fine series of estate plans unequalled in their day for clarity and precision, as Plates 3, 4 and 7 show.

At Whatborough the task of the map-maker, Thomas Clerke, was to identify the bounds of Whatborough Close, 407 acres of pasture lying to the north of the road from Leicester to Oakham which passes just south of Whatborough Hill. A sketch-map might have sufficed, something like the crude diagrams attached to other sets of depositions in the Elizabethan Exchequer, but Clerke's plan was the equal of the other College estate plans made by Thomas Langdon, although not on so large a scale as the individual field-plans of Padbury, Salford or Maids Moreton.[20] The summits of the little hills

[20] There are three Whatborough plans at All Souls: one in the Hovenden portfolios, one listed in Martin as No. 219, and a third formerly in the Bursary.

were indicated by sketches of hillocks; the springs which rise on What-borough Hill had their size exaggerated: but the position of roads and hedges, and the internal detail of the fields can be transferred to a modern six-inch map with only minor corrections. Clerke swore on oath that the plan was

> made in figure and resemblance . . . in proportion and scale,

and in the verdict returned in 1587 the jury found [21]

> that the figure or plott to them exhibited is a true plott and proportion.

When Clerke visited Whatborough for his survey the open fields were no longer farmed by Whatborough villagers. His map shows a great hedge thrown across the former Furlongs, indifferent to their course, sometimes straddling the middle of a Furlong (Plate 11). On the west, some of the Whatborough Furlongs had been added to the fields of Halstead, which were still unenclosed in 1586. On the east the hedge had severed a great close, *Whateborough Close*, which had been converted to pasture. The sheep grazed over the site of the village where only the shepherd's house stood above ground, and the new hedge kept them from trespassing on the sown acres of Tilton and Halstead.

The course of this hedge over the old open-field strips was noted by more than one witness:

> parte of the furlongs lie within the hedge and parte withoute, and are to be seene at this day to prove this.[22]

What sign convinced the men of 1586 that there had once been open-field furlongs at this point? Thomas Clerke and the witnesses took it for granted that ridge-and-furrow was sufficient proof that the hill-side had once been broken up into the pattern of Furlongs which we encountered at Maids Moreton and Salford in Chapter 3. Clerke sketched in finely-spaced lines to show the direction of the "grain" and used heavier lines for the Furlong boundaries. The meadowland he left plain. The lines of his plan correspond with the line of ridge and furrow on the hill-slopes of Whatborough to-day.

Within the park of Launde Priory, enclosed about 1538, Clerke used similar words, writing on the plan (Plate 11, bottom right).

> theise groundes doe also lye ridge and furrow

and in another place

> theise groundes have like wise bene arable.

[21] All Souls, Whatborough MSS., No. 111: *Verdict.*   [22] *Ibid.*, No. 145, f. 3.

The experienced local farmers who were called as witnesses used the same terms. John Tarrie of Owston, a husbandman of 74, said:[23]

> the greatest parte of Whadborowe lyeth by ridge and furrowe,

and in a later lawsuit in the Court of Wards (1609) some villagers from Tilton and Halstead[24] were able to identify other land which had been enclosed for fifty years by its "ridge and furrowe". In the lawsuit of 1586 the hedge cast up between Whatborough Close and Halstead was described by more than one witness[25] as

> set . . . right over ridge and furrowe.

What of the village whose husbandmen had once tilled these fields? Clerke's plan shows in a central open space

> the place where the towne of Whateboroughe stoode

and the short lines which fill the rest of this space may be his attempt to show the earthworks of the houses and crofts. In a childlike, roof-door-and-window sketch he showed "one little howse nowe stand-inge" where Christopher Typtape (or Tiptoft), the shepherd, was still living, his sheep grazing where

> apparent signes and tokens yet seene

indicated[26]

> that there hath bene there sometyme a village or towneshippe which hathe bene decayed long synce.

In 1525, four of the oldest men of Halstead had set their names to a description of its bounds, and along these they came to Whatborough Oak,[27]

> nye there as the houses of the same town stood.

In 1586 there was no one alive who remembered the old village, but it had lived in the gossip of the old men. Valentine Allen, aged seventy-two, a husbandman from South Marefield, said[28] that he

> hath hearde by his auncestors that there was a hamlett or village there whereof some signes or likelihoods appear at this daye.

[23] All Souls, Whatborough MSS., No. 111, f. 12.   [24] *Ibid.*, No. 195.
[25] *Ibid.*, No. 111.   [26] *Ibid.*, No. 147.   [27] *Ibid.*, No. 86.   [28] *Ibid.*, No. 111.

This cautious testimony was backed by that of the other witnesses, whose ages ranged from fifty-four to eighty.

Clerke's plan is one of the very few to indicate a deserted village site until the archaeological interests of one of the Ordnance Survey officers caused some of the North and East Riding sites to be marked on the first edition of the six-inch sheets in 1850-54. In 1625 John Norden crossed the site of East Lilling (Yorks.) and noted[29] that

> it hath been a hamlet of some capacity, though now utterly demolished,

but his plans did not show the site (p. 220).

The dispute which brought Whatborough into the courts and Clerke into its fields was both protracted and complicated. It began with an Exchequer action in 1586 and only ended in 1605 when the Privy Council appointed a committee of seven Privy Councillors to arbitrate.[30] The College attorney then noted that the action had cost the College £2,000 besides the loss of rent. Things were not made better by the political commitments of their adversary, the Lord Cromwell, a descendant of that Thomas Cromwell who had served as a Commissioner for the suppression of the monasteries. It was noted in the College records[31]

> this terme, Michaelmas 1598, nor after duringe the life of Queene Elizabeth, little or nothing could be donne in this cause, but all was stayed by reason of the Lord Cromwell his going and being in Ireland. And his trouble in England after his coming from thence.

This is a generous understatement. Cromwell had been sent to the Tower for his complicity in Essex's rebellion and was only released in 1601 after paying a fine of £6,000.

It is difficult to sum up the contentions in a case which kept so many lawyers busy for so long, but the origin of the trouble was the College practice of leasing out their land at Whatborough for long periods at a time. It lay distant from Oxford, and the College found it convenient to take a fixed money-rent. In 1458 the houses and field-land were leased from the College by the abbot of Launde

---

[29] B.M. Harleian MSS. 6288; Ingram's copy is T.N. MSS. B 417391, lacking the plans.

[30] All Souls, Whatborough MSS., Nos. 156-57; side-issues were raised later in the Court of Wards, ibid no. 195.

[31] *Ibid.*, No. 145, f. 1.

whose Priory adjoined Whatborough on the south-east and who already had three properties in the village. In 1504 and 1531 the lease was renewed, each time at a higher rent to keep step with rising prices. The abbot was well able to pay, for the whole village was enclosed in 1494-95. The lease from the College and a purchase of six cottages from another neighbour, Owston Abbey, had given Launde control of the whole township.

Yet, by the time that the term of the lease expired, the monasteries of Owston and Launde were no more, and the Launde lands had passed to Thomas Cromwell, who had been one of the principal agents in the suppression. The enclosure had confused the old boundaries and when the College came to renew the lease they found that the Cromwells denied them possession of Whatborough Close. Naturally, the College lawyers had to clear up the tangled history as well as the confused boundaries, and several of the questions in their interrogatories sought to draw from the local witnesses what had happened to the village.

> The Pryor of Launde, being possessed of Wateberge by force of the leases from the Colledge . . . and having purchased divers freeholds, in king h[enry] 7. time depopulated the towne of Wateberge and enclosed the fields thereof

say Hovenden's notes,[32] and in the pleading in Carter *v.* Cromwell the College attorney stated[33] that

> the said Pryors depopulated the Towne . . . which stoode in the greate Close . . . as by the foundacions of howses may appeare, and suffered the Mannor House of Whadborowe and all the edifices of Buildings thereunto and all the Cottages and coppiehowld tennents to fall to utter Ruine, one little howse nowe standinge except.

Christopher Tiptoft's house showed that the shepherd and his dog did in truth have all.

The top of Whatborough Hill is not one's ideal choice for a village site, and Launde Priory could have had only a small hamlet on its hands in 1494-95, which is the date given by another document for the enclosure of Whatborough Close. In 1086 there were fifteen households; there was a chapel in 1220, but it disappears from the record soon after.[34] In 1334 the tax assessment of 5s. 6d. was small,

[32] All Souls, Whatborough MSS., No. 145, f. 3.   [33] *Ibid.*, No. 147.
[34] *Ibid.*, Nos. 1, 3, and 145, ff. 44, 65 and 78.

and in the fifteenth century large reductions in this small sum were being allowed by the tax-collectors. Whatborough had a dozen taxpayers[35] in 1377 when its neighbour (the now-depopulated) Owston had twenty-nine, and Withcote, also deserted, had forty-five. Halstead, which still survives, had sixty-four.

In the early days of its settlement any advantages which Whatborough possessed were defensive rather than agricultural: from its hill-top vantage point, the approaches through the tracks and clearings of the Leicestershire forest could be scanned. Of the two elements in the name, *wheat* and *burh* (= fortified earthwork), the second seems to have been the determinant advantage when the site was first being occupied: the crops felt all the disadvantages of a high wind-swept site. The township now contains only one farm, as it did a hundred years ago when the Census enumerator of 1851 recorded a grazier, his wife, two children and an elderly pauper as the sole inhabitants.[36] No public footpath crosses the site of the village and permission to visit must be obtained from Whatborough Farm. The visit is rewarding: there is a good view in all directions, Rutland to the east, the Nottinghamshire Wolds to the north, Northamptonshire to the south and Leicestershire to the west. The immediate surroundings are well wooded in hedgerow and plantations: this is not the virgin timber which faced the Anglo-Saxon settlers who first chose this site. As their clearings extended into the valleys the timber went down before the plough: the timber seen hereabouts is the timber of Leicestershire parklands which in turn supplanted so many ploughs; it is the timber of the squire and the gamekeeper and not the timber of the woodcutter and the swineherd.

At Whatborough the perimeter of the village site is easy to find.[37] The level, ploughed field surface and the corrugations of pasture suddenly cease. There is a low rampart of an earthwork to be crossed, and inside it the characteristic pattern of streets, crofts and houses. The hollow-ways which mark the former streets are clearer than any of those visited earlier in this chapter; the individual houses are represented by saucer-shaped depressions adjacent to, and a little higher than the streets. There is not much shape in these house-

[35] P.R.O. E179/133/24.

[36] P.R.O. HO107/2080.

[37] W. G. Hoskins, *Essays in Leics. History* (1950), 94-98, with air photograph of the site; an enlargement of part of this photograph is printed in Beresford, Plate 5.

earthworks: the fallen rubble and the accumulation of soil and grass would need to be cleared by the spade before the plan of the houses could be recovered. The streets have received their share of washed and blown soil but, even after their sides have been smoothed and their road surface submerged, the streets are markedly deeper than the general level: the constant passage of men, animals and carts wore away the soil, and the rains continued the erosion, which has only been checked by the protective shroud of turf after the men had given way to sheep and cattle.

Whatborough has no fishponds at the village: for those the streams near the Priory and castle must be examined, but it has natural springs at the south of the village, and streams which join on the lower slopes. In 1586 Clerke drew these rather like a two-headed snake, the heads resting inside the village perimeter. The water has now been piped away, but in very wet weather the channels down the hill-side are full again, swirling past the crofts, through the small piece of meadow, and breaching the outer boundary of the village before joining forces to run down between the furrows of the plough-lands. It rained on a party of us who surveyed the site in April, 1947, but April is a notoriously cruel month; perhaps Thomas Clerke, the commissioners and the jurymen were no more fortunate in 1586: for wheat prices were unusually high that autumn, suggesting that it had been a bad summer. It could not have been worse than another day in July, 1954, when I sat miserably in a car waiting for the rain to clear and the sun to come to aid of the camera.

NOTE. Since this chapter was written, Dr. M. E. Finch has brought together an account of the rise of the Spencer family in her *Wealth of Five Northamptonshire Families, 1540-1640* (Northants. Record Soc., xix [1956]).

5

A JOURNEY TO NEW TOWNS

HEDON, YORKS. E.R.

RAVENSEROD, YORKS. E.R.

WYKE UPON HULL, YORKS. E.R.

> *If the place, whereto men are drawen through the Authority of any, afford them no commodityes they will not abyde nor tarry there.*
>
> G. BOTERO, *Delle Cause della Grandezza delle Città* (*in the translation of R. Peterson, 1606*).

Chapter Five

A JOURNEY TO NEW TOWNS

IN the 250 years following the Norman Conquest the population of England multiplied some threefold, rising from about 1,100,000 to about 3,700,000. One consequence of these extra mouths and hands has already been seen, for they brought about that steady increase in the area of cultivated land which spread the open fields across the English plains. But the same 250 years witnessed an expansion in the number of towns and town-dwellers, and in the next two chapters we shall be visiting towns which were created in this period. The object will still be the same: to detect the finger of the past in the present landscape and to show how topography—even of streets and squares—is still the child of history.

The towns in which Elizabethan surveyors worked were the product of many centuries' growth. In these centuries some towns had prospered steadily, and in particular London, Newcastle and Bristol; others, like Dunwich and Stonar, had flourished and faded; others were beginning to mourn their past glories and look for scapegoats and remedies. Whatever their difference in size, most Elizabethan towns had several features in common beside antiquity and tradition. They were the possessors of "liberties", privileges which marked their citizens off from the general run of country people. They had market-places and fairs. Many of them had been fortified and some still retained their defences. Their townsmen displayed great extremes of wealth, and in recurring periods of bad trade the living standards of many were pushed below the poverty line. Towns had more inhabitants than a village and their populations were more densely housed.

Thus, a borough at the end of the Middle Ages was marked off from the countryside not only by a superior legal status but by the satisfying achievements built upon it. To the tax-collector this means that a higher rate of tax can be levied from townsmen whose incomes exceed a peasant's. To the mason and carpenter a town is a place whose houses are more numerous and more substantially built than those of a village. To the lord's bailiff a town is a place of diverse skills where he can hope to find craftsmen to tackle jobs beyond the capacity of a jack-of-all-trades village smith. To an officer of a noble household it is a place not only of purchases on a larger scale than in a village but of commodities coming from far beyond, their presence engineered by the initiative of the town's specialist merchants. In the largest towns the lady of the household may hope to find the rare things of the known world fashioned to her taste, but even in the smallest market-town the country wife edges among the stalls, hesitates beside some talkative huckster and fingers the pennies she got an hour ago for the chickens already on their way to the pot in the crowded inn.

The more usual sequence in a town's history is typified in the next chapter by two old-established English villages which first acquired a distinctive colour of town life in the thirteenth century when certain legal privileges were bestowed on them. In the present chapter the Humber estuary is visited to examine some of the "new towns" of the Middle Ages, created in open country where there was no village before. If the act of creation proved successful, there was soon little to distinguish this "new town" from one which had developed more gradually, and most Elizabethan antiquaries surveying the towns of England would have found it difficult to say which were "gradual" and which "planted". Yet, as this chapter will show, the two types of town are likely to have different street-plans and different parish shapes.

What they had in common, both in the thirteenth and sixteenth centuries, was the possession of a legal status which marked them off from their village neighbours. In some towns it was merely the right to hold a market; in others there was also the right to hold fairs; and in others the distinctive possession was the existence of burgesses and burgages. The townsman who could call himself a burgess was a free man at a time when the majority of Englishmen were subject to customs and duties of the manorial system. If he paid his rent—which was usually a known and unchanging sum—he was secure in possession of his land, free to sell it and dispose of it by will, and not liable to be called upon for service at the lord's plough or on the lord's estate. His wife and family were also free.

128

PLATES

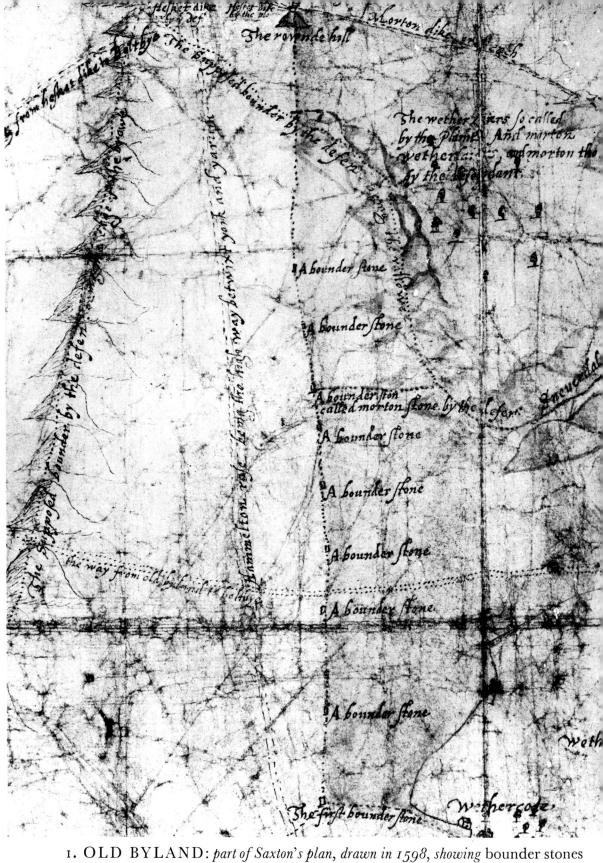

1. OLD BYLAND: *part of Saxton's plan, drawn in 1598, showing* bounder stones *on the western edge of the parish, the disputed* Wetherlaiers (top right) *and the* rownde hill (top centre). (*Cp. fig. 4.*)

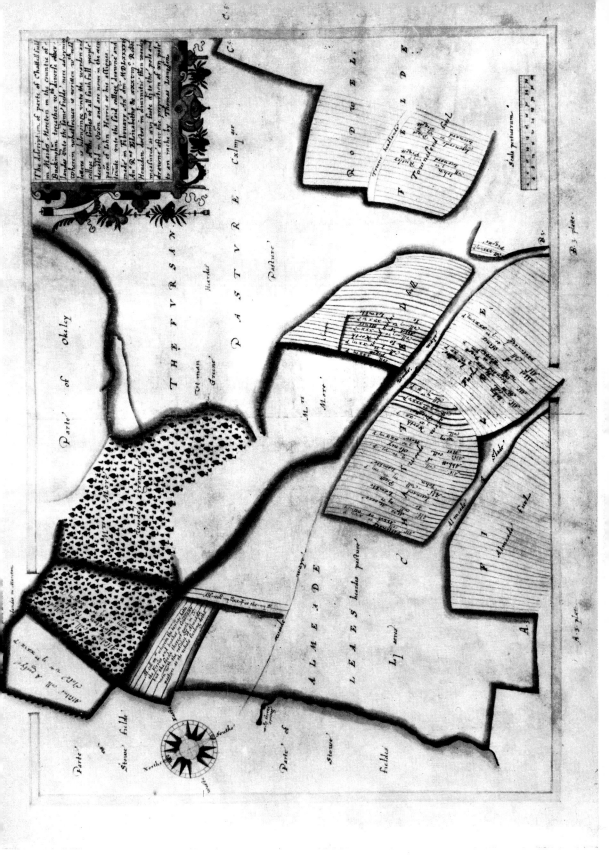

2. MAIDS MORETON *in 1596. The N.W. portion of Langdon's plan, with wood, pasture, and fragments of open fields. (Cp. fig. 5.)*

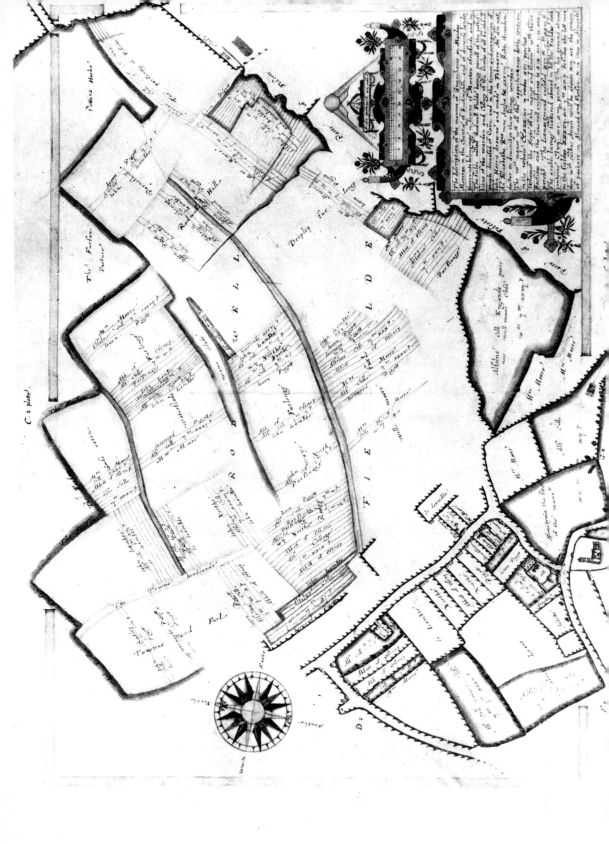

3. MAIDS MORETON *in 1596. The village centre with the church*, 'site of the manor', *some enclosed fields, and part of* Rodwell Fielde. (*The blank areas indicate land which did not belong to the College.*)

4. MAIDS MORETON: *a cottage on the west of the main street, shown in 1596 at the head of its croft, belonging to John Lamberte;* (below) *a view down* Balles Crosse Waye *which divided the two open fields, Meade and* Hollowwaye. *The buildings are those of College Farm, built in the newly enclosed fields in 1801.*

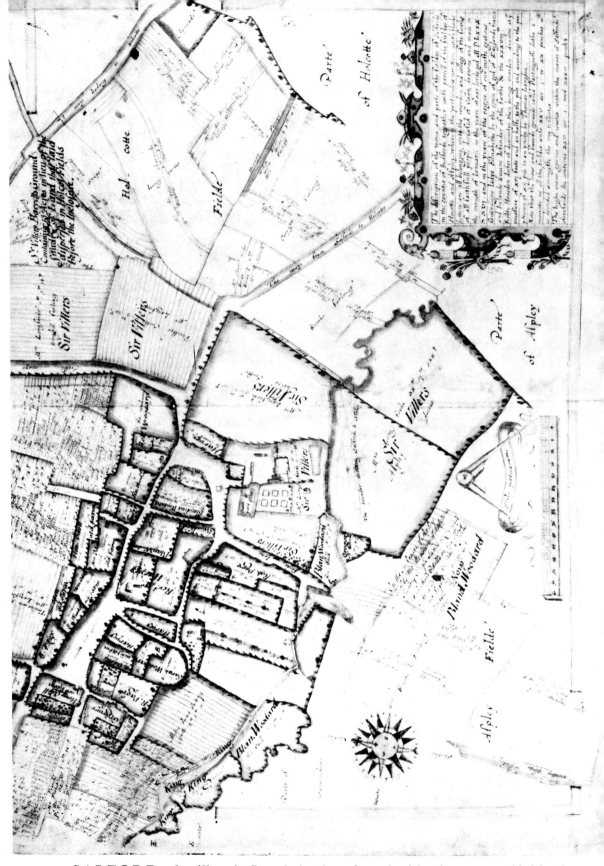

5. SALFORD: *the village in Langdon's plan of 1596 with other names added by the College bursar at a partial enclosure in 1769.*

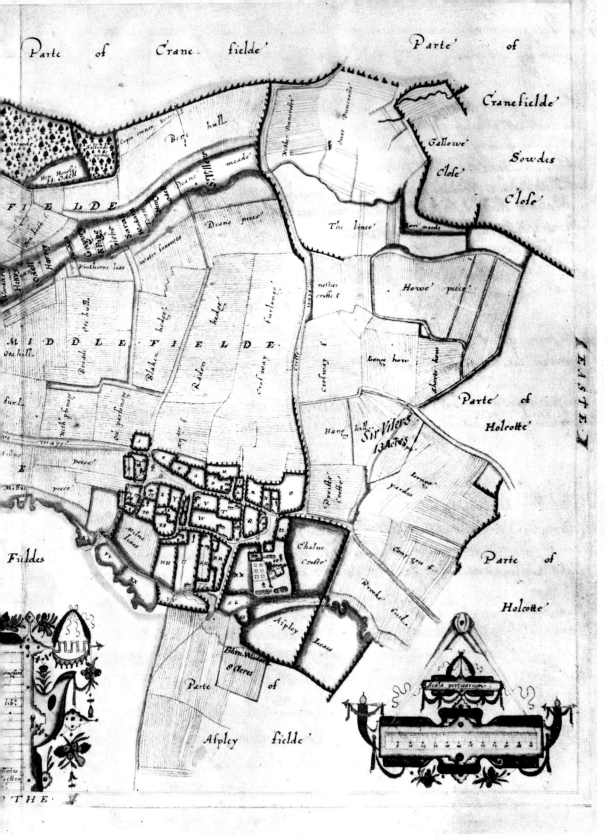

6. SALFORD: *part of the open fields in 1596 with 'Sir Vil[l]ers' added in 1769 when a partial enclosure was agreed.*

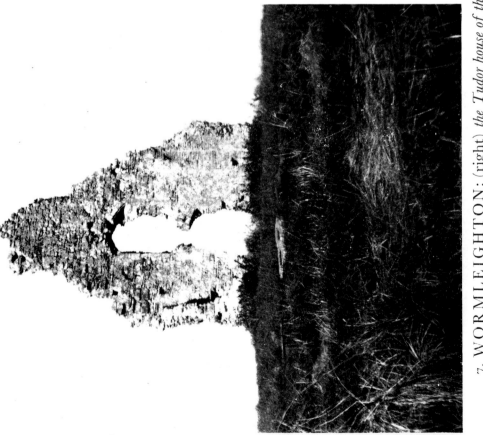

7. WORMLEIGHTON: (right) *the Tudor house of the enclosing squire;* MIDLEY: (left) *the ruined church of the depopulated village on Romney Marsh.*

8. WORMLEIGHTON: *sheep graze over the village site. The depressions are the village fishponds;* (below) FAWSLEY: *two tombs of the Knightley family, the sheep-masters who destroyed the village.*

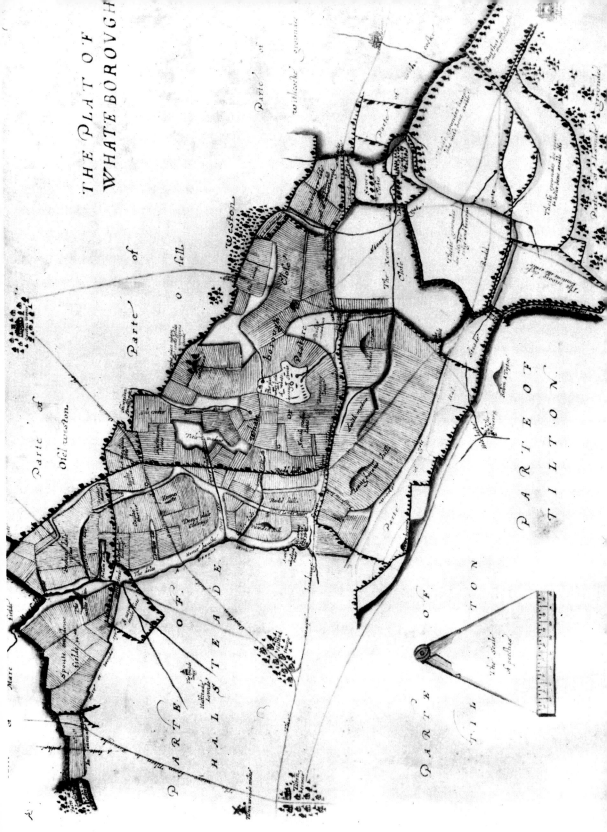

9. WHATBOROUGH: *part of Thomas Clerke's plan of 1586, showing the hedge thrown up in 1494 when the western portion of Whatborough fields was added to Halstead, and the remainder thrown into one large close.*

10. WHATBOROUGH: 'The place where the towne of Whateboroughe stoode': *looking from Halstead parish boundary eastward to the hill-top site of the deserted village. Compare the hedges in the 1586 plan, Plate 9.*

11. WHARRAM PERCY: *the ruined church, with excavation of the north aisle about to commence;* (below) *a fifteenth-century peasant house, excavated on the hill-side above the church: wall foundations, on top of which was a wooden superstructure; the group of stones near the centre of the interior was a hearth; opposing doorways can be seen near far end of longer sides.*

12. HEDON: *the grass-grown market-place, and St. Augustine's, the only survivor of the three churches.*

a. The market place
b. The scyte of y^e olde castle
c. The church & church yarde
e. The Colledge
f. a new inclosure of m^r Hughes
g. the backe lane
h. the Comon hill
+. the p^{r}sonage
k. the scholehouse
l. m^r Ruddes

2 The way to Itleborro
3 The way to Higham parck
4 The way to Bedford
5 The ways to Rushden
6 The ways to Raun

Comune

13. HIGHAM FERRERS: *John Norden's plan of 1591.*

Feyld ĸs.

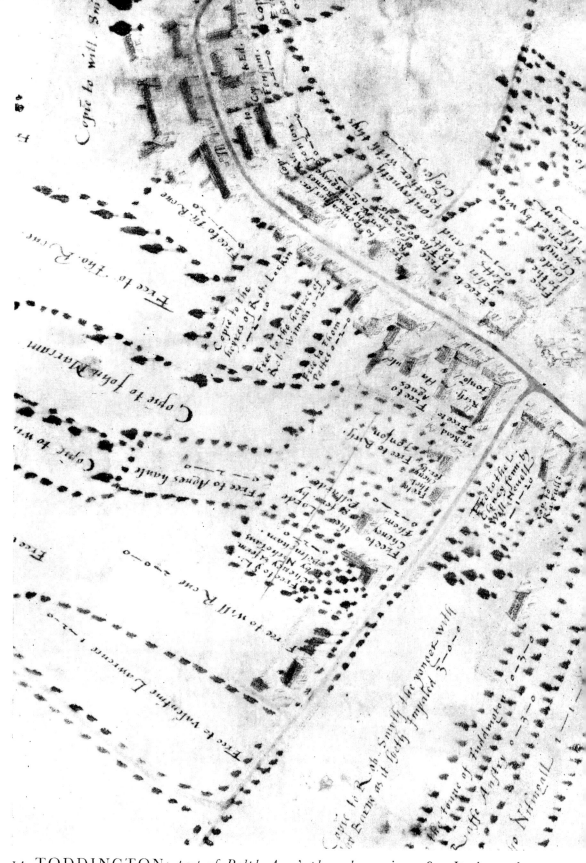

14. TODDINGTON: *part of Ralph Agas' plan, drawn in 1581. It shows the market-place, church, and the site of the Norman castle* (right).

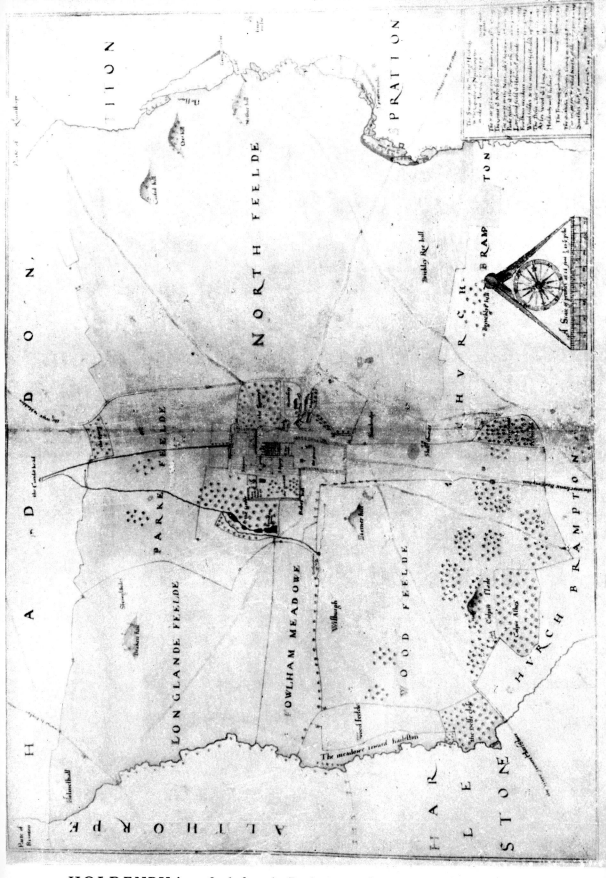

15. **HOLDENBY** *in 1580 before the Park was made.*

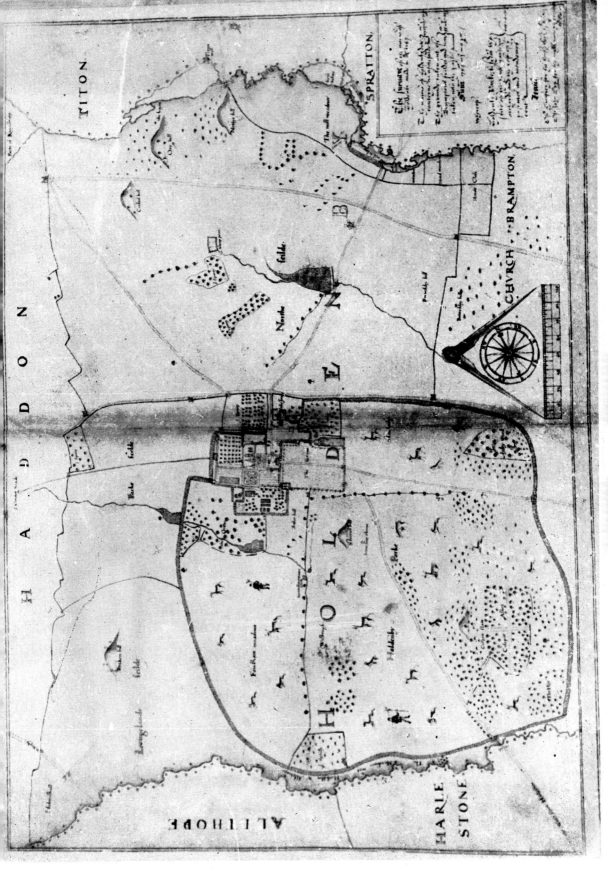

16. **HOLDENBY** *in 1587 after the Park was made.*

17. PARKS OF NORTHAMPTONSHIRE: *Saxton's plan of 1576 with the parks ringed by little pales. Higham Park is shown at the foot, and Fawsley top centre.*

This freedom was an immense advantage in the pursuit of any occupation and it was the attraction which steadily drew men to the towns. Even in agriculture, which formed a side-line in most boroughs, the freeman was more able to specialize and was free from the awkward summons to work on the lord's land, where such services were still exacted, or free from payment when the lord was one who chose to take cash in lieu of personal labour. But it was in the non-agricultural occupations that the townsmen needed personal freedom most. The freeman kept what he earned: the villein was himself his lord's chattel and his possessions were vulnerable to exactions both during his life and at death. The freeman could follow the time-table which best suited his craft or his trade without fearing the reeve's summons into the field. He could move freely from market to market seeking his raw material cheap and making contact with those who bought his finished product.

It was the incomes earned by free men in these surroundings which induced even the most conservative manorial lords to grant charters to their villages. The sums which were paid and the promises of future regular payments were tempting additions to a lord's rent-roll, earned effortlessly in comparison with the profits of a home farm. The further step of allowing a borough to be self-governing and to elect its own officers was a much more serious concession to make, and was not everywhere made. In many boroughs the main concession remained the improved legal status of the burgess himself, and on that base—together with a market and fair—many towns were able to build prosperity.

The planned towns of the Humber estuary were the product of the years following the Norman Conquest. Even the widespread grants of borough status to old-established villages proved insufficient to meet the demand for towns, and at least seventy-five[1] of these new plantations were called into existence between 1086 and 1350. After that date economic conditions did not encourage any further additions and the towns already established were more than adequate for a population reduced by the plagues.

Even when the period between 1540 and 1640 brought a great revival of industrial activity in textiles, iron and coal, the new

[1] The English were at the same time responsible for new towns in Gascony, Normandy, Ireland, the Welsh border and Wales. I hope to make these plantations the subject of my next book.

industries were based in the countryside and their workers lived not in new towns but in old villages. It was only in the late eighteenth century that another great increase in population and another industrial revolution spread houses, factories and streets far out beyond the old centres of population and created new towns of coal, iron and steam.

The "New Towns" of our own day, the product of a central planning agency, have much in common with the new towns planted in the medieval countryside. Both are rooted in an outside authority which provides land, building-plots and certain services. Each displays a regularity of street plan more disciplined than that which results from years of piecemeal growth and a slow transition from village to town. In neither medieval nor modern New Towns were commerce and industry already waiting for house-room and shop-space: the medieval burgess had to be attracted as did the modern industrialist. A medieval landowner who miscalculated the attractiveness of his site paid the penalty in empty streets, as even Edward I found at Newton on the Isle of Purbeck. It looks as if the growth of industry and trade between 1086 and 1350 was sufficient to permit the establishment of new towns in the gaps between the old: but only a limited number and not everywhere. The projected borough of Bere, Merioneth, was never built; the new town of Cause outside Cause Castle, Shropshire, was in decay by the mid-fifteenth century; and the Northumberland borough of Warenmouth was so unknown to the Elizabethan Chancery that its charter was ascribed to Wearmouth.[2]

If there was a right place and a wrong place there was also a right time and a wrong time to plant a medieval New Town. Most unfortunate were the members of the order of St. John of Jerusalem who thought that they saw an admirable site for a new town in Lincolnshire, halfway between Lincoln and Newark on the busy Foss Way. There was no village on the road in the whole sixteen miles of this section, and the Knights' manor of Eagle abutted on the road at the halfway point. The king was petitioned, the money paid and a charter granted. Yet to-day there is no town, no village and no hamlet at this point, nor any earthworks to show that building ever

[2] Newton: Hutchins, i, 462 and 652; Bere: E. A. Lewis, *The Medieval Boroughs of Snowdonia* (1912), 23 and 282; Cause: (Anon.) *Trans. Salop. Arch. Soc.*, liv (1951-52), 45-68; Warenmouth: *Northumb. County Hist.*, i (1893), 194; *Cal. Chart.*, i, 320.

began.[3] The fault was not in the acumen of the projectors who—on paper—had as good a chance as the projectors of Baldock, Buntingford and Royston, New Towns with very similar positions on important north-south roads. The misfortune was in the time. New Towns flourish best on new opportunities and an expanding volume of trade. Some historians have seen certain signs of a general economic depression in the fourteenth century with roots back in the early years of the century. But the cruellest blow was struck by the events of the years following the Eagle charter: they saw the Black Death and the reduction of the English population by perhaps 25-30 per cent. With empty warehouses and empty shops in the old-established towns and with the population all over Europe so drastically reduced, the chances of promoting another community to live by buying and selling were less than promising. But not all the New Towns of the twelfth and thirteenth centuries have melancholy histories: one of them, Boston, was probably the tenth largest town in England in 1377, while such well-known towns as Portsmouth and Liverpool had their origin in this period.[4]

II

The Humber estuary forms a natural outlet to the North Sea both from the Midlands via the Trent and from the Yorkshire Pennines and plains via the Ouse and its tributaries. Yet in Domesday Book the estuary is strangely empty of towns. The oldest large town east of York was Beverley, an administrative and commercial centre as well as a port but relatively hampered by its position on the river Hull, nine miles up from the Humber, far from the sea and with a hinterland restricted by the Yorkshire Wolds on the west. On the sea-coast itself, the older ports nearest the Humber were Scarborough, Bridlington and Grimsby but these ports had no waterways leading inland which could compare with the Humber rivers.

The Humber estuary was a natural place for shelter from storms and pirates and for transhipment of goods off river barges to larger vessels for the voyage coastwise or across the North Sea. Near the

---

[3] T. Hugo, *The History of Eagle* (1876), 14-21.

[4] Boston: M. R. Lambert and R. Walker, *Boston, Tattershall and Croyland* (1930); A. M. Cook, *Boston* (1948), 1-15; Portsmouth: *V.C.H. Hants.*, iii, 172-202; Liverpool: *V.C.H. Lancs.*, iv, 1-57.

sea the estuary has shoals and shifting banks, so that the two main medieval ports, Hedon and Kingston on Hull, developed twenty miles up river where the coast became firm and the tributary rivers gave shelter from the open and tidal estuary.

The development after the Norman Conquest of these new Humber ports depended not only upon their geographical advantages as havens but also on the economic development of the hinterlands

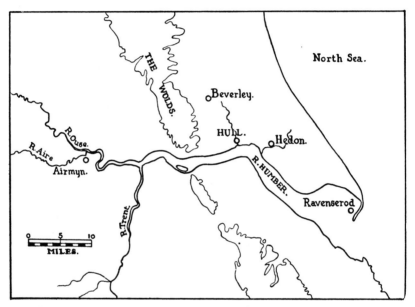

Fig. 13. The New Towns of the Humber with the old town and port of Beverley.

drained by the rivers which flow into the Humber. Just as the post-Conquest development of King's Lynn and Boston mirrored the growing economic potentialities of the east Midlands and Lincoln-shire, so the new ports of the north-east (from the Humber to Hartlepool, South Shields, North Shields, Alnmouth and Berwick) show the increased importance of the produce of the north-eastern counties, particularly in wool, raw hides, lead, leather, grain and cloth. On the southern and south-eastern coasts of England where the hinterlands had been earlier developed there were old-established ports with good Continental connections and only a very limited need for new ports. The New Towns of southern England were therefore, in the main, inland market towns catering for more intensive exploitation and vigorous exchange within developing areas of old colonization.

The four New Towns of the Humber were situated in the territory of important landlords. The small river port of Airmyn stood at the junction of the Ouse with the Aire and was planted, probably in the reign of Henry I (1100-35), by the abbot of St. Mary's, York, who also derived a substantial income from the tolls of the important ferry at this point near where Booth Ferry bridge still provides the lowest crossing of the river for traffic coming from the Midlands to the East Riding. The site of the new town was a river bank on the edge of the parish of Snaith.[5]

Like Airmyn, the settlement at Wyke, the forerunner of Edward I's town of Kingston upon Hull, does not appear in Domesday Book and the earliest known documents bearing its name date from 1160-80, that is within a generation of the foundation of Airmyn. Wyke was more than a river port. A natural resting place for passing traffic and placed at the junction with the river route to Beverley, it was also set where the Humber was deep enough to satisfy the needs of sea-going traffic. The ground on which permanent houses were first built was, like Airmyn, on the edge of a parish. The town lay within Hessle parish and by 1200 had obtained a dependent chapel of its own, the mother church of Hessle being four and a half miles away to the west.[6]

In 1301 the Archbishop of York was on a visit here and noticed that the townsmen had to take the bodies of their dead along the banks of the Humber for burial at Hessle, often at great risk in floodtime. The Archbishop decided to allow the town to have its own burial ground alongside its chapel of Holy Trinity, and in 1302 the king granted a vacant plot on the west of the chapel for this purpose. In 1304 he gave more land for the use of the Carmelite Friars whose old building in Monkgate was

> too small for their divine service and for the people of the town and others coming there from divers countries,

[5] W. Farrar, ed., *Early Yorkshire Charters*, i (1914), 270; P.R.O. Curia Regis Roll 151 m.27d. (1253): "there was no town here till the abbot's predecessors founded the town."

[6] The documents are brought together in J. Billson, *Wyke on Humber in 1293* (1928).

but it was not until the seventeenth century that the chapel of Holy Trinity became independent of Hessle and a full parish church.

The New Town of Wyke lay within the manor of Myton which was the property of the Cistercian abbey of Meaux, seven miles to the north among the low lands of Holderness. In 1279 the abbey was granted the right to hold a weekly market and an annual fair at Wyke. The fair was to be held on the eve, day and morrow of the feast of the Holy Trinity and on twelve days following. The choice of date is significant and is matched in many other places where fairs were held at the very season when men had been long accustomed to congregate for the patronal festival. At Hedon the annual fair, granted seven years earlier than at Wyke, was held at St. Augustine-tide. The great parish church of Hedon dedicated to St. Augustine can be seen in Plate 12.

No doubt the abbey at Meaux found the port of Wyke convenient for their own provisioning, rather as Alnwick abbey had a share in the planting of a port at Alnmouth for its supplies. The port of Wyke also served for the shipment of the most valuable of the crops of the Meaux estates, the fleeces of Holderness. In 1193 the wool contributed by the Cistercian houses of Yorkshire towards Richard I's ransom was collected at Wyke ("portum de Holme") and the port must then have been already well developed, for in 1203-5 it ranked sixth among English ports when a tax was levied from merchants.

It is sometimes said that Edward I founded the town of Kingston upon Hull. In fact, he acquired the town at Wyke from the abbot of Meaux in 1293 and an impressive programme of public works began. Between 1297 and 1302 the King's Quay was built and by 1334 a Hall of Pleas had been erected at the south end of the present market-place. These were also the years, it will be recalled, of the new cemetery (1302) and the new house of Friars (1304). Edward extended the duration of the fair to six weeks and set aside $7\frac{1}{4}$ acres of pasture to be a permanent site for it. In 1299 he gave the town the status of a self-governing borough. The king renamed the town *Kingston* and certainly engineered an expansion in the number of building-plots, although some were still vacant in 1320. Yet there is no doubt that he found a town already in existence alongside the Humber and that it had been created by the abbots of Meaux.

The town of Hedon, with which we are principally concerned

here, has features in its development which recall Wyke and Airmyn.
It was planted on the edge of an agricultural parish, probably on
uncultivated ground, by the side of the small river or creek which
flowed into the Humber a mile to the south.[7] It had the advantage
of being nearer the sea than Wyke and this advantage probably
accounts for its earlier development. While there is no mention of it
in Domesday Book, the town and its tolls first appear in a document
written between 1138 and 1142, about the time of the foundation of
Airmyn. By 1167-70 it had a borough charter, more than a century
before Wyke. Yet the up-creek position was bound to prove less
attractive as the size of ships and the volume of traffic grew, and by
the late thirteenth century Hedon was feeling the rivalry not only of
Wyke but also of another port, the fourth of the Humber New Towns,
planted even nearer the sea, just off Spurn Head at Ravenserod.[8]
In 1280 a local jury reported to the Exchequer that

> the men of Hedon are straitened and poor; many of them wish to move
> away on account of being tallaged here every year; and they have
> near them two other good towns, Ravenser and "the Hul" which have
> good harbours and grow day by day, and if they go there they can
> dwell without paying tallage [i.e. the tax which the lord of a town
> could levy on townsmen at will].

It is curious that the lord of Hedon should have wanted to treat
Hedon harshly, for he was also the lord of Ravenserod. Both these
New Towns owed their existence to the earls of Aumale, lords of
Holderness, and it is worth turning aside to Ravenserod before
visiting Hedon, since its sudden rise and fall underlines rather than
contradicts what has been said about the advantageous positions of
Hedon and Wyke, west of the shoals, and in some respects its origin
and early years are better documented.

A visit to Ravenserod is not possible: it has been under the
sea for nearly 600 years. One can only stand on the desolate shore
of Spurn Head and look westwards into the estuary towards the
traditional site, described by the chronicle of Meaux abbey in these
words:

[7] The documents in their original Latin are printed in J. R. Boyle, *The Early
History of Hedon* (1895).

[8] The documents in their original Latin are printed in J. R. Boyle, *The Lost
Towns of the Humber* (1889).

the town of Ravenserod, occupying a position in the utmost limits of
Holderness between the waters of the sea and the Humber, is distant
from the mainland a mile or more. For access to it there is a sandy
road no broader than an arrow's flight yet wonderfully maintained by
the tides and the ebb and flow of the Humber.

The interest of Meaux in Ravenserod was not, as at Wyke, that of
the landlord who had sponsored the town, but merely of one
proprietor among many. Between 1241-49 the third William de
Fortibus, earl of Aumale, had given them a plot of land in his new
borough to

> construct buildings suitable for a store of herrings and other fish.

About the same time as this gift to Meaux the earl obtained a
charter from the king for a Thursday market and a sixteen days' fair
in the new town. No document from the actual year of foundation
has survived, but in 1274-76 and again in 1290 the complaints of
Ravenserod's rivals included an account of its origin.

In 1274-76 the Hundred Rolls give the following story.

> Forty years and more ago the casting up of the sea caused sands and
> stones to accumulate, and on them the earl of Aumale built a town.

This account would make the town about fifteen years old when the
market charter was granted in 1251. Another story was told in 1290
when the king was investigating complaints from Grimsby that trade
was being captured by Ravenserod, and in this version the town
appears very small in 1251.

> In the reign of king Henry [1216-72] the father of the present king, at
> first by the casting up of the sea, a certain island was born which is
> called Ravenserod. And afterwards fishermen dried their nets there
> and men began little by little to dwell and stay there, and afterwards
> ships laden with divers kinds of merchandize began to unload and sell
> at the town. And now, inasmuch as the island is nearer the sea than
> our town of Grimsby and as ships can unload more easily, nearly all
> ships do stay, unload and sell there.
>
> Asked what time men had lived at Ravenserod, the jury say: forty
> years ago [i.e. about 1250], a certain ship was cast aground at a place
> where there were no houses built, and a certain man took the ship and
> made a cabin out of it to live in and dwelt there, selling food and drink
> to merchants whom he received there, and so others came there to

dwell, but thirty years ago [i.e. about 1260], there were not more than four dwellings.

And now Isabella de Fortibus, countess of Aumale, is the lady of the island and takes the profits there, and men freely buy and sell. The market is not held on any fixed day. The men of Ravenserod also take tolls as if the place was really a borough.

The men of Grimsby were unsuccessful in preventing Ravenserod from trading, and within ten years the taunt "as if the place was a borough" could not be used, for in 1299 the men of Ravenserod paid the king £300 for the privilege of a borough charter: by it the fair-days were extended to thirty a year and a second market day added. In 1304 the borough was duly summoned to send its two representatives to Edward I's Parliament.

Within another thirty-six years the chronicler of Meaux was recording the flooding and destruction of the town. An Exchequer inquiry of 1346 reported two-thirds of the town washed away and burgesses moving elsewhere. In 1347 another inquiry reported more than 200 houses washed away since 1334, and the borough's tax assessment was reduced to 100*s.* Within twenty years there was no borough to tax at all.

All men daily removing their possessions, the town was swiftly swallowed up and irreparably destroyed by the merciless tempestuous floods.

Writing the town's epitaph, the chronicler pointed a moral.

This was an exceedingly famous borough devoted to merchandise and very much occupied with fishing, having more ships and burgesses than any borough on this coast. But by wrongdoing on the high seas it provoked the wrath of God beyond measure and was destroyed to its very foundations.

III

Ravenserod is now under the Humber, and Wyke has been submerged in the bricks and mortar of modern Hull. One must go to Hedon to see the pattern of streets and havens created by the foundation of these Humber towns, and there it is the very misfortunes of the port in the later Middle Ages which have been responsible for preserving the earthworks of the medieval town in the fields and lanes around the small, compact area of the modern Hedon.

As it happened, I made my first visit to Hedon and Hull after an appropriate prelude. The date of a broadcast from the London studios in June, 1954, was rather suddenly rearranged, and Clifford Farrar, who had promised to take my photographs of Hedon, agreed to drive me to London and back along a route which would take in some of the other New Towns which I had identified by then. On our way from Leeds to London we photographed the church and market-place of the new town which the Knights Templar had founded at Baldock, although we were a little hampered by the midday traffic on the Great North Road as we sought for the best camera-angles; on our return journey we saw Buntingford, St. Ives and Market Deeping—all post-Conquest foundations—before spending the afternoon in Boston, the most successful of the early plantations. We viewed its crowded Saturday market-place from the tower of St. Botolph's Church, Boston Stump.

Had I not been harried by an appointment at an examiners' meeting on the Monday, we might have behaved as medieval travellers did by going westwards via the Witham and north up the Trent to Airmyn on Humber, there to pay tribute to the abbot of St. Mary's, York. But time pressed and Airmyn had to have a later visit of its own. We reached the East Riding not by the bridge at Booth Ferry near the old Airmyn ferry but by the car ferry from Barton to Kingston on Hull.

As the car drove away from the slipway in search of a hotel for the night we passed Holy Trinity Church, with its graveyard added by king and bishop for the convenience of the fourteenth-century burgesses, and the parallel streets at the core of the old settlement. We did not examine them, for we were anxious to find a hotel manager who did not think it suspicious or mad to want to be up at 6 a.m. the next morning. Experience in Baldock and elsewhere had taught us the value of early, uncongested streets for leisurely photography. The weather forecast was good and it seemed worth sacrificing a Sunday morning lie-in. As it happened, we had no difficulties. The first hotel we tried was sympathetic and co-operative: had other historians and photographers of Hedon prepared the way for such an un-English hour of Sunday rising? We felt less like pioneers. But the manager explained that our request was nothing unusual. We had forgotten that we were in a port, and that ships sail at all hours.

In the thirteenth century we would have found it difficult to travel to Hedon by land from Hull, for the intervening country was marshy and intersected by creeks. The natural way would have been by river: the only landward routes into the gates of Hedon came from the villages on the east and north. But the eighteenth-century turn-pike road has obscured this fact, and it was along this straight high-way past the docks of Hull and the suburban factories that we drove until the tower of St. Augustine's and the narrow, intersecting streets told us that we were in Hedon.

In its earliest years Hedon was unrivalled: Ravenserod had not yet risen from the waves and Wyke was small and further from the sea. But by the mid-thirteenth century Hedon was seriously affected. From the customs duties of 1203-4 it can be seen that Wyke was paying six times as much duty as Hedon and at the end of the century the tax collectors assessed the merchants of Hedon at only two-thirds of the sum of Ravenserod. The petition of 1280 which described the departure of burgesses from Hedon because of tallage suggests that the earls of Aumale were more interested in Ravenserod than Hedon, and by the time that Ravenserod had proved a poor investment it was too late for them to re-invest in Hedon. The position of Hull was too secure. Nor would the general condition of trade during the fourteenth century pestilences encourage attempts to revive Hedon. In 1334 Hull was assessed at three times the tax of Hedon and at two-thirds of the tax of Beverley, the great clothmaking town. Even after the plagues, in 1377, the tax-paying population of Hull was three times that of Hedon and had reached just over half that of Beverley.[9]

Thus, the Market Hill at Hedon is now grass-grown and the great parish church, once one of three, towers over narrow lanes which still bear the names of medieval crafts. Beyond the gardens and allot-ments the parallel streets of the old port survive only as lanes leading down to the banks of the Hedon river. Three artificial Havens once ran parallel to these lanes, bringing ships into the heart of the town, but they are now silted up and grass covered. The casual passer-by is as unlikely to envisage wharves and warehouses alongside the hedges as he would parish churches on the empty sites of St. James' and St. Nicholas'. (Fig. 14.)

Although there are only seven trains on a weekday it is worth

[9] 1334: P.R.O. E179/202/52 (Hull, 667s.; Hedon, 213s. 4d.; Beverley, 1,000s.); 1377: E359/8b (Hull, 1,357 taxpayers; Hedon, 482; Beverley, 2,663).

using the rail approach to Hedon. From the distance the town first appears as an island of trees and houses in very flat and undistinguished countryside with the tower of St. Augustine's Church rising above them all. The railway only runs through Hedon for a matter of 300 yards, the station lying in the little rectangle which

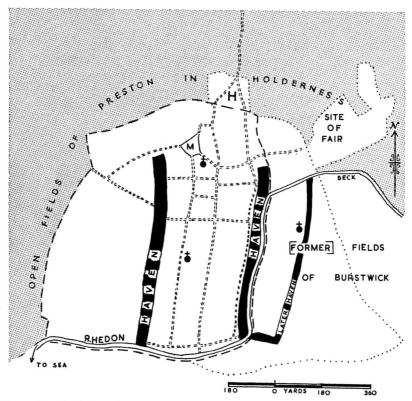

Fig. 14. The New Town of Hedon laid out in the fields of Preston, which still surround it. M: Market Hill; H: extra-mural Hospital land; — — — indicates original borough bounds (c. 1140); . . . . . . indicates eastern extension (before 1200).

projects from the north end of the borough like the button on a station-master's cap. On either side of the station the track runs through the parish of Preston in Holderness, the village a mile north of Hedon in whose fields the earls planted the new town. As one stands on the station platform watching the little train continuing its

140

journey eastwards to Withernsea the two worlds are on either hand: on the left the agricultural world of Preston not greatly changed through the centuries, and on the right the commercial world of Hedon now only a shadow of its medieval self.

The vantage point of the railway platform enables one to see an even more curious monument to the past. By the side of the Preston road on the north of the station is a brick building, the disused goods-shed of the station, with an inclined embankment leading up to it where rails were once laid. This shed, built by the railway company when the line was made in 1854, is also a child of the Middle Ages, however squarely Victorian its brickwork. An examination of the map shows that it is the only part of the station to lie outside the bounds of the borough.

There was room on all sides to spare. Why build the goods shed out there? the medieval privileges of the borough supply the answer. The right to take toll from all goods unloaded within the confines of the town was an important part of the burgess' privileges, helping them to collect the money for those annual payments which they had promised their lord when he gave them their charter. The Hull and Withernsea Railway Company saw no reason why the same tolls should be levied in the nineteenth century for the benefit of a shrunken borough and from merchandise which did not come up the Hedon River and which used a form of land transport not envisaged in the charter of 1170.

The New Towns, the creations of kings, abbots, bishops and magnates, show the recognition even by feudal overlords that it might sometimes pay to release a man from feudal servitudes. The interest of lords and townsmen ran in the same direction: if the recruits to the New Town were left free of the villein obligations customary in villages they could then pursue their self-interest and from the proceeds be able to promise a contribution to the lord's purse, a flow of money which would come into him regularly and effortlessly. This had attractions compared with the risks of agricultural production, but the beauty of a New Town in the lord's eyes was that he could have the best of both worlds. There was no question of balancing gain and loss, of deciding how many men of a particular agricultural village could be enfranchised; the loss of villeins did not have to be balanced against the advantages of having an additional trading centre. The New Town gave all these advantages, not instead of, but in addition to the old-established profits of village lordship.

Those who lived in Hedon after 1170 were not obliged to obey the reeve of Preston when he summoned the villeins to work in the fields nor to do other services for the lord of the manor: their freedom rested securely on a grant from the earl of Aumale which Henry II later confirmed in a short charter.

> Know ye that I have granted to William, earl of Aumale free burgage in Hedon to him and his heirs . . . that his burgesses may hold freely and quietly in free burgage as do my burgesses of York and Lincoln.

The burgesses who took up the building plots in the New Town now had to pay only a small money rent, usually 6d. or a shilling; villein services were not due; the burgage-plot and its house could be sold, sub-let and disposed of by will; no question of heriot or merchet arose; the courts of the manor of Preston and of the hundred of Holderness were replaced by a special borough court for Hedon alone.

Not all the modern implications of "borough" must be read into the charter of 1170. The burgesses of Hedon had not acquired self-government. There was no Mayor and Corporation, and the town's second charter bought from King John in 1200 went no further. The important-sounding privileges "of York and Lincoln" were probably only the right of associating in a guild-merchant (that is, a trading society) and the right to take toll from the lading of ships and to be free of tolls elsewhere in the kingdom. A market also began to be held at this time twice weekly and the Earl of Aumale obtained licence for a fair on Magdalen Fields outside the town (c. 1155-62).

Privileges had to be paid for: it was thought worth while to pay John £46 13s. 4d. for confirming Henry II's charter, and the Earl of Aumale went pledge for the payment. In 1203 the burgesses made another payment to the king in order to continue selling dyed cloth. In 1272 the Earl of Lancaster, who had succeeded to the seignory of Holderness by marrying the Aumale heiress, obtained a charter from Henry III for an eight-day fair in Hedon itself to be held at Augustine-tide, from August 20th to 27th.

Edward I, a good friend of towns and merchants, must have seemed to the burgesses a likely man to grant a further stage in independence of status, and in 1280 they petitioned to "farm" their obligations, that is to render a fixed sum direct to the Exchequer, excluding the sheriff from the town's affairs. But although Edward I became Lord of Holderness there was no significant change in the status of Hedon until 1348 when a long charter granted the "farm" and other privileges. A sentence at the end of another document of that year suggests that the town had long enjoyed many of these privileges by tolerance but that the generality of the words in Henry II and John's charters was causing concern. It will also be remembered that by 1348 the town's general fortunes had already been seriously challenged, and the extension of privileges may have been a late attempt at remedy. As a symbol of incorporation a seal was struck: a ship in sail with two oarsmen, a pennant flying at the masthead and a crown below it.

IV

Like other New Towns created at this period, both the bounds and the street-pattern of Hedon emphasize the circumstances of its origin. The grid-pattern of parallel streets with intersections at right-angles indicates a planned lay-out of building plots similar to those which Edward I was to set out on the hill-top above drowned Winchelsea to accommodate the merchants of that Sussex port. The New Town of Hedon had an additional artificial feature in its plan, the Haven which was dug parallel to the streets and leading up at right-angles from the Hedon river.

New Towns often indicate their relatively late arrival on the medieval landscape by the regular alinement of their bounds and by the relation of these bounds to those of the surrounding rural parishes. As we have seen in Chapter 2, the countryside was partitioned into parishes well before the Norman Conquest and it was to the advantage of the incumbent that these should not be encroached upon: we have seen the townsmen of Wyke carrying their dead to burial in the parish church 4½ miles away. Hedon was fortunate: those who lived in the borough were provided with their own parish church, St. Augustine's, probably before 1190. The present bounds of Preston parish show where the parish of Hedon has been cut out on the southern flank. The 300 acres taken out are not the regular rectangle of a New Buckenham or a Flint, but the slightly curving east, north and west sides probably had to follow an older watercourse or drain through the fields of Preston, and the southern boundary was the river Hedon itself. (Fig. 14, p. 140.)

143

It is also noticeable that the area of Hedon parish is small: compare its 300 acres with Preston's 5,000 or Burstwick's 4,300. The earl had not anticipated that the townsmen would need field-land: the houses had gardens, but the crop which the townsmen were expected to sow was one whose profits would enable them to buy all the food they needed without the aid of plough or livestock. The only animals a trader would need were horses for riding where a boat could not carry him, and a small area of common grazing was allocated in the west part of the town, behind the Haven; burgesses could keep pigs, and there was a pinder and a pound for strays.

The boundary moat of the town is now dry except for a short length on the east side of the North Gate. The road from the railway station into the town crosses the former moat near the Station Hotel, the site of the North Bridge. On the east the Humbleton Beck, which had long acted as the frontier between the Preston fields and the Burstwick fields, continued in service as the boundary between Hedon borough and Burstwick.

The earl provided the land—perhaps the easiest step for him. He offered good terms to settlers; and he obtained a charter of confirmation from the King. It is not known whether he also helped to pay for streets, buildings and harbours, but it is unlikely that individual immigrants could have afforded this capital expenditure.

Not all the available space was taken up by houses, streets, havens and churches: north of the churchyard was the open triangle of ground where the Wednesday and Saturday markets were held; in the early days of the town the churchyard was probably also used. On the north-east of the town and on the way to Burstwick, an important centre of administration for the Lords of Holderness, were Magdalen Fields, the site of the first Hedon fairs.

The House of Pleas, or Court House, also stood in the Market Place; it had a prison in its basement and near it stood the pillory and stocks. There was also a ducking stool and the Horse Well lay conveniently to hand on the west; the town's main drinking well was a few yards further south at Stockwell. The town had frequently to warn its citizens against washing clothes here. The housewife had little choice: the local streams had been diverted into the town ditch and the Havens were too deep and probably too dirty.

Apart from the market-place the medieval streets of Hedon were narrow. Many of the streets were named after the crafts which were practised in them, and their narrowness indicates the pressure on building land when they were first laid out. Before the end of the twelfth century this pressure was sufficient to cause another piece of land to be added to the borough on its east flank, taking in about eighty-six acres from the fields of Burstwick. The Humbleton Beck now ceased to mark the eastern bounds of the town and a fourth artificial Haven was dug to connect with the river and extend the length of the wharves. Alongside it a third parish church was built and dedicated to St. Nicholas. (Fig. 14, p. 140.)

The extension of the built-up area, the new Haven and the new parish church all indicate a rapid rise in population as well as in wealth. Unfortunately, the only occasion on which the numbers can be estimated is in 1377, after the mid-century pestilences, and in the town's declining days: the poll tax receipt shows 482 persons over the age of sixteen years, perhaps 750 souls in all. If the estimate of one-third for the plague death-rate is accepted, this would give about 1,125 for the early fourteenth-century population.

It is very unlikely that the rise in population in the twelfth and thirteenth centuries had come from a natural excess of births over deaths. As well as the initial migration of settlers to the earl's building plots there must have been a continuing stream of immigrants anxious to live in a town and confident of making a living there. Similar townwards migration was occurring all over England, and indeed all over Europe. It was bringing about the expansion of old-established towns and the continued foundation of new ones.[10]

Thus, even in its earliest days, Hedon could not have recruited solely from existing towns. The purpose of the new towns was not simply to beggar their neighbours by capturing trade and luring away craftsmen and merchants: it was to increase the number of English craftsmen and merchants by providing new and additional centres for their activities. A core of experienced recruits must have been sought and no doubt the privileges of York and Lincoln guaranteed in Hedon's charter were something of a bait. Yet poaching on a large-scale would have aroused powerful opposition. Where else could a lord look to fill his empty building plots?

[10] Germany: Hans Planitz, *Die Deutsche Stadt im Mittelalter* (1954); France: the basic study is still M.A. Curie-Seimbres, *Essai . . . sur les Bastides* (1880); see also P. Lavedan, *L'Histoire de L'Urbanisme*, i (1926), 281 *sqq.*; C. Higounet in *Moyen Age*, liv (1948), 113-21 and lvi (1950), 69-84; O. de St. Blanquat in *Annales*, iv (1949), 278-89; and J. P. Trabut-Cussac in *Moyen Age*, lxx (1954), 81-135.

He might hope to lure a few foreigners to take up residence in England under his protection and to contribute their skills in crafts or their knowledge of foreign coasts and markets. But the principal source of new townsmen must have been the same expanding and migrating rural population which was causing fields to replace forests. There may not have been direct migration of peasants, for the freer (and probably wealthier) life of the town would attract men of the type of village traders or small craftsmen who had already some idea of what making and selling were about; their place in the village might be taken up by less experienced countrymen and younger sons with no hope of succeeding to their father's estates. But the free air of the town would also attract all those whom manorial burdens irked, and while one man might go off to the margin of cultivation to carve out a new living, another might come to a Hedon or a Hull as an unskilled labourer hoping, as opportunity served, to carve out for himself in turn a better living of a new sort. In this nothing succeeded like success, and there was no stronger recruiting sergeant than the reports of success which rumour carried back to the countryside.

The mobility of the townsmen is indicated in the Hedon petition of 1280 which declared that many burgesses were considering moving on to Ravenserod and Hull, where the taxes were lower; and about 1360 the chronicler of Meaux described how the townsmen of Ravenserod scattered before the floods.

> Those former inhabitants of Ravenserod coming together to the town of Kingston on Hull determined to construct and build there a suitable place for themselves and their merchandise at Drypool, across the water of Hull in the countryside of Holderness. But the lords of that fief not giving them a speedy and peaceful consent they determined to move instead to Kingston itself and to any other borough or maritime town where the spirit led them.

In the villages, the lords of manors seem to have had no difficulty in the thirteenth century in finding a tenant to replace the migrants: conditions were favourable to the simultaneous expansion of cleared land and the growth of towns, without injury to either. Indeed, the growth of a new town depended very largely on an expanding and more varied agricultural output to feed its market and on prosperous landowners and countrymen to purchase the goods which it brought from overseas. So long as these conditions were maintained there was room for new fields, new villages and new towns. In the Hedons of England the houses and the parish churches multiplied. When these conditions were not maintained—as, by and large, they were not in the fourteenth century—the founding of new towns ceased and parish churches began to decay.

Two hundred years earlier, in the first prosperous years, Hedon burgesses had founded three parish churches. The foundation and endowment of hospitals were also proper objects of piety both for an individual wealthy townsman and for the town guilds. Hedon had three, and the land where they stood was considered part of the borough even where it lay outside the moat. Fig. 14 shows two protuberances, a small one on the north (near the railway) where St. Sepulchre's Hospital stood, and a larger area on the north-east alongside the Burstwick road. This was part of the field-land of Preston which the Earl of Aumale gave to endow a hospital for lepers, the poor and the infirm. Between 1155 and 1162 the king granted the Hospital the right to hold a fair on the feast of its patron, St. Mary Magdalen, and on the seven days following. This was the main fair of the year for Hedon and seemingly the only fair until the grant of the Augustine-tide fair in 1272. This second fair was held inside the town, in the Market Place and the surrounding streets, a rather cramped position. The larger English fairs of the period were in less confined conditions, more like those of the Magdalen fair at Hedon: Cambridge fair straddled Sturbridge Common and St. Bartholomew's spread across Smithfield outside London Wall.

The third Hedon Hospital, St. Leonard's, lay inside the borough on the west bank of the Fleet alongside the timber merchants' yards. It was founded by Alan Fitzherbert of Preston. But the largest monuments to burghal piety were the parish churches. All three were so organized as to be closely bound to the communal life of the town. Their churchwardens were elected in the borough court and their accounts were presented for audit there; when St. Nicholas' and St. James' churches decayed, the sites were treated as town property and their documents have survived as part of the borough archives. The principal town guild, that of Holy Cross, had its meetings in St. Augustine's Church and it was on their feast day that the Mayor made his formal procession from the church to Market Hill to proclaim the byelaws and the penalties for unlawful trading (p. 173). The oldest surviving part of this church dates from the late twelfth

147

century, but this is a south transept and the core of the church may
have been older. The architecture shows that about 1240 there was
a pause in the building programme, and when it was resumed the
scale was less expensive. The second church, St. James', seems to
have been in use until the last quarter of the fifteenth century. New
stalls were bought in the last year of the surviving accounts, 1476; a
reference to it as "outside the town" in 1448 suggests that the mer-
cantile buildings in that quarter were then in decay, but the church
is not definitely known to be ruined until 1546. The accounts of St.
Nicholas come to an end in 1475, but a new missal was bought that
year and the final collapse must have come later. No stone of either
church is still standing.

In the original plan for the new town, besides building plots, a
market-place and a parish church, there were three harbours. One
was formed by the main Hedon river on the south of the town; the
artificial West Haven was excavated; and the Humbleton Beck, the
eastern boundary of the town, was deepened to make the Fleet.
These three harbours were 440, 650 and 450 yards in length, respectively. The extension of the town eastwards before the end of the
twelfth century made room for a fourth Haven, the East Haven dug
parallel to the others and extending for 830 yards. It was alongside this
new Haven that St. Nicholas' Church was built. (Fig. 14, page 140.)

No document has yet been found which dates the disuse of the
Havens, whose present condition can be seen in Plate 12. It is
clear that Ravenserod and Hull stole a good deal of the town's trade;
the establishment (*c.* 1300) of a port at Paull Fleet, where the Hedon
river joins the Humber, looks like an attempt to remedy the decaying fortunes of a town which was dependent on the relatively small
Hedon river. Its epitaph as a port is provided by John Leland's
description of the town,[11] written about 1536.

> the Se Crekes parting aboute the sayde Toun did insulate it, and
> Shippis lay aboute the Toun: but now men cum to it by 3 Bridges,
> wher it is evident to se that sum Places wher the Shippis lay be over
> growen with Flagges and Reades, and the Haven is very sorely decayid.

Compared to some of the other towns founded at the same time,
Hedon's life was short, although not so short as Warenmouth (Northumberland), Skinburness[12] (Cumberland) or Newton (Dorset). For

[11] Leland, i, 61-2.   [12] *Cal. Chart.*, iii, 2 and 55.

a few centuries the Earl of Aumale's judgment paid good dividends, and even in the sixteenth century Hedon had a role as a local market centre. The New Towns were not alone in knowing decay: some towns older and larger were left high and dry by the silting up of estuaries or washed away by the sea. Inland towns did no better: of the twenty-three boroughs—only one of them a New Town—which were chartered in Lancashire between 1066 and 1372, only four retained established borough status at the end of the Middle Ages, while some—like Warrington and Manchester—had lapsed into manors again.

No founder of a town could force traders to come to an unattractive spot or to remain there after trade was in decline, however advantageous the terms he offered. Soldiers could be forced to hold a castle in an unpeopled wilderness, but professional traders stood or fell by the society of other men and the coming together of buyers and sellers. Like Shakespeare's Glendower, a founder of towns might call spirits from the vasty deep—but would they come for him?

6

A JOURNEY TO ELIZABETHAN MARKET-PLACES

HIGHAM FERRERS, NORTHANTS.
TODDINGTON, BEDS.

You have no good cytie, towne nor vyllyage but London.

THE FRENCH HERALD in JOHN COKE'S *Debate of the Heralds* (1549)

Chapter Six

A JOURNEY TO ELIZABETHAN MARKET-PLACES

I

WE must now follow the Elizabethan surveyors, whom we left in the fields of Maids Moreton, into the market-places of two small country towns. By the reign of Elizabeth several hundred towns, large and small, possessed charters and ranked as boroughs. Only a few were the result of a deliberate act of plantation such as that of Hedon described in the previous chapter; the majority had followed the normal progress which led small villages to grow into large ones, and then to seek the economic and legal privileges which carried them over the border between the large village and the small town.[1] Two such promoted villages were Higham Ferrers and Toddington, selected here because each was surveyed by well-known Elizabethan surveyors, the one by John Norden, the other by Ralph Agas. In the numbered key which went along with Norden's plan of Higham the first place was given not to the castle, church or college, but to the market-place; in Agas' plan of Toddington the medieval castle was no more than a curious mound in a field to the east of the town; the lord of the manor had built himself a new mansion out in the heath, well to the west of the town, and the central position in the plan is taken up again by a market-place. Although some other features of town plans will be touched upon in this chapter, the market-place will stand at its centre as it did in the daily life of the Elizabethan town.

The Elizabethan map-makers worked principally in the countryside, passing their working day on the road between country house and country house or in the fields of their patrons' estates. Their field-work over, they returned to their house in a town in order to

---

[1] For an account of a larger (but not very large) Elizabethan town see W. G. Hoskins, "Elizabethan Leicester" in J. H. Plumb, ed., *Studies in Social History* (1956); for the larger towns, W. G. Hoskins, "English Provincial Towns," *Trans. Royal Hist. Soc.*, 5th ser., vi (1956), 1-20.

complete the work and to wait for messages from the next client, but it was in the countryside that they received most opportunity to exercise and sharpen their skills. In a town there were fewer disputes over property boundaries and fewer projects to change the use of land so that a commission for a town plan would often have to await a publisher realizing the sale for an engraved and printed map. Naturally, it was the larger and more famous towns—London, Norwich, Bristol, York, Oxford and Cambridge—which first attracted surveyors to them, and by 1600 each of the six mentioned had been surveyed.

Yet neither Toddington nor Higham Ferrers was large and famous. What brought two celebrated London surveyors to their streets? plans of small country towns are rare enough even in the seventeenth century—why should these two small places receive the attention given to London and York? The answer lies in the presence near by of two important country gentlemen. The plan of Toddington in twenty sheets was commissioned from Ralph Agas by Lord Henry Cheney in 1581. While most of the twenty sheets show open fields and pasture similar to that on the All Souls maps described in Chapter 3, one sheet is very different. It shows the mixture of rural and urban features which one associates with a small country town even to-day.[2]

The second plan, that of Higham Ferrers, was executed by a surveyor as famous as Agas, John Norden the elder, who mapped Higham in 1591 in order to convince his patron that a county-by-county survey of England was useful and possible. A description of Northamptonshire together with an annotated gazetteer and county map were prepared as a sample; two large-scale plans were appended, one of Peterborough and one of Higham Ferrers.[3] The patron, Lord Burghley, was suitably impressed and recommended the Queen to protect Norden against literary pirates by granting him the sole right[4] to publish during the next ten years

[2] B.M., Add. MSS. 38065.
[3] The MSS. was located by Dr. Y. M. Goblet in the Bibliothèque Nationale, Paris: MSS. 706 Anglais, Acq. Nouv. No. 58. It was briefly described by E. Heawood in *Geog. Journ.*, xcvi (1940), 368-69. In a letter of February 9, 1954, I was informed that the MSS. is again lost. The British Museum Map Room possesses a photographic copy: Maps c.7 b.20.
[4] P.R.O. C66/1382 (May 1592). On January 27, 1593 the Privy Council granted him a pass asking J.P.s to afford him help in his travels for topography: A. W. Pollard, *Library*, 4th ser., vii (1926), 235-36, 242.

a booke called Speculum Britanniae or a description of England and Wales with Cartes and Mappes thereof . . . which book was by himself made and compyled.

The volumes for Middlesex and Hertfordshire were published within the ten years but the Northamptonshire section remained in manuscript until 1720 when an enterprising London publisher issued it,[5] but without the town plans, probably using a revised text later than that which Norden made for Burghley in 1591. Burghley's copy was only rediscovered in 1939 when Dr. Y. M. Goblet found it among the English manuscripts in the Bibliothèque Nationale in Paris. In 1953 attempts to find it there again failed, but photographic copies had been deposited in the British Museum, where Agas' map of Toddington already rested. The Paris manuscript still lacked the plan of Peterborough, but Mr. E. Heawood has argued convincingly that it was used for the inset plan of the town on the well-known county map which John Speed issued in 1610.

When Norden presented a copy of his Hertfordshire volume to Queen Elizabeth I in 1598 he added a dedication in his own hand on the page facing the title.[6]

I was drawne unto my simple endevors by honorable Councellors and warranted your royall favour,

he began, recalling the Queen's letters patent of 1592, and the support he had had from the two influential Northamptonshire councillors, Burghley and Sir Christopher Hatton. It was probably Burghley's local connections which prompted Norden to begin with Northamptonshire. He looked to the right patron, for Elizabeth's principal minister was a methodical man, interested in the logical arrangement of his speeches, the setting out of argument in column and counter-column, the collection of statistics and of all forms of political intelligence from the provinces, realizing that the art of governing rested on knowing well the governed and the potential governors among the country gentry, a class which held a key place in the rapidly changing and often turbulent economic scene.

Sir Francis Walsingham, another of Elizabeth's ministers, had been of a similar opinion, and in his notes on the proper conduct of a

[5] John Norden, *Speculum Britanniae Pars Altera or a Delineation of Northamptonshire* (1720).
[6] This copy is now in the British Museum: Grenville 3685.

Queen's Secretary (drawn up in the same year as Norden's patent) he wrote:[7]

> A Secretarie must likewise have a . . . booke of the Mappes of England with a particular note of the divisions of the shires . . . and what Noblemen, Gentlemen and others be residing in every one of them; and what Citties, Burrows, Markett Townes, Villages . . .

A volume which was at once a Who's Who, a gazetteer, an atlas and an economic assessment might well be expected to appeal to Burghley, and it was a composite work of this kind which Norden projected. It was to be called the *Speculum*, a "Mirror" of England in words and maps. It is interesting to see what Norden had in mind, for his topographical description and plan of Northamptonshire stand almost at the beginning of that type of English book. Saxton had moved on from local plans like those of Old Byland (Chapter 2) to a complete county atlas in 1574-79, but there was no accompanying commentary to his maps, and no town plans. Had Norden published all his volumes according to the original scheme there would have been a set of English town plans twenty years earlier than those of Speed in 1610.

The ambition of the project was matched by Norden's industry. In 1598 he was able to tell the Queen

> I have spent above a thousand markes and fyve years tyme. . . . Onlie your Majesties princelie favor is my hope, with out which I myselfe most miserablie perish, my familie in penurie and the work unperformed, which being effected shalbe profitable and a glorie to this your most admired Empire.

In another part of the dedication Norden described the *Speculum* as

> mine intended labours, the description of famous England

and when in 1596 he published a pamphlet[8] answering some of the critics of the *Middlesex* volume, a similar phrase was used

> I, the most unworthie being imployed (after the most painful and praiseworthie labours of M. Christopher Saxton) in the redescription of England, and having thereof exhibited some simple beginnings . . . have yeelded attention to the sundrie censures of men.

He acknowledged the growing skills and numbers of his profession—

---

[7] Conyers Read, *Mr. Secretary Walsingham* (1925), i, 423.
[8] *John Norden's Preparative* (1596).

there are many men of rare perfection in Geographie and of the Mathematikes in this land and by the industry of many they increase dayly, whose kind reproofes I accept as necessary documents unto me—

and their aid was invoked in his "topographicall and historicall purposes." The purpose was "historicall" because it was part of Norden's scheme to note antiquities where he found them, in the manner of Leland and Camden, and to preface his topographical description of the county with a summary of its history. The comprehensiveness of the project is reflected in the title which Robert Nicholson conferred upon Norden in the poem dedicatory to the Middlesex volume,[9] "Cosmo-choro-poly-grapher".

If Norden chose Northamptonshire because it was Burghley's native county, why did he take Higham Ferrers and not the county town for his specimen town plan?—

> I have set downe this former plott of Higham Ferrers, my right honourable good Lord, to thende that it might please your Honour to consider whether it might be expedient that the most principall townes Cyties and castles within evrry Shire should be breefly and expartly plotted out, in estate and forme as at this day they were.[10]

This small country market-town was probably chosen because it was part of the Crown estates, having once been the property of the dukes of Lancaster. Indeed, in the same summer that Norden drew his plan, the Duchy surveyors had made a full *terrier* (that is, written survey) of the Higham properties[11] and Norden may have been able to draw upon this, or may, indeed, have been an assistant to John Worthe, the surveyor whose name appears upon it. In the dedication to the revised version of *Northamptonshire* (not printed until 1720) Norden said as much:

> I tooke occasion in my Travaile in these Parts to performe it after this poore sorte, being otherwise imployed in surveys there,

and it is known that between 1588 and 1590 he was surveying the monastic estates granted to Sir Thomas Heneage in the same county.

The form of Norden's *Mirror* differs from the old-fashioned type of

[9] John Norden, *Speculum Britanniae, a Historical and Chorographical Description of Middlesex and Hartfordshire* (1723).
[10] British Museum: Maps c.7 b.20, f.42 (September 20, 1591).
[11] P.R.O. DL42/117 (July 1, 1591).

survey drawn up by Worthe. The *Mirror* was not concerned with the details of tenure, rents, decays, boundaries and arrears but with a broader view, less economic and more literary. The county plan was large enough to indicate the main roads, churches, country seats and park pales, but too small to indicate any of the property boundaries with which the large-scale estate plans were concerned. Norden did not think that parish boundaries could be included:[12]

> as touching the conceite of some that would have the distinction of the limits of every parishe I holde it not so needefull as impossible, and I thinke the most of iudgement will affirm the same.

Of large-scale town plans he was less certain, and as the note to Burghley shows, he was anxious to see whether his patron approved of more plans on the model of Higham.

The manuscript plan of Higham is only roughly drawn (Plate 13). Unlike Agas' Toddington, one could not set it alongside a modern large-scale plan and fit feature to feature exactly. It combines something of the linear accuracy of a field-plan with some elements of the pictorial and perspective. It would better match an air photograph taken obliquely than an Ordnance Survey plan. There is an attempt to picture the fallen masonry and grass hillocks of the ruined castle on the right of the church; the former moats are accurately drawn; and the layout of the gardens behind the College is shown in detail: but there has been some distortion in the position of the lanes which come into the town from the countryside, and the houses and gardens in the bottom left-hand corner have been pushed round to fit in with the rectangular frame of the page: finally, the magnetic north shown in the little compass at the foot has a wild deviation from true north of about 110 degrees. In fact the main street, the long axis of the plan, is almost due north and south. The church, with its east end facing the reader, is accurately placed and contradicts the compass.

II

Perhaps this would be a convenient place to draw the reader's attention to the main topographical features on Norden's plan whose historical significance will be considered in the pages which

[12] *John Norden's Preparative* (1596).

follow. The main street running across the plan widens in the centre to form the market-place, which is distinguished by the market cross; below it and separated by a row of houses are the church and the Bedehouse, with the vicarage to the left. The bottom right-hand quarter of the plan is occupied by the ruins and moats of the castle. Small houses line the main street and are set back in small enclosures behind it. A twisting back lane runs behind the houses on the top of the plan and a similar straight lane divides the castle from the fields at the bottom.

The market-place had been encroached upon by the erection of several buildings. Norden sketched in the steps which led to the first floor of the stone Moothall on the left of the cross, and behind it, almost obscured, is a row of cottages which reduce the upper part of the market-place to a narrow alley known since 1276 as *Behind-the-sty*. The only other important feature is Archbishop Chichele's College on the top (west) of the main street (right), halfway between the market-place and the end of the town. Norden shows the gateway opening on the street, an inner quadrangle surrounded by buildings, and formal gardens beyond. Enveloping the whole town are the *comune feyldes*.

The central position in the plan is taken by the market-place; jostling it for attention and exceeding it in size is the *scyte of the olde castle*. The eye can move from one to the other and take in both together at a glance more easily than can the pen. The simplest course is to begin with the castle, the symbol of a great feudal overlord, built to serve in baronial warfare and no longer maintained in the more peaceful days of Elizabeth. From the castle we pass logically to its lords, the architects of the town's prosperity. In 1251 a lord freed the villeins and made burgesses. A lord promoted the market village to a borough with two market days a week, twelve fair-days a year and (for a while) its own Members of Parliament. The villeins-turned-burgesses bring the narrative back again to the market-place from which the important medieval buildings of the parish church and College can be seen, and from there it is only an arrow's shot to the fields, meadows and riverside mills, and thence southwards to Toddington and Ralph Agas' plan with which the chapter ends.

In the descriptive text of *Northamptonshire* Norden wrote of the castle ruins and the moats:

159

there was sometime a very fayre and lardge castle, a mansion house now raysed downe to the grounde whose rubble and olde foundations argur the same to have bene very great and stronge. About the same at this daye are very fayre fish pondes replenished in some measure with fishe.

Things were much changed when a castle moat was valued most as a fishpond. To-day the moats are filled with brackish water which discourages all but the most optimistic small boys from fishing in them. There are grass-grown mounds covering some of the "rubble and olde foundations", and nearby the trenches for new houses were turning up pieces of medieval pottery when visited in 1953. The castle mounds are hidden from the main street by houses and even where they are open to view from back lanes there are trees and undergrowth which do their best to conceal. The castle is the most insignificant of the remains of medieval Higham.

In Norden's day, like many medieval castles, it had no value to the Queen except the few pence a year which could be got from letting out its grassy mounds and courtyards for grazing. Any stone which was useful for building had been taken away in 1523 to repair Kimbolton Castle, so that when the antiquary John Leland visited Higham in the 1530s he noted[13] that the castle was

now of late clene fallen and taken downe.

Norden could see only

the foundations and ruyns which doe declare that it hath bin a place of some accompt.

It had indeed. At the time of the Norman Conquest the manor[14] belonged to the Countess of Hereford, the wife of one of Edward the Confessor's nephews. It was already an important village, for in 1086 Domesday Book records a market, and it was also the centre of a

---

[13] John Leland, *The Itinerary*, ed. T. Hearne (1710-12), v, 94.
[14] The descent of the manor is set out in *V.C.H. Northants.*, iii, 263-79, with an account of the town and borough. Documents cited, unless otherwise footnoted, are from R. M. Serjeantson, "The Court Rolls of Higham Ferrers", *Associated Architectural Societies Reports and Papers*, xxxiii (1915-16), 95-146 and 326-72; xxxiv (1917), 47-102; and W. J. B. Kerr, *Higham Ferrers* (Northampton (?1925)) which represents 15 of the 51 chapters of his original work. No publisher would take the remainder of the MSS, which the author then burned (*ibid.*, v). The work extant shows most thorough use of the Duchy of Lancaster manuscripts and a heavy price has been paid for the local indifference of a generation ago.

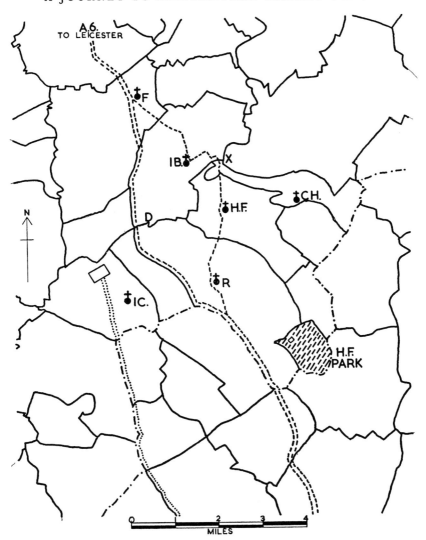

Fig. 15. Higham Ferrers (HF), its Park, neighbours and local road system. (i) *Left*, the Roman road to Irchester (IC), (ii) *centre*, the old London-Leicester road crossing the Nene at Ditchford (D), (iii) *right*, the diversion through Higham Ferrers crossing the Nene at Higham bridge (X). N.B. also the long tongue of Chelveston (CH) parish giving access to the river and meadows. R: Rushden.

unit of Anglo-Saxon local government, the hundred. After the Conquest the estate was given to William Peverel in whose family it remained until seized by the king in 1155. Two years later it was granted to Robert, Earl of Derby, whose family name of Ferrers has been used ever since to distinguish this Higham from the other Northamptonshire *high-ham*, the villages "set on a hill."

Saxon Higham was distinguished from other villages of the locality by having a market; it was singled out in this way probably as a result of its geographical position. It stood on a hill above the valley of the river Nene, and within the parish the river is crossed by the main road northwards from London through Bedford to Leicester, the route now followed by the A6; two miles to the west of Higham the main railway line from St. Pancras to the north crosses the Nene; within sight of the viaduct is the site of the Roman town of Irchester alongside the Roman crossing of the same river. (Fig. 15.) Between Higham and Irchester, at Ditchford bridge, there is a significant alinement of parish boundaries coming from the south which suggest that once (probably before the Norman Conquest) the main road from London to Leicester left the present A6 south of Rushden, following the bridle road through Wymington and Manton Spinneys down to the Nene crossing. No documents reveal when the road moved eastwards to the present crossing by Higham Bridge, the earliest reference to which is in 1227.

It would be natural for a village in such a position to be a gathering point for the surplus agricultural produce of the neighbouring countryside. Travellers themselves would eat and drink at the inns and buy necessities for travel; the traveller who was also a dealer would be on the look-out for goods that he could profitably take away to the larger centres like Bedford and Leicester; travellers who had things to sell would be able to tempt the peasants to bring out their hidden stores and encourage trade by the oldest of examples, a bargain. There would also be a traffic in small river boats coming down from Northampton and up from Peterborough. It is on such simple beginnings that the highly organized markets and fairs of medieval Higham were built.

The market of 1086 was no more than an adjunct to a village whose way of life was still tied to the fields and to the servitude of manorial custom. This was the position for more than 150 years after the Norman Conquest. It was the great-grandson of Robert Ferrers,

William fifth earl of Derby, who was the principal benefactor of the village with which the family had become closely associated. The substantial area of the castle grounds indicates something of the importance which the manor had for its lords: it was again the Nene crossing and the London road which directed the building of a castle at this strategic point. With the castle garrison and a household now to be fed and equipped there were additional inducements to barter and sell at its gate, and additional coming and going of potential customers.

William de Ferrers was of the same cast of mind as the lords who planted towns, but in his case there was no need to colonize a riverside meadow or fields on an open road. The potential town was at his gate and the site was already proven. In the short seven years of his earldom (1247-54) this favourite of Henry III obtained the two necessary additions which transformed Higham: in 1250 the king allowed him to hold a fair each St. Botolph's-tide (June 16-18) in addition to the old market each Saturday; and in December of the next year the King confirmed the charter by which the earl had created the free borough of Higham and thereby freed ninety-two of his villeins. The charter, dated March 12, 1251, has an unusually long entry in the modern printed *Calendar of Charter Rolls*,[15] for it includes the names of all the freed villeins

> who shall hold the lands by free burgage tenure which previously they held at will.

The freed villeins were to be the first burgesses of the new borough and the free status was to descend to their offspring. Thirteen of the villeins were women and three of these, widows. Since there are seventy-nine men's names, these women must have been single, the married women being passed over in silence. The men's names include some with surnames of local villages, showing that they (or their forebears) had once come from outside Higham, and also eleven with occupational names—"the butcher", "the cobbler", "the fisherman", "the skinner", "the baker", "the miller", "the smith", two "clerks" (probably clergy) and two "cooks". The list of simple specialisms is in keeping with the trades needed in a large market village.

The new borough which had been created out of the large village

[15] *Cal. Chart.*, i, 372-73.

did not occupy a compact area which took in the whole town in the fashion of a Hedon or a Hull (p. 144). It was merely the place where the ninety-two burgesses had their dwellings, making up 53¾ acres in all. Most of these burgages were grouped together around the Market Place and along both sides of the main street, the London road. From a document of 1313 the measurements of one burgage plot are known: it extended from the highway, where it was 14 feet wide, to the edge of the fields where it was 16 feet wide. Its length was 110 feet. Within this plot stood the burgess' house itself with its outbuildings, and the remainder of the space was available for a garden. It was in fact a villein croft of the type shown on the village maps in Chapter 3.

There were other houses in Higham in 1251 occupied by families which were not freed by the lord's charter. These "manor" houses were interspersed with the "borough" houses. The borough was too small to maintain full-time specialists in trade and crafts, so that both burgesses and manorial tenants were concerned in the cultivation of the remaining 1,900 acres of the parish. In law, all the townsmen except the burgesses were still the tenants of the lord's manor, and the courts of the manor continued to be held for them in the castle while the burgesses' court met in their new Moot Hall set in the market-place. When, in the later Middle Ages, personal freedom spread to the descendants of all villeins the distinction became less important, but even in Norden's day the two courts were held and the tenure of land in the fields and of houses in the town still preserved the distinction between the 101 free burgages paying their fixed rents and the various customary and leasehold tenures of the other townsmen's properties. It was important, therefore, to know where the borough began and ended, especially when—as will be seen later—certain buying and selling could only take place "within the borough". Thus, the charter of 1556 defined the borough bounds by naming the crosses set along them. Worthe's survey[16] of 1591, on which Norden may have worked, gives the bounds within which the burgage houses are to be found—from Spittell Cross to Malleries Cross—and the sum of its rents, £15 19s. 5½d. But the manor brought in £41 11s. 9d. in rents, showing how valuable the land outside the old borough had become, while the manorial mills brought the Queen £22 3s. 4d. a year.

[16] P.R.O. DL42/117; also SC12/3/31 and SC12/13/33.

In some English towns the promotion of a village to a borough involved some adjustments of the lay-out of streets and houses to meet new needs, particularly for an ample market place and for new building plots to accommodate those whom prosperity attracted to the town. In Higham there is no sign of any of the rectangular aline-ment of streets and of straightened-out curves which often indicate these second thoughts. The main street, as the London road, stretched out into the country and new house-sites could be set along it; Norden's plan shows that a few other houses had been set behind this main frontage along lanes leading into the fields, but there were no buildings outside the two Back Lanes which encompassed the town and divided it off from the field-land.

The founder of the new borough did not need to set out space for a market place, for the market was already at least two centuries old, and had made elbow room for itself by a slight broadening of the main street, perhaps taking in what had once been the village green. Like most English towns Higham had probably held its earliest markets in the churchyard itself. What more natural a place for buying and selling than at the place of frequent assembly conveni-ently set near the castle gate? The idea was only slowly accepted that a churchyard was an improper place for such secular dealings and it needed a statute of 1285 to ban fairs and markets from church-yards "for the Honour of the Church."

The open market-place at Higham begins at the churchyard wall, and in the cobbled, tree-lined triangle shown in Plate 14, the market cross still stands, 14 feet high. It was erected round about 1280, that is, within a generation of the first borough charter. The weekly Saturday market was supplemented in 1251 by the three-day fair at St. Botolph's-tide; and in Norden's day there were four fairs a year, twelve days in all, and a market each Monday and Saturday making more than a hundred days a year when booths and stalls occupied the streets. In this central open space were the sinews, heart and lungs of the town.

By Norden's time, some of the stalls recorded in medieval docu-ments had turned into permanent shops. His plan shows two blocks of buildings set like islands in the market-place in addition to the town-hall and the bakehouse adjoining. The block furthest from the reader made a narrow alley already referred to as "Behind-the-sty". Many English market-places have had their area reduced by the encroachment of buildings in this fashion. In some towns the buildings are so numerous as to leave only narrow streets remaining. It is an interesting exercise to leave the reduced area of a market square and follow the neighbouring alleys to see whether the bounds of the

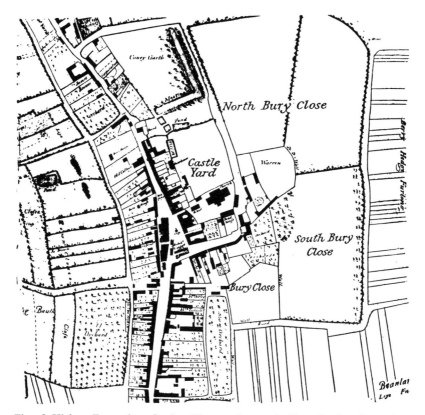

Fig. 16. Higham Ferrers in 1789 (cp. Plate 13 for 1591). Note the four Bury closes, possibly outlining the Saxon 'burh'. The strips of the open fields appear on the right.

original open square or triangle are still discernable. The narrowness of Behind-the-sty and the block of buildings near the Moot Hall prevented Norden from obtaining a good bird's-eye view of Higham and his plan errs in making the Market Place a rectangle. A more accurate plan is that made for the Duchy of Lancaster[17] in 1789 and

[17] P.R.O. MR205, by T. Bainbridge.

reproduced in part in fig. 16. This plan admirably shows the un-interrupted line of the old street frontages behind the encroachments on the west of the market-place and the simple open triangle of ground which existed before the various encroachments confused it. The plan also shows the back lane running behind all the house-gardens on the west of the town, probably another feature preserved from the old village. There is a shorter back-lane on the east sepa-rating the castle, church and manor from the fields.

Some new towns which were founded about the time when Higham was promoted to borough status were equipped with gates and walls. There is no sign that Higham had either, for it was too small to need walls, and the earl's castle afforded a place of retreat in troubled times. When the town needed a meeting place for the borough court there was room for a new building in the market-place alongside the old common bakehouse of the manor. When a bedehouse and a chantry chapel were needed they were set inside the churchyard itself. When Archbishop Chichele needed ground for his new College in 1422 he acquired tenements in the main street and built on their site, placing his College gateway on the same line as the other house fronts. There was a bad fire in 1410 and for sixteen years the King allowed the burgesses a rent reduction of 16 per cent. to offset their losses, yet the rebuilt burgages were placed within the old boundaries. Norden's plan consequently shows, undisturbed, the characteristic lay-out of a market-village of the mid-thirteenth century. Freedom had descended on the villagers as they sat in their homes, and here a new borough was but an old village writ large.

One other feature of the 1789 plan deserves notice, for the tele-scoping of detail at the edge of Norden's plan tends to obscure it: below, that is to the east of, the town are four closes sharing the name, *Bury*. The outer boundary of these four fields is suspiciously regular, and the Rev. W. J. B. Kerr, the most informed of the town's historians, suggested that together they outline for us the Saxon *burh* which protected and contained the houses of Higham in the days before the first Norman castle, which was built in the north-west corner of this same rectangle. It seems likely that the great moats shown on the plans of 1591 and 1789 mark out the defences of a second castle intended to replace the early Norman mound, but never completed, for in 1314 this area of ground was already valued only as a *coneygree*, a walled rabbit-warren, with a small boat to fish in the moats now turned from defences to a placid fishpond. The "ruins" of Norden's plan—to the south of these moats—lie in the three acres marked as *Castle Yard* in 1789, and would be those of a third castle, the stone buildings whose repairs figure large in the long series of Duchy account rolls until the last quarter of the fifteenth century; and it was these buildings which were ransacked in 1523 by the building contractors from Kimbolton looking for stone and lead.

It is significant that the fields of the *Bury* contained not only the medieval castle but also, outside its gates, the enclosed part of the lord's home farm, the demesne. Near the small field marked "warren" in 1789, stood the buildings from which the lord's open-field holdings were worked: the Great Barn (part of whose walls now support a factory roof); the Hay-barn; the Ox-house; the Cattle-sheds; the Sheep-house; the Malt-kiln and the Horse-stables which recur so often in the repairs-accounts of the manorial officers.

The manorial lords who took the profits of this farming were not always the de Ferrers. After the baronial revolt of 1264 the king took the estates and awarded them to the Earl of Chester who in 1267 became Duke of Lancaster; they came permanently to the Crown when the House of Lancaster obtained the throne in 1399 and this royal connection probably accounts for the Parliamentary franchise exercised by the townsmen from 1557 until the Reform Act of 1832. From Higham the officers of the well-organized Duchy administration directed their other local estates, holding their courts in the castle, keeping its records there and living there a good part of the year. The castle formed a convenient stopping place for journeys to Leicester and Northampton and both dukes and kings often stayed here.

There is no record that Higham castle was ever engaged in any major military operation, and by the time of Edward IV the spending of money on maintaining its defences seem to have lapsed. In the civil disorders of Northumberland's rebellion (1553) Higham rendered some service to the orthodox cause but whether with arms or money does not appear. As a reward for the townsmen's loyalty Philip and Mary issued a new and more ample charter[18] in 1556, for

the old letters patent partly from want of safe custody and partly by mishap have been mislaid and lost.

[18] *Calendar of Patent Rolls, Philip and Mary*, iii, 200-3; P.R.O. C66/904, m.27.

This charter went much further than the Earl of Derby's grant of 1251. His charter did little more than emancipate certain villagers and leave them free to dispose of their property as they willed; their personal freedom also gave them opportunities to develop their skills as craftsmen and tradesmen, should they wish to divert their energies away from the cultivation of the common field; nothing was said in 1251 of self-government. In 1556 the government of the town was entrusted to a Mayor, seven aldermen and thirteen other chief burgesses, but there are records of a "mayor" as early as 1350 and it would seem that the lords of Higham had long allowed a good deal of latitude to the burgesses.

In Norden's day the presence of the lord of the manor did not make itself felt in the exaction of the old villein services, even from the descendants of those who had not been among the ninety-two in 1251. Perhaps even in 1251 the lord was already allowing his villeins to give him cash instead of services in the field? Certainly in 1298 the documents show that he was receiving 2d. from each tenant instead of harvest-works, and with the money he was hiring seventy-five carts and paying out for 828 man-days of hired labour with which to get the harvest from the 266 acres of arable land which made up his demesne.

There were, however, certain profits of overlordship which the Duchy still enforced, even on the borough tenants. The townsman was reminded of one as soon as he came in the market-place, for alongside the town-hall was the Queen's bakehouse at which all were forced to bake, and to pay for the baking; similarly, and a source of many lawsuits in the Elizabethan courts, the Queen still took her toll of corn which was ground at the two mills, each with its three pairs of stones turned by the waters of the Nene. Nor could a townsman without fear of prosecution grind elsewhere to escape the toll, and there were many fines and quarrels. In 1570 the borough court agreed that the toll should be "but a pecke in a quarter", and in 1604 the miller was fined for demanding his measures heaped instead of level (or "razed"). The mills also gave the Queen a small income from the letting of the meadow around the mill-pools which were themselves another source of dispute,[19] since the boatmen complained if the sluices cut off too great a volume of water in dry seasons. In 1578 a jury of townsmen assembled by the mill-dam on

[19] *Ducatus Lancastriae, Pars Quarta—Calendar to the Pleadings*, Part III (1834), 206.

Rogation Day to measure the height of the gates to see if they exceeded the "fore foutt and halfe" agreed upon in 1570. A third, and small, reminder, of the presence of an overlord, even if the castle was decayed, lay in the dove-cote which still stands in the outer courtyard of the castle, now the grounds of the Green Dragon. The keeping of doves was a seignorial monopoly; in 1577 the tenantry were forbidden to keep doves for themselves and there are many cases in the Duchy courts of men fined for snaring the Queen's birds which were a menace to the crops as well as a delight for the table.

There were other regulations affecting the lives and conduct of those who came into the market-place of Elizabethan Higham which did not derive from the vestiges of feudal overlordship. These regulations were made by the burgesses assembled twice a year in their court, for which a special hall was erected in the market-place at least as early as 1381 and possibly earlier. Norden's plan shows a flight of steps outside the building leading up to the first floor, which may originally have been supported on pillars in the fashion of other medieval town-halls, leaving an open space at ground level to serve as a shelter for open-air debate and haggling. In 1444 there is a record of a shop under the hall, but it is not clear whether this was a stall or a permanent building. Norden's "common hall" has no open colonnade, and the present hall at the south end of the market-place is a new building erected in 1808. This place of assembly met the needs of a self-governing commercial community as effectively as a castle met the needs of its royal and baronial owners. The walls, gates, towers and moats protected the castle from assault. In the Moot Hall the burgesses sought the best strategy in the unending war of commerce, defending themselves against the privileges of rivals; against the fraudulent dealer; against the thief and the slanderer; and against the unscrupulous and non-conforming dealers among their own number.

The regulations sometimes irked certain townsmen, and there was often the temptation for someone to break them and make money, but in general they were tolerated as made by the authority of the borough and designed to protect the good name and efficiency of the market. In addition there were other regulations deriving from the Commons in Parliament assembled—and among the Elizabethan Commons was the member for Higham. It was not possible to do as one liked in Norden's market-place; and, indeed, it never had been, for many Elizabethan regulations were simply medieval rules of commercial conduct taken over wholesale.

The paragraphs which follow are based on the many orders formally agreed upon at meetings of the borough and manor courts at Higham during the reign of Elizabeth, and upon the court-cases against law-breakers in the same period.[20] The principal use of these documents is to reveal something of the range of activity among the townsmen of Elizabethan Higham. Legal records can be misleading as a source of social history. No one would consider that the *News of the World* would make an ideal source for the history of our own day, but it would be wrong to see the prosecutions in Elizabethan courts solely as the hunting down of criminals. So many townsmen, even mayors and aldermen, appear as offenders that it is clear that the notion of crime cannot be pressed too hard. Rather might we think of the fines as payments akin to a licence. The object was not to prevent people doing something but to make sure that their action was registered and public and paid for. As an example, nearly every-one was fined annually for keeping a dung-hill outside his door: the Queen, as lady of the manor, was really taking the opportunity to augment the rents. Nearly every brewer was regularly fined for "illegal brewing of ale": it is difficult to believe that they all regularly overcharged and watered the beer; they were in fact paying a concealed licence fee.

Some of the Elizabethan regulations were designed to protect all those who dealt in the market, and others aimed to give a special advantage to townsmen over "foreigners", by which was meant not the occasional Flemish, French or Dutch merchant, but anyone from outside the town. The market-place was not—and never had been—an open forum run solely as a public service. It was a place where trade could be canalized for the more efficient levying of tolls. In the time of Domesday Book the tolls had yielded the first Norman lord of Higham 20s. a year; in 1298, on the death of Edmund, Earl of Lancaster, a valuation of his estate assessed the profits of the Saturday market at nine times that amount, while an additional £4 was de-rived from renting the space for twenty stalls in the market-place. It

---

[20] Serjeantson, *op. cit.* The original rolls from the borough archives are now at the Northamptonshire Record Office, Lamport Hall. They were briefly noted in Hist. MSS. Comm., *12th Report*, App. ix (1891).

is idle to ask whether men thought these payments reasonable—for they had no choice: the market-places of England were local monopolies each backed by its charter or an immemorial custom. In the reign of Elizabeth there were also new statutes which forbade the sale of important commodities outside a market or fair: the medieval privileges were still thought worth maintaining. This opinion was not only held by those who took the profits of tolls. The towns themselves, living in a situation where the balance of economic power was held by hundreds of local monopolies, could see no other way than to maintain and strengthen their own privileges.

III

The physical appearance and setting of the English country market-place derive from these historical origins. The natural development of buying and selling wherever men came together is indicated by the churchyard market and the over-spilling into the street. The wide street indicates a compromise between a highway and a market-place which emphasizes the periodic nature of markets: they were not held every day, for there was not enough local produce to sell, and many of the traders were moving around the district to towns with markets on other week-days. When the market-day closed, the stalls were removed to make way for the next day's traffic. In Elizabethan Higham it was the duty of the mayor's bailiff to

kepe the markett place *pure et pulchre*

The transition from removable stalls to permanent shops and shambles was a slow one. Higham had some permanent stalls by the end of the fifteenth century and their heirs are the stone buildings which encroach on the market-place in Norden's plan. To a man who owns a permanent shop, trade has ceased to be a minor adjunct to agriculture, but not all who traded in the market-place of Norden's Higham had gone so far towards specialization. There were still the temporary stalls rented by people from outside the town and by townsmen who were not full-time traders. There were still bargains which could be struck without stalls, especially the sale of animals on the hoof, just as at the annual hirings prescribed by the Statute of Artificers (1563), men and women sold their own services for the coming year. But the Elizabethan market-place retained two medieval features. It was held in an open space with the maximum of publicity for dealings, and the venue was so placed that traffic coming to it could be easily supervised, goods inspected and tolls levied. The publicity was achieved by confining dealing to fixed hours and by legislating against private bargains before hours and outside the market-place. The central position of the market-place, with all the country roads leading into it, ensured that no one would pass unseen by the collectors and searchers.

The organization of a market was not solely in the interest of toll-collectors. There was a strong public opinion which looked un-kindly on certain trading practices and supported the authorities in their regulation. It was natural to have inspection of weights and measures. Inspection of quality was more difficult because of the more uncertain yardstick involved. Higham had its tasters of ale and victuals, its searchers of leather and its regulations against some of the craftsmen's commoner deceits. The interests of the toll-collector and the customers sometimes ran in the same direction. The markets were still haunted by the fear of scarcity, and the bad harvests of the years 1593-97 resurrected old bogeys. The enemies of good order were the men who bought only to re-sell when prices were higher and the men who bought in large quantities to corner a commodity and exploit a local monopoly.

The middleman was unpopular: by buying only to re-sell the same goods at a higher price somewhere else he seemed to do nothing productive. Thus, calves bought in Higham could not be re-sold under five weeks. A man who kept and fattened stock for that period was not re-selling the same goods that he had bought: but a man who bought on Saturday to sell at Northampton on Monday was a notorious "re-grator", fit for punishment and the pillory which stood only a few yards from the market-cross. From the steps of the cross the Queen's proclamations and the orders of the local courts were read aloud.

Very similar regulations were proclaimed[21] each Holy Rood Day (September 14) by the Mayor and the Twelve principal burgesses of Elizabethan Hedon (p. 147), who

> with ther best apparell [shall] make proclaymaicion in the Merket Plaice that men shall occupie [i.e. use] trewe weightes and sell no decytfull stouff;

[21] J. R. Boyle, *The Early History of Hedon* (1895), lxxix and xcii.

while the proclamation to be read at the fair included these admonitions:

> no person shall sell any manner of cattle or other wares until they come within the said fair, and then to sell them openly and not in corners nor yet in secret places; no person shall take away any goods before they shall have answered for the toll; offenders shall be punished who shall sell bread, ale or other victuals corrupt or harmful to men's bodies or at unreasonable prices or any ware that is deceitful: as flocked cloth, wool butts, shoes of evil leather, unlawful pots or other brazen or pewter vessel; or who sell by unreasonable names and weights to the deceit of the liege people.

As the eye strayed from the crier at the foot of the market-cross to the pillory near by, both townsmen and countrymen were reminded of the fate of those caught in their trespasses, and "Amen" and "God Save The Queen" were cried the more fervently.

It does not appear from the court cases and regulations that Higham market was famed for any one single commodity either in the Middle Ages or in the sixteenth century. Rather was it a typical all-purchase, local market taking the agricultural produce from a score of surrounding villages and giving the peasants an opportunity to purchase whatever they could not make for themselves. Some of the goods brought into Higham market-place by carts, men and pack-horses were used in the town's own shops and workplaces. The brewers, bakers, butchers, poulterers, fishmongers and chandlers had land in Higham fields where they could grow some grain and feed some stock, but beyond this they needed to buy whatever the country-man could offer, particularly in years of bad harvests and animal disease. Other goods passed from the market stalls to be loaded and taken away to the larger centres of manufacture and export. The middlemen from Northampton came to Higham to buy up what their own market had not supplied sufficiently.

The countryside around Higham was fitted to supply most agricultural products. In Norden's day the majority of villages in this part of the county were still unenclosed and grain-producing, although within the next forty years there was to be much enclosure by agreement and conversion to grass. A minority of local villages were already enclosed for pasture and carrying the flocks whose wool went off to the looms of the clothing towns. There is no evidence of a textile industry at Higham and a townsman hearing of more grass-land here and there would probably think not of sheep but of cattle. The fertile meadows of the Nene valley had for long maintained large herds of cattle providing meat and leather, and the pasture enclosures of the sixteenth century enabled cattle-breeding to extend among the villages on the higher ground. They were able to make this change partly because animal products commanded a good price relative to grain, and partly because a more integrated system of inland markets was removing the necessity to keep land under corn as an insurance against starvation in a year of dearth: only the run of bad harvests in the 1590s and in 1606-7 stirred this old fear; but the danger passed.

The local industry in the Higham Ferrers district to-day is shoe-making,[22] but there is no record of any specialization in footwear in the county before the mid-seventeenth century. Every English village of any size would be expected to maintain a shoemaker alongside the smith, the baker, the brewer and the carpenter. The antecedents of the modern industry can be traced no further than the widespread tanning found in Elizabethan Higham and other local centres. The raw material lay near by: there were cattle in the meadows and water in the Nene; oak-bark for the tan-pits and wood-fuel for heating could be got near by in the surviving North-amptonshire forests (such as Rockingham, north of the Nene, and the long chain of woods south of the river which still spread continuous green across the map on the Northamptonshire-Bedfordshire border).[23]

The borough court annually appointed a *scrutator* of hides who should see that only good skins and thorough processes were employed. In 1586 their oath ran:

> ye shall see whether it be lawfullie tanned accordinge to the statute, and then to seale it; no lether be here sold before it be searched and sealed.

There were leather-users among the Higham craftsmen of Norden's day although we cannot be sure that they were all shoemakers. The leather-users were anxious that the fame of Higham leather should not result in it all being snatched up: in 1582 it was ordered

> no tanner shall come to this markett to bie any hide except he brings cloute leather with him to sell,

[22] *V.C.H. Northants.*, i, 317-31.   [23] See fig. 24, p. 217 *infra*.

and in 1570 butchers were ordered to bring all their hides and tallow openly to market and not make private sales.

From the market square it is only a step to the four other buildings which remain from the medieval borough, and there is no space here to do more than mention them. Three are in the churchyard: Norden's plan shows the east end and spire of St. Mary's Church immediately below the market-place and next to the castle ruins; to the right of the church he drew the miniature Jesus Chapel, a fifteenth-century building now restored for worship; and on the left, adjoining the vicarage, Norden shows the roof of the Bedehouse, a building of the same period as the Jesus Chapel. The core of the present parish church dates from the mid-thirteenth century and it is tempting to attribute the rebuilding to the de Ferrers who was giving the town its fairs and freedom at that very time. The interior of the church has the roodscreen and stalls given by a famous native of Higham, Archbishop Chichele. The screen and stalls bear the arms of his see of Canterbury and of Henry Chichele himself; the same arms appear on the decorated Hovenden estate plans (Plates 3, 4, 6, 7 and 11, above), for the archbishop was the founder of All Souls College, Oxford. In his birthplace he bought land to build and endow a college of a different sort, a community of seven chaplains, four clerks and six choristers at whose head was a Warden who also served (until the dissolution of the monasteries) as vicar of the parish church; one of the priests took over the teaching in the grammar school. After the well-preserved church and Jesus chapel the remains of the College are scanty: when I visited it in July, 1954, the Ministry of Works had begun excavating the foundations of the buildings which lined the inner quadrangle; the chapel has been serving as part of a farm; the street-façade, with the gateway, is seen in Plate 14 with the three empty niches where, before the Reformation, stood the images of the three saints to whom the College was dedicated in 1425: St. Mary the Virgin, the patron saint of the parish church; St. Thomas the Martyr, the saint of Chichele's Canterbury; and St. Edward the Confessor, the uncle of the lady who held the Saxon manor at the time of the Norman Conquest. Norden's plan shows the original design of the courtyards and garden as yet unchanged, although in his day the College had been closed for sixty years and its properties—houses, field-land and market-shops—sold to augment the royal revenue.

Nor must we linger long in the fields of Higham, our principal concern being with the market-place. Norden's plan was equally selective. He contented himself with writing 'Comune feyldes' at the end of the town gardens. John Worthe's assessment of the field-land, made in the same year, was favourable:

> the arable land whereof [is] somewhat fertile with reasonable good medowes and commons.

The open fields which resulted from the progressive clearance of the Northamptonshire woodland had the same features as the villages studied in Chapter 3, and they were not enclosed until between 1800 and 1838. Norden's plan giving no indication of how the strips and furlongs ran, we must wait until 1737 when a large-scale plan of the still-open fields was drawn for the Duchy, giving each strip a number and setting occupiers' names against the number in an accompanying terrier or schedule. Another plan of the same type was made in 1789, probably in connection with the projected enclosure.[24] In both 1737 and 1789 the strips cover almost all the 1,900 acres of the field-land. By chance a very full terrier of open-field holdings has survived from a period even earlier than Norden and Worthe's surveys: for years the Duchy stewards must have used a terrier made in 1567 by one Edmund Twyniho, keeping it up to date by entering fresh names and noting when two or more strips were brought under one man and consolidated. The much-erased and interlined notebook was re-copied in 1728 and has now come with Earl Fitzwilliam's manu-scripts into the same Record Office at Lamport as the borough court rolls.[25]

Twyniho's survey was of the old-fashioned sort, the sworn testi-mony of a jury of fourteen inhabitants who proceded to take Furlong by Furlong and strip by strip until all the four Fields (Brooke, Middle, Handcrosse and West) were covered. There were, for example, 150 strips in the first Furlong: the medieval patchwork was slightly modi-fied, for five adjacent strips had been brought into one man's hands here and, elsewhere in the Furlong, four others; there were also four blocks of three strips and twelve blocks of two, leaving 105 single strips. There do not seem to have been any grass balks marking off

---

[24] 1737: Fitzwilliam (Milton) MSS. vol. 48 with terrier (Lamport Hall, Northants. Record Office); 1789: P.R.O. MR205.
[25] 1567 and 1728: Fitzwilliam (Milton) MSS. vol. 47. (Lamport Hall).

strip from strip: at Higham, as in some other Midland villages, the word "balk" was reserved for the grass lanes leading in among the furlongs. Only here and there are strips noted as "next a balk", when they abutted on such a grass way. Had each strip had a boundary balk it would have been necessary to say it in each case. In one Furlong the "balk" is explained: the strip lies

> next a balke being a Drift [i.e. Drove] Way for cattle from Chelston way to the brooke.

The absence of grass balks gives point to the order of the local court in 1577

> noo man shall yncroche uppon his neybors ground nether by eyrynge [i.e. ploughing] or other wayes.

This terrier of 1567 shows that the burgesses of Elizabethan Higham were not wholly divorced from the fields which surrounded their borough on all sides. In this, Higham resembled even the largest Elizabethan cities. Even London had near-by orchards and fields where citizens could take their pleasure. Norden's contemporary, the topographer and historian John Stow, relates how as a boy he brought back to his City home the milk still hot from the cows, and there was as yet no town where one could climb on the wall and see houses to every horizon, although there were pessimists prophesying this fate for Stow's London. York had its common pastures, the Strays, at its very gates; the fields of Norwich began at the walls; at Newcastle the Town Moor was hard by. In Higham, Worthe's survey recorded the pasture rights of 1591: every ancient cottage carried with it the right to turn out "two bestes and a breeder and ten sheepe". The freehold and customary tenants of the manor who held land in the fields had more substantial rights: everyone who held a yardland (here about 30 acres) could turn out forty sheep, four horses or other plough-beasts, and eight horned-beasts.

Finally, how many people were living in the town of 1591, maintained by these fields, these shops, these workplaces and this market-place? Norden's plan shows 140 buildings but his draughtsmanship is too rough to show whether any of these contained more than one separate household, and not all buildings may have been dwellings. The roughest estimate, then, at four people to a house would give 560 souls. If another rough-and-ready estimate is calculated from the parish registers—which show nineteen baptisms between March, 1592–March, 1593, and the same average for the next fifteen years —a population of 570 (thirty times nineteen) is arrived at.[26]

These two estimates cannot be linked continuously with the medieval town because the fifteenth century shows many houses decaying and never rebuilt, and the plagues of the fourteenth century also stand between 1592 and the establishment of the borough, when the ninety-two burgages can scarcely have housed fewer than 400 souls (without any account of the "manor" tenants, of whom there were at least twenty in 1313). In the poll tax of 1377—after the plague years—the receipt given by the collectors shows 258 persons over the age of fourteen, perhaps 400 souls again. More useful than these very rough estimates, perhaps, are comparisons with other places in the vicinity. In 1377 the borough of Northampton had 1,477 taxpayers, nearly six times as many as Higham; Peterborough had 850 without counting the suburban villages near by; Raunds, across the river from Higham, had 555 taxpayers and more than a score of Northamptonshire country villages were as large as Higham. In terms of numbers the borough was inconspicuous. Any two neighbouring villages added together could have mustered as many taxpayers.[27] It is the market place of a typical small country town that we have been visiting, a community only just missing the category of "large village" by the privileged legal status conferred on it by the Earl of Derby in 1251.

IV

The account of the town and market-place of Toddington, in Bedfordshire, will be shorter, partly because the essential basis of the economy in the two towns was the same, despite their different legal organization and status, and partly because there is no series of accounts, surveys and court records to rival those for Higham preserved among the archives of the Duchy of Lancaster. Yet there are some interesting comparisons and contrasts between the two towns which cannot be passed over, and even if Toddington is poor in manorial documents[28] it has Ralph Agas' magnificent set of plans,

[26] The parish registers are in the custody of the Vicar and churchwardens; Mr. A. N. Groome kindly lent me his transcripts.

[27] P.R.O. E179/155/28

[28] V.C.H. Beds., iii, 439-42 for the manorial descent; also J. H. Blundell, Toddington (1925), cap. i.

equalled only in their day by the estate surveys of All Souls and the Percies.

Toddington lies twelve miles south of Bedford and halfway between Dunstable and Ampthill. Thus it lay on the road from Bedford to London which took the Luton gap over the Chilterns: the Duchy of Lancaster officials on their way from London to Higham Ferrers must often have passed through its market-place. There is every chance that John Norden rode through it, but it is impossible to say whether he knew the great twenty-sheet plan of the parish which Ralph Agas had drawn for Lord Henry Cheney in July, 1581, ten years before Norden went to Higham.[29] He would certainly have known Agas' plan of Oxford and must have seen the advertising bills with which he sought to make himself known to the country gentlemen who were in London during term-time. In 1596 Agas wrote a pamphlet with the same title as Norden's apologia of the same year, a *Preparative*. Agas' pamphlet was designed to publicize the "new and scarcely established" techniques of surveying with the theodolite, and the survey of Toddington would have served as an excellent credential. It can now be seen in the Manuscripts Room of the British Museum. It is perhaps unfair to compare it with Norden's Higham which has no scale and was probably not measured out on the ground. Norden's plan was intended for engraving at the size of the page of a book, probably no larger than the map of London which prefaced his *Middlesex*, about 30 square inches. Agas' plan covers some 80 square feet on a scale of 40 inches to the mile (8 perches to 1 inch), and it bears comparison with the Ordnance Survey plans.

At Higham the parkland of the Manor was remote from the town (Fig. 24, p. 217) but at Toddington it lay rather nearer, and had heathland around it. About three-quarters of the remainder was under open-field cultivation. Thus the main concern of the cartographer was to obtain information by questioning the twenty-four townsmen who made up a jury of survey similar to those summoned when Twyniho and Worthe had gone to Higham in 1567 and 1591. The questions[30] dealt principally with the field-land: how much did a man hold? where were its strips located? on what tenure did he hold it? what rights of common were enjoyed? The open-field strips and

[29] B.M., Add. MSS. 38065.
[30] Details from the elaborate cartouche of the plan.

enclosed fields are so carefully drawn and on such a large scale that Agas must have made an instrumental survey; even the trees in the hedges are shown in their real position and not merely pictorially.

Toddington was a large parish of 3,535 acres, but the town, which occupies about one-third of one sheet, was somewhat smaller than Higham Ferrers. There are sixty-two tenants named on the map

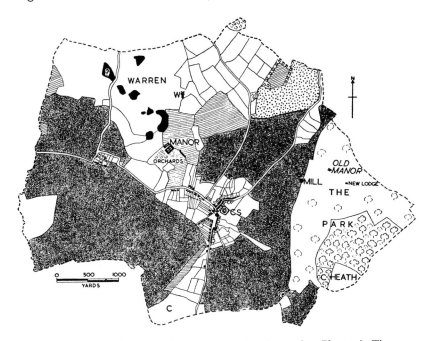

Fig. 17. Toddington in 1581 with detail from Agas' map (cp. Plate 15). The open fields are stippled and the meadow line-shaded. The open ground north of the Elizabethan Manor was heathland with scattered ponds and a windmill (W). On the right of the map is the thirteenth-century Manor and Park. CS in the village indicates the Norman castle mound. C: commons. (The dotted area in the N.E. was not included in Agas' map.)

itself and sixty-six families were reported to be living here in 1563 when the Privy Council collected figures from the bishops.[31] At Higham Norden's plan shows 190 buildings, not all of which can have been houses, and Agas' has 133 red-tiled roofs.

The history of Toddington is less distinguished than that of Higham. Its most distinguished proprietor was an Earl of Pembroke,

[31] B.M., Harleian MSS. 595.

at whose suit the market and fair were granted in 1218. But his widow married Simon de Montfort, and after the barons' revolt the manor passed to a local family, the Peyvres (or Pevers) who never rose higher than a knighthood. The peer who was Agas' patron had inherited the estate through a female line.

The lords of the manor did not construct any elaborate medieval stone castle. The earth mound of the Norman castle is shown as a dark heap on the right of the church in Agas' plan. It was then a rabbit-warren, *Conger Close*, a "coneygree" like the banks of the old Peverel castle at Higham in 1313. But whereas the lords of Higham had built themselves a second castle nearby, at Toddington the lord preferred a mansion described in 1251 by the chronicler Matthew Paris[32] as

> like a palace and environed with orchards and parks in a manner which, with its chapel and other outbuildings roofed with stone and lead, astonished all beholders.

The earthworks of *Conger Close* do not match this description, and this manor house was placed at Wadelove in the east of the parish. It in its turn had been replaced by the great Elizabethan house and gardens of Agas' patron on the west of the town. It is now the home of the Association of Fish Meal Manufacturers. (Fig. 17, p. 181.)

Like Higham's, the market-place at Toddington is formed as an extended triangle. There were fewer encroachments at Toddington and the church standing at the head of the triangle is able to dominate the picture, its tower looming over the low houses which cut off the churchyard from the market-place. One of these, now restored, was the Town House, the equivalent of the Moot-house at Higham, a meeting place for the townsmen. On the right of the churchyard, where the Georgian rectory now stands, Agas drew a "Town Kitchen", the equivalent of the manorial bakehouse at Higham. Right in the middle of the market-place were the "Town Shambles", the roofed shops of the butchers. In 1681 there were sixteen butchers' stalls set out each week here.

Agas' plan also shows the "markett cross", a maypole, and two men carrying water by shoulder-buckets from the common pump in the centre of the market-place. There is a rectangular pool for watering beasts shown in the bottom right-hand corner of the plan.

[32] Matthew Paris, *Chronica Majora*, ed. H. R. Luard (Rolls Series, 1880), v, 242.

Seven roads lead into the market-place, and it would seem that the roads from Dunstable and Luton which pass this pool have been widened, probably to take an overflow from the market.

Toddington market was first chartered in 1218, thirty-three years before Higham became a borough. It was held on Thursdays until 1316 when it was moved to Saturdays, probably to avoid a clash with the Thursday meeting at Ampthill, chartered in 1219. When Agas came to Toddington in 1581 the markets were still active: the roofed market house had only recently been constructed out of the materials from the demolished hospital of St. John the Baptist, founded in 1443 to house a chaplain and three poor men who would pray for the souls of the king, Thomas Peyvre (lord of the manor) and Mary, his wife. On a smaller scale, this endowment recalls Chichele's College founded in Higham in 1425.

In the mid-eighteenth century, Toddington market was still thriving. The prosperity of the town in this period is witnessed by the many Georgian buildings which face the green, having replaced the houses sketched by Agas. But in 1799 the market house was pulled down and in 1803 there was no market held at all although three fairs a year were still held. The market was revived in the second decade of the nineteenth century but—like so many—it languished when the Railway Age transformed rural communities and strengthened the larger markets at the expense of the smaller. The area in which country produce could be bought and sold was now much widened, tempting buyers and sellers to frequent only the large urban centres. There was no railway to climb the hill to Toddington and the town lost place to Bedford, Luton and Dunstable. In 1912 the chief occupations were "the plaiting of straw and the breeding of poultry". The condition of the market-place in 1954 is shown in Plate 16. The pool from which the townsmen took water has become an ornamental pond; the market house and shambles have gone; the sole encroachment in 1912 was a smithy, now become garage and petrol pump. There is no maypole visible and the disused market-place has sunk even further than Higham's in the economic scale. At Higham the cobbles serve for a car-park, but at Toddington the broad triangle is indistinguishable from any Chiltern village green.

7

A JOURNEY THROUGH PARKS

MILTON ABBAS, DORSET

WILSTROP, YORKS. W.R.

HOLDENBY, NORTHANTS.

HIGHAM FERRERS, NORTHANTS.

SHERIFF HUTTON, YORKS. N.R.

WOOTTON UNDERWOOD, BUCKS.

SUTTON COLDFIELD, WARWS.

> *Expresse the Parkes (if any be) with the number of Deere therein; what number of Aunteller and what of rascall Deere . . . having before you the rough plot of the whole Mannor.*
>
> AARON RATHBORNE, *Surveyor* (1616), p. 221

Chapter Seven

A JOURNEY THROUGH PARKS

I

THE field-worker must always be doubly grateful to parks. In their own right they are significant historical documents pointing to a characteristic man-made landscape created by social tastes and a concentration of wealth which are unlikely to return to England. The second virtue of parks to an historian is one which was not intended by their creators: the virtue of fossilizing older landscape features within the park.

It is true that landscape architects have diverted rivers, dammed valleys, drowned villages and done everything except remove mountains. Yet these massive renovations could only affect a fraction of the area brought into a park, primarily the area nearest to a Hall. Further away, the planting of avenues, the building of Follies and the throwing up of little hills disturbed only a few acres of ground. Elsewhere in the park, a sight of greensward was sufficient, and as a result—even in parts of England which have been otherwise greatly transformed by enclosure and intensive ploughing—the parkland is often able to show in its grass a pattern of medieval fields and field-roads. More than this, for, as we have seen in Chapter 4, some parks have preserved the sites of medieval villages and the earthworks of streets and houses, including one village (Tusmore) which was destroyed by the Black Death in 1349.

Other medieval earthworks such as abandoned fishponds, windmill mounds and animal pounds can be found within parks. Nor is the archaeology of parks confined to agricultural remains: one Yorkshire park (Cawthorne near Barnsley) has an excellent array of medieval iron-pits preserved by the trees which have grown up over them; and a Lincolnshire park (Hovenden House, Fleet) has as good a set of circular saltern mounds as anywhere in the fens.[1]

[1] The pits at Cawthorne lie in the woods on the north of the park: O.S. 1" sheet 102, GR 281100-289095; the Hovenden salterns lie near the road: O.S. 1" sheet 124, GR 396261.

For Roman and prehistoric archaeology parkland has done good service as a protector of earthworks during the centuries before the Ancient Monuments Act. Not only small earthworks, such as barrows and camps, lie in English parks, but also well-preserved lengths of some of the great cross-country earthworks and of Roman and prehistoric roads. In Sutton Park, to be considered later in this chapter, the Roman Ryknild Street runs across open heath for a mile and a half, while the parks at Stanwick and Forcett (Yorks. N.R.) had so effectively incorporated a great circuit of mound and ditch that these were firmly believed to be the pale of a medieval deer-park until Sir Mortimer Wheeler descended on them in 1951 and proved them to be the earthworks thrown up at the last stand of the Brigantes against the Romans.[2] The parkland had confused the historical issue, but it had at least preserved the mounds against the levelling bulldozer.

In this chapter we shall be considering parkland as a landscape feature in its own right. Parks of different periods will be cited in order to illustrate the different motives of park-makers and the different raw materials from which parks were made; visits will be paid to some parks where it is also possible to use the technique of previous chapters and set old maps against the modern appearance of the same areas; and the final journey will be to a Warwickshire park which can make the rare claim of being almost entirely "natural".

In modern England the word "park" brings to mind two different landscapes, one rural, one urban. In and near the towns a park is an open space which has been preserved from building; it is usually laid out formally with concrete paths, flower-beds, children's pools, shelters, waste-paper baskets, public conveniences, football pitches, bowling-greens and the like; at its entrance municipal authority and custodianship are commemorated in a notice-board which proclaims the hours of closing and a formidable list of bye-laws and unlikely nuisances.

In the larger cities these municipal parks sometimes derive from the gardens and grounds of a large Victorian suburban house. Death duties, local patriotism and the desire to fly from the sight of encircling suburbs have transferred ownership to the local council for the benefit of the citizens. Elsewhere, particularly in the north where

[2] Sir Mortimer Wheeler, *The Stanwick Fortifications* (1954); Stanwick lies 6 miles WSW of Darlington, O.S. 1″ sheet 85, GR 185120.

moorland still encompassed the little industrial towns in the early nineteenth century, the parks are vestiges of old common grazing grounds saved from the builder. Leeds provides me with parks of both kinds: in Roundhay Park whose slopes were once a medieval deer park I can watch cricket in the grounds of a nineteenth-century mansion, while on Woodhouse Moor I can take a walk after lunch and before lectures across one of the old common pastures of medieval Leeds. There is another type of urban park which reflects the conscience of town councils in the last fifty years, concerned to leave some open space for recreation among the spreading housing-estates. In these cases the Park is simply a piece of preserved land which, if left in its "natural" state, will retain the features of its previous use, usually grass pasture.

Municipal parks of these three types are important amenities to have and to retain. Historically they are an interesting reflection of the English townsman's desire to keep something rural by him even after he had given himself up to a working life cut off from the fields. Like the window-boxes of the skyscraper flats and the privet-hedged suburban gardens it represents a characteristically English wish to have something of both worlds, urban and rural.

In the countryside itself the word "park" conjures up a quite different landscape of grounds surrounding a country-house. It is true that some features of the country-house were imported into the grounds of the Victorian suburban mansion—shrubberies, flower-gardens, orchards, paddocks, stables, kitchen-gardens and lawns—but the fundamental characteristic of spaciousness was impossible near a town. The "spaciousness" of the country park is not simply a matter of acres: with enough money these could be bought, even near Victorian Birmingham and Bristol. It derives from the fact that that parkland merges into the "working" countryside. There is no limit to the landscape: beyond the park wall we see more open spaces, the fields, and not simply the edge of a town or the rhododendrons of the next villa.

A country park is part of the rural landscape. It has mellowed until it matches its surroundings so perfectly that the passing traveller might assume that the park is as old as the fields and the House as old as the village. That such a thought is possible is a tribute to the skill of successive landscape gardeners whose sleight of hand produced the parkscape. As in so many other deceptions daily practised on us, it is familiarity and repetition which bemuse us into accepting parkland as a "natural" part of the countryside. Parks, large and small, are so frequently encountered: there can hardly be a sheet of the Ordnance Survey map which lacks the speckled grey symbols of parkland; on some Midland sheets almost every second parish has its manor house set in a park; even the motorist who never leaves a main road will have his fill of park-lodges, park-gates, avenues, lakes, plantations, grazing animals in grassland peppered with oak-trees—and all seen over a wall or through the characteristic iron palings.

If so few parks are natural, does it follow that all others have been created by taking land from its natural and wild state? Was there a process of emparking akin to the assarting described in Chapter 3, except that instead of fields it was parkland for which men were cutting down trees and grubbing up roots? Or was there an inter-mediate position, so that the order of events is wasteland—fieldland —parkland?

The answer depends very much on where the would-be park-maker lived and in what century. Park-making has been in process in England since at least the eleventh century and by the time of Elizabeth I even the smaller gentry, the one-manored men, could hope to achieve in miniature what kings, lords and bishops had achieved much earlier at Windsor, Warwick and Devizes.

In those parts of England where agriculture had not already sub-dued the parks and heaths, the Elizabethan gentry had to adapt wild and open country, very much as kings and bishops had done earlier. Tastes were changing. A certain sylvan elegance was becoming fashionable, but the natural landscape was able to provide most of the essentials. But the places where a "natural" landscape lay ready at hand were few and scattered. Generations of land-hungry villagers had seen to that. When Lord Henry Cheney came to make a new park at Toddington in 1563 he was exceptionally fortunate, for the unclaimed heathland of the Woburn sands was still there for the taking, but in the greater part of the English plains it was only possible to create parks by converting one landscape into another, by taking over land which had been meadow, pasture and arable. What had to be done was not the conversion of natural scenery into a man-made landscape, but the conversion of one man-made land-scape into another. A landscape fashioned by the economic needs of local farming was being refashioned to meet the squire's wish for a decorative and even flamboyant setting for his home. In the eighteenth century the Capability Browns went even further and proceeded to attack the natural landscapes of wood and heathland in the service of their patrons and fashion. If native trees were of the wrong type or if the natural position of a wood was ill-adjusted to the view from a drawing-room window, then it became necessary to cut down some woods and to plant others elsewhere.

As we shall see later in our visits to parks, it was not only fields and trees which were liable to removal, for a village itself was not too great a barrier for the energetic craftsman. If it stood in the way of a vista or if it crowded too intimately at the back-door of the Great House, then let it be moved! In their own way the emparking squires of the eighteenth century could be as revolutionary in the transformation of landscapes as William the Conqueror had been in the destruction of villages to enlarge his New Forest.

II

It should not be difficult to establish the antiquity of any particular park. Private estate-records from as early as the thirteenth and fourteenth century are slender, but parks both private and royal are well represented in certain classes of the public records.

Both "forest" and "park" had original meanings which must be noted. The royal "forest" was not a continuous belt of woodland, but simply an area of jurisdiction, a man-made island in which the special measures necessary to protect the interests of the royal chase could be enforced.

In the twelfth and thirteenth centuries there was considerable pressure on the king to reduce these claims. The fields of villages in and near the "forest" were extending and villagers did not relish having a barrier against assarting, and losing crops when the forest animals broke into their fields. From the king's side, in addition to the wish to preserve hunting-grounds there was the economic advantage of maintaining a claim to forest jurisdiction since "fines" could be collected for permission to assart. The "forest" in its legal sense was at its widest about 1190, although the progress of assarting had already made large inroads upon the woodland recorded a century earlier in Domesday Book. In Magna Carta (1215) and the

Charter of the Forest (1217) the king promised to abandon forest law over any areas not already forest in 1154, but the local inquiries which followed upheld some remarkably exaggerated claims for exemption which were in their turn successfully challenged when Henry III came of age, and there were more disagreements under Edward I. The final settlement came only with Edward III (1327-77). These controversies have left a great mass of unpublished documents[3] among the *Forest Proceedings* at the Public Record Office.

The essence of a "park" was that it was separated from the surrounding land by some physical division. In this original sense, "park" could be used to describe small enclosures from the open fields which had been banked and ditched to mark them off from the remaining common land. In Devon and Wales this sense of the word is preserved in modern field-names. Elsewhere the sense has narrowed to one particular kind of enclosure, where the purpose of the bank and ditch (or other barrier) was to preserve land for the beasts of the chase. The *bestiae sylvaticae* were the wood-lovers, those (like the hart, wolf, wild boar and hare) who needed rousing and drawing by packs of hounds. The *bestiae campaticae* were found grazing in open ground among the trees—the fallow and roe deer, the fox and marten. The *deor falds* of some Anglo-Saxon charters may have been parks. The forest *parks* and *haiae* of which there is mention in Domesday Book (e.g. at Weobley, Herefordshire), were marked off from surrounding woodland in order to keep out the destructive wild animals and to prevent the beasts of the chase from escaping or damaging crops when there were near-by villages with cultivated land.[4]

The king himself often had a park, in this sense, as the core of a wider area of forest in which he hunted animals released from the park when the huntsmen were ready. Woodstock Park was one of these. If a private person wished to make such a park for himself within the broad bounds of the royal "forest" the new park would cut off the royal hunt and limit the feeding ground of the herds, so that royal permission was necessary. Even outside the royal "forest" a new park might take in woodland where some other person had

[3] Used by Miss M. L. Bazeley, "The Extent of the English Forest in the 13th Century", *Trans. Royal Hist. Soc.* (4th ser., iv, 1921), 140-72.

[4] For forest laws see Intro. to G. J. Turner, *Select Pleas of the Forest* (Selden Society, xiii, 1901). The Domesday references are brought together in Darby, 125, 180, 234 and 298; and Darby and Terrett, 84-5, 151, 247 and 437.

common rights such as wood-gathering or swine-feeding. Thus, in the class of records arising from the inquisitions *ad quod damnum* (what loss will there be) the local jury was empanelled to inform the king whether the proposed park would infringe the rights of the king or of any other person.

A park might also produce the diversion of a road, and this interference with public rights was also a matter for a jury—as a footpath diversion may be to-day at Quarter Sessions. There are dozens of places where the main road swings out of its direct course along the curving edge of a park and a diversion can be presumed, although not always documented. Sometimes the old course of the road is visible in the park as a depression. Not all these diversions are medieval, for there was a good deal of road diversion in the seventeenth and eighteenth centuries, but the road around the north edge of Tusmore Park, Oxon, has already (p. 97) been shown to date from the creation of the park in 1357. The park at Little Bolton in Wensleydale in 1314 similarly caused the diversion of an old road running from village to village, parallel to the river.[5] Another diversion which has left its record in an inquisition *ad quod damnum* is that of the road from Whichford[6] (Warws.) moved outside the park in 1252; in 1445 the road through Hunsdon Park (Herts.) from Eastwick was diverted;[7] in 1256 two paths through the deer park at Hodnet (Shropshire) were diverted:[8] the A53 and the A442 now make a semi-circle around the park edge.

The arrival of a private park on the landscape may sometimes be dated from the appearance of the park in the inquisition *post mortem,* held by the king's officers to establish the value of the deceased's estate. For royal parks, the appointment of keepers and orders for repairs are frequently encountered in the Letters Patent and Close, while in the accounts returned to the Exchequer the building of pales and the erection of lodges offer other clues to the progress of emparking.

The existence of a park also left its mark on the social obligations of local tenants. Since feudal landowners prized their hunting, there existed a range of minor feudal services which were originally

[5] *Cal. Pat. 1313-17*, 80 and 260.
[6] *Cal. Close*, vii, 174; *Cal. Chart.*, i, 431; *V.C.H. Warws.*, v, 205.
[7] P.R.O. C143/450/32.
[8] P.R.O. C143/2/5.

intended to make the holding of land dependent on performing some personal act when the superior landlord came to hunt. Thus the bishop of Lichfield had a castle at Eccleshall, eight miles north-west of Stafford; near by was the manor of Bromley where the lord was the bishop's tenant: for his manor he paid his overlord 10s. a year, and had to find four men three times a year to serve the bishop when he came to chase in Eccleshall Park. Land at Hole in Devon was held by the service of finding the king three arrows whenever he hunted in person in Exmoor Forest; another Devon manor, Bud-brook in Drewsteignton, was held by the service of a bow and three barbed arrows, but by the early fourteenth century the lord was able to make instead the more convenient but less picturesque payment of 5s. a year. Obviously the king was not hunting in person on Exmoor very often. The Oxfordshire manor of Bletchingdon was held by the service of finding a roast of pork when the king was hunting in Cornbury Park, something of an insurance against a poor day in the field and an empty spit. When the king hunted in Savernake Forest near Marlborough the lord of the manor of Grafton (Wilts.) had to provide a horse for carrying two packs laden with the king's wine. Fifty-two acres in Eastwell, Kent, were held by the service of leading two greyhounds on a leash, and the limit of the service was strictly defined: it should be for as long as a pair of shoes worth $2\frac{1}{2}d$. would last. These incidental services, and many like them, will be found among the records of feudal obligations (such as the *inquisitions post mortem*) in addition to a great number of ordinary keeper-, forester-, falconer-, and hawker-services.[9]

The progress of agriculture made it increasingly difficult for the lord of a manor to create or enlarge his park solely at the expense of waste land. Many thirteenth-century licences to empark include arable, pasture and meadow in their description of the land which is about to be enclosed. The Statute of Merton (1234) made it impossible to take in land on which freeholders had common rights without compensating them elsewhere, and there are numerous disputes in the central and assize courts where the new parks were challenged by litigants.

The builder of a castle, in particular, was tempted to imitate his betters by giving his castle the setting of parkland. Yet the strategic position for building a castle might not be among woodland and

[9] See indexes to the 14 vols of *Cal. I.P.M.* under "Services".

heaths: and the park could then come only at the expense of agricultural land, and the later the date of the park, the more likely it was —even in the wooded parts of England—that some disturbance of agriculture would be necessary or that rights of common within the park would have to be acknowledged and tolerated.

There are many places where a park bears signs of the older agricultural uses to which the land had once been put. At Bolton in Wensleydale we have already noted the diversion of roads when the Low Park was made in 1314. As the great terraces in the High Park still show, the making of the Castle Park in 1379 also saw the end of arable husbandry. Down in the Chilterns the monks of Ely had been given the manor of Hatfield by King Edgar (959-75) to be a source of building timber for them. Subsequent bishops of Ely used the manor as a hunting seat, but in the thirteenth century the bishops had to concede to their tenants the right of still pasturing horses, cattle and pigs within the thousand-acre Great Park. When Edward IV proposed to enlarge Windsor Park in 1467 he had to compensate the townsmen for the loss of land, and when he extended his park at Castle Donington (Leics.) in 1482 he gave 402 acres of his demesne fields to his tenants in order to persuade them to extinguish their common rights in the park, a mile from the town, where he was proposing to build a new house.[10]

III

Like a castle, a monastery of wealth and dignity often surrounded itself with an enclosed home park. Perhaps the best preserved of these is the Home Park of Fountains Abbey. The abbey itself had a precinct of gardens, orchards, outbuildings, tan-pits, water-mill and valley-side woodland; the surrounding wall still stands in some places to the height of 7 feet, and can best be seen to the south of the abbey on the east side of the Ripley road. Separated only by this road is the beginning of a much longer wall which made the circuit of the Home Park. The "Monk Wall" of the Ordnance Survey 6-inch sheet marks its course (fig. 18), but in places it has fallen down and the bank is ploughed level. The best-preserved

[10] Castle Bolton: *V.C.H. Yorks. N.R.*, i, 268-73; Hatfield: *V.C.H. Herts.*, iii, 99-100; Windsor: P.R.O. C66/516, m. 1 and *V.C.H. Berks.*, iii, 1-70; Castle Donington: P.R.O. DL43/6/3-5, letters patent of March 1, 1482 cited.

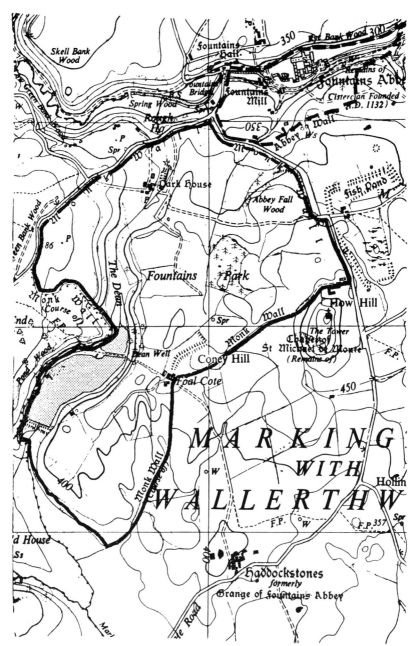

Fig. 18. Fountains Park, the home park of the Abbey, bounded by the *Monk Wall*. *Abbey Wall* marks the Abbey precinct.

portions lie on the edge of the wood north-west of the great lake which looks just like the work of some ambitious landscape gardener of the eighteenth century but is in fact the creation of the monks who dammed the valley with a great earthen bank. Just below the dam, where the stream is crossed by the Monk Wall, there is the original bridge designed to let water escape while retaining the animals with which the park was stocked.

In this part of Yorkshire it would have been possible for the monks to make a park in the early thirteenth century without encroaching on anyone else's property and without disturbing agriculture. Elsewhere, the frequent signs of ridge-and-furrow in the grass suggests that former arable fields had been taken into the park. At Jervaulx, for example, the abbey received part of the demesne lands of the lords of East Witton when the monastery was first built and in the course of time acquired all the present civil parish of East Witton Without, as well as a good deal of land in East Witton Within.

After the dissolution of the monasteries the home parks could be transformed into the parks of the country houses which the new proprietors might build, often from the stones of the monasteries. Thus, at Jervaulx, the modern park is simply the monastic home park as described in the dissolution surveys and in the early seventeenth-century estate plans.[11] Where the new proprietors were not interested in building a residence there was less reason to preserve the park, and if a good rent could be got for it as farm-land the park would be dissected into fields. Even in these cases, the outer limits of a former park are often shown on a large-scale plan by a succession of field-boundaries curved to follow the old park pale. One of the reasons why curving field boundaries of this type have lasted so long is that many pales were reinforced with a ditch which either from its size or from its utility as a drain has been an obstacle to re-shaping the fields.

If an abbey did not pass into a gentleman's park it could usually expect destruction or neglect. The Cistercian Houses, being remote, were usually immune from any later encroachments upon their surroundings by builders, but the Yorkshire abbey of Kirkstall is an exception. Mildly remote in the twelfth century, the valley of the Aire became the seat of industry in the eighteenth and nineteenth,

[11] *V.C.H. Yorks. N.R.*, i, 280-6; plans of 1627 by William Senior: Jervaulx Estate Office, seen by kind permission.

and the suburbs of Victorian Leeds lap around it. They have not totally submerged it, for the park has undergone a transformation. It is now neither a setting for a gentleman's residence like Jervaulx, a Ministry of Works show-place like Rievaulx, nor farmland like Fountains: it has passed into the custody of Leeds Corporation and is the responsibility of its Parks Department. With its asphalt paths, railings, wooden-benches, waste-paper baskets and official closing time it marks as emphatic a social change as the more common sight of the parkland of a Hanoverian peer housing the offices of an insurance company.

IV

Some abbey parks were insufficient for their Tudor owners and had to be enlarged. At Milton Abbas in Dorset, however, the medieval park seems to have satisfied the owners of the Abbey until the time of Joseph Damer, the Whig M.P. who was created Baron Milton in 1762 and Earl of Dorchester in 1792. The former monastic park lay to the north and west of the Abbey, of which in 1762 only the church remained, serving as the private chapel for the owners of the Abbey House and as a parish church for the market-town of Milton Abbas. The town had grown up outside the abbey gate, so that some of the houses backed on to the park wall as they do at Windsor and Woodstock. The enlargement of the park was perhaps the most audacious piece of landscape engineering in the whole eighteenth century. Other landed proprietors (such as the lords of Stowe, Castle Howard and Nuneham Courtenay) had removed villages which blocked a clear vista, but none of these transplantations involved more than a score of houses.[12] At Milton Abbas a whole market-town stood in the way. More than a hundred houses can be counted on a plan of the town drawn about 1769, when the earl's ambitious scheme was in its early stages.[13] It took twenty years to achieve; not all the tenants were willing to move to the new village that was being built in a side-valley, out of sight of the Great House. In the fifteenth

[12] For these (and other emparkings) see D. Stroud, *Capability Brown* (1950).
[13] A re-drawn extract from the original plan was published by H. Pentin, "The Old Town of Milton", *Proc. Dorset Nat. Hist. and Ant. Soc.*, xxv (1904), 1–7; the original plan came to light in 1955 and has been presented to the Brotherton Library, Leeds, by the Rev. C. K. Francis Brown. It covers the emparked parish of Milton and the open fields of the Winterbornes.

century an impatient lord might have evicted, but in the 1770s that was impossible. The due forms of law had to be observed, and until the leases expired the tenants were safe. On the 1769 map the length of the unexpired lease was written in each plot. A few houses were already "in hand", but the majority had one, two or three *Lives*. Plot 25, for example, at the south end of Broad Street, was leased to Mr. William Harrison for three lives, that is until all three persons named in the lease had died. Harrison was stubborn, as the interesting plan (Fig. 19) shows. This second plan was discovered among the drawings which the architect James Wyatt made for his patron in 1776 and is of about that date. It shows a landscape of the most curious kind.[14]

At the north is Lord Milton's house adjoining the old church of the Abbey. Just outside the churchyard wall were: an isolated group of houses, all that remained of the market-place; the School House; next to it the George Inn; and, across the street, the King's Arms. Of the ordinary village houses only two remained, both belonging to Mr. Harrison, one in High Street and one in Broad Street. There was, however, one sign that time had passed since 1769 and that Lord Milton would soon be able to give Capability Brown his final orders. The "three lives" of the first plan were now only "one life". By 1786 the transformation was complete, and a new church was opened in the new village street whence the Jacobean almshouses had also been moved, perhaps out of fear of the Commissioners for Charitable Uses. The School House was re-established in Blandford.

In the plan of 1776 there are continuous plantations of trees on the hillsides on the east and west of the valley where the ground rises steeply. The western belt is continued along the stream, right up to the west door of the Abbey church, and there are scattered trees both in the old pastures north of the church and in the new landscape to the south where Capability Brown's workmen had levelled the houses and sown their lawns. A kitchen garden and an orchard will be seen, left centre, but the other enclosures—L on Fig. 19—which break up the smooth pattern of the oaks and grass are simply the scattered property of the steadfast William Harrison. Harrison was a local solicitor and knew his rights, casting himself in the role of a village Hampden, and successfully maintaining the part for twenty years.

[14] Royal Institute of British Architects, London: MSS. plans and drawings, uncatalogued.

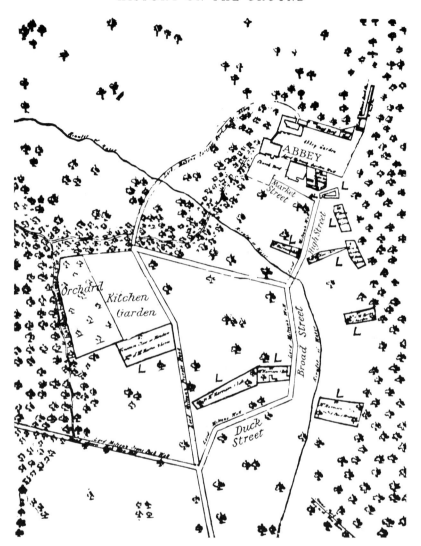

Fig. 19. Milton Abbas in 1776 with only a few houses from the old market-town, and the new parkland planted with trees.

Only after Harrison's death could Lord Milton complete the removal of the town.

In 1798 Sir Frederick Eden published his great survey of poor law administration in the English provinces. Of Milton Abbas he wrote:[15]

> the town is now converted into a fishpond. The Earl of Dorchester [Lord Milton] pulled down the houses as the tenants died off and removed the church to a distant spot where he erected very substantial cottages for such of the inhabitants as could not procure a more substantial habitation.

In 1770 Oliver Goldsmith published his famous poem, "The Deserted Village", in which the destruction of a village named "Auburn" was described and criticized. "Auburn" has never been satisfactorily identified either from the internal evidence of the poem or from the sea-side landscape of the engraving on the title page of the first edition, but in his *Preface* the author was at pains to emphasize that this was not a poetic fiction. He had seen real-life Auburns.

> I know you [Sir Joshua Reynolds] will object that the depopulation it deplores is nowhere to be seen, and the disorders it laments are only to be found in the poet's own imagination . . . I have taken all possible pains, in my country excursions, for these four or five years past, to be certain of what I alledge, and that all my views and enquiries have led me to believe those miseries real, which I here attempt to display.

It is unlikely that Milton Abbas itself could have been in Goldsmith's mind, for the first leases were only just beginning to fall in when the poem was published and when

> now the devastation is begun,
> And half the business of destruction done;

but there is one passage which fits admirably:

> The man of wealth and pride
> Takes up a space that many poor supplied;
> Space for his lake, his park's extended bounds,
> Space for his horse, his equipage and hounds;
> The robe that wraps his limbs in silken sloth,
> Has robbed the neighbouring fields of half their growth.

[15] Sir F. M. Eden, *The State of the Poor* (1797), ii, 148.

The cross in Milton Abbas at the junction of Market Street and High Street marked the site of a market which had been held since

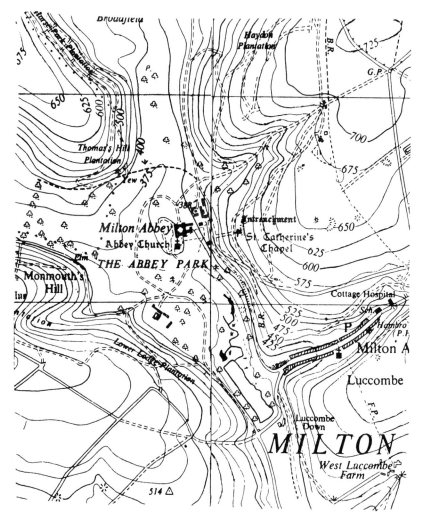

Fig. 20. Milton Abbas, the park to-day with the new village lining a valley out of sight of the Abbey House.

the charter of Athelstan, king of the West Saxons in the second quarter of the tenth century. It is shown on the plan of 1769 and also on the emaciated plan of 1776. It is said that the base of the cross may still be found in the roots of a shrubbery, but a cursory examination in July, 1953, did not reveal it to me.

The park is still private, although visitors are permitted to visit the Abbey Church. From there, one can look northwards up the forking valleys where the old monastic park lay and southwards down the valleys to the lake, the eye crossing the parkscape created for Lord Milton at so much cost and trouble. The lake is within 200 yards of the new village and well outside the area of the old town, so that the remains of eighteenth-century Milton Abbas do not have to be sought beneath the waters like the drowned villages of the Derbyshire and Welsh reservoirs. In 1863 it was said that ruins and foundations of houses were still visible,[16] but I could not see any sign of the former town in the park grassland, a tribute to the hard labour of Capability Brown's diggers. The streets have been erased as effectively as the houses and gardens, and only on the very steep hillside to the east did I think that I could detect the remains of divisions between the gardens which in 1769 are shown running up the hill behind the houses in Back Street; in fig. 19 five of these gardens alone remained on the edge of the new woodland.

V

To retain the animals of the chase and to exclude marauding animals and poachers it was necessary in deer-parks of all periods to have a high fence, reinforced sometimes with one ditch, sometimes with a pair. As such modern deer-parks as Woburn show, an effective fence has to be as high as 8 or 9 feet. The strongest fence was of oak paling fastened vertically and with a sharpened top. These made up the "pale", the boundary of the park, and can be seen in the sketch-plan of Elford, Staffs., made in 1508 (fig. 21). The Lord of Elford had a small park of 300 acres on the north edge of the common Fields, one of which was named after the *Park*. Licence to enclose Field-land, meadows and pasture had been given by the king[17] in 1386. The pale appears again in the Elizabethan plan of the new park at Holdenby, Northants. (Plate 20) and a pale was also taken as the symbol of the park in Saxton's small-scale county plans (Plate 17).

[16] Hutchins, iv, 382.
[17] Plans: Birm. Ref., Elford MSS. 49 and 55; Licence: *Cal. Pat. 1385-9*, 110; original in Birm. Ref., Elford MSS. 32.

When the making of a park evoked protests from those who were
excluded, the commonest way of expressing resentment was to pull
down these palings. Matthew Paris relates how William de Valence
came from Hertford Castle in 1252 to hunt in the Middle Park at
Hatfield, a Hertfordshire manor where the Bishop of Ely had a

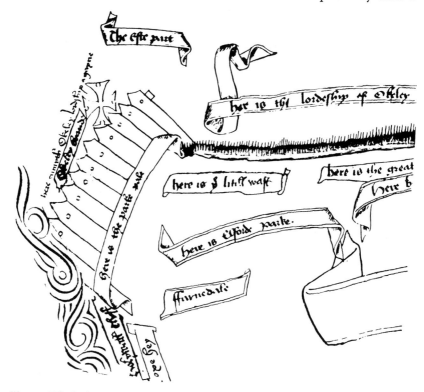

Fig. 21. Elford, the park pale from a plan drawn in 1508: "here is the parke pale" says
the scroll (left), and in the centre: "here is Elforde parke."

hunting-seat (p. 195). This park was claimed by the bishop as
private, and in 1251 he had obtained the grant of "free warren"
from the king, giving him the sole right to hunt within it. De Valence's visit was probably a challenge. He came, says the chronicler,
"despite the king's prohibition". His party tore down the fences,
hunted the animals, broke into the bishop's house, demanded a better drink than ale, smashed the buttery doors, knocked the taps of

the casks of wine and distributed it to the grooms as if (says Matthew Paris in horror) it were water or common ale.[18]

About 1490 the Wilstrop family, who took their name from a York-shire village near the junction of the Nidd and Ouse, had enclosed the fields of that village and evicted the villagers. The disgruntled villagers joined forces with other local gentry, who seem to have had a running feud with the Wilstrops, and attacked the park. In the course of a case heard in the king's court of Star Chamber it was alleged that a Wilstrop

> dydd caste doune the town of Willistrop, destroyed the corne feldes and made pasturs of theym, and hath closed in the commen and made a parke of hytt.

In April 1497 a party of eight came

> and there riotoselie pulled and bet doon ralys and pale

(that is "rails and pale") at the order of Sir William Gascoigne, a neighbour and rival. The next day they assembled on Marston Moor and marched to Wilstrop Park with a crowd of 200 people intending

> to pule doon the pale of the parke aforesaid.

The next January a larger crowd of 400 people came by night

> and there rioutously pulled down nine score roods [1,000 yards] of pale of the said parke.

Miles Wilstrop repaired the pale soon after, but a crowd of 200 people came and made assurance doubly sure: they

> pulled doonn the said pale, and therwith not being content cruelly cutt all the said pale bordez [pale boards] in sonder, and also hewid and kit doonn 100 walnottreis, and appiltreis grafted ii or iii yere before, and also distroid the same length of quickwood where the same pale stode.

Apparently there was a quickwood hedge running alongside this park pale. In October of the same year, after other destruction, a party invaded the Wilstrop rabbit warren and destroyed the bur-rows. Finally, in January, 1489, a party of 100—all tenants of Sir William Gascoigne—cut down another 200 yards of pale, hunted Wilstrop's deer, took away the venison and sought Wilstrop in his own house,

[18] *V.C.H. Herts.* iii, 99-100.

conspirying his utter distruccion, oppynly sayng that they wold repare agayn to the said parke and dwellyng place of ye said Miles; and make serch for hym, and if thei myght fynde hym to sle hym.

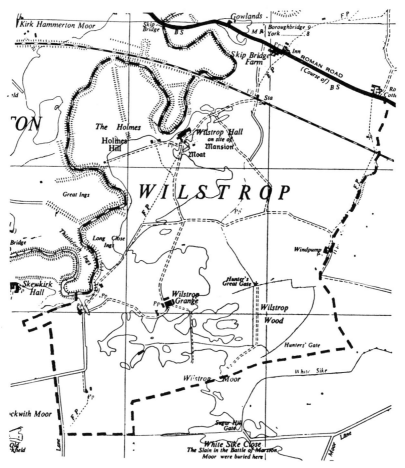

Fig. 22. Wilstrop, the medieval village and the Tudor park both now submerged into farmland. The site of the village was south of the railway and north-east of the Hall.

The park of Wilstrop, like Marston Moor itself, has now been cut up into farmland, but the visitor can still see a number of scattered oak trees. The fields are rather larger than normal—often a hint of early enclosure—and the grass fields near the Hall do not seem to have

206

been ploughed since they were enclosed by the Wilstrops, for the field-ways and ridge-and-furrow of the medieval ploughlands are well marked. On the east of the Hall, near the river, are the undisturbed earthworks of the houses and streets of the little "town" which the Wilstrops "dydd caste doune", an action which no doubt contributed to the violence of local feeling and to the repeated casting down of the park pale itself.[19]

In very similar circumstances only a few years later, but with more control of local opposition, the Duke of Buckingham pulled down the greater part of the manor house on his estate at Thornbury, Gloucs., and rebuilt it as Thornbury Castle.[20] Leland, who visited Thornbury after the Duke's execution, reported that the park had been enlarged by taking several hundred acres of "faire ground, very frutefull of corne."

Between 1350 and 1450, even in the regions of old settlement, the opportunity for making or enlarging a park was widened a little as the pressure of population on land eased, but towards the end of the fifteenth century the fortunes of agriculture revived and the man who planned to make a park found himself competing with others for available land. Some competitors wanted to enlarge their pastures for more cattle and sheep, others to grow corn on a commercial scale. Not all the monastic parks which came on the market in the 1540s escaped disparking (that is, conversion into farm-land), and even by the time of the first county maps in the reign of Elizabeth there were some medieval parks in the Midlands which had already disappeared.

The park at Studley (Warws.) which had been made by Simon de Montfort had already disappeared; it was disparked early in the sixteenth century. In 1520 the stone from the castle in the Duke of Bedford's park at Fulbrook near Warwick was taken to build the new house at Compton Wyniates on the edge of the Cotswolds, and Fulbrook Park was turned back to farmland between 1551 and 1553. Burghley bought the old royal park of Kings Cliffe near Peterborough from the Earl of Essex and promptly disparked it. When Leland visited this district fifty years earlier the park wall was already tumbling down and the royal hunting lodge was in disuse. The park at

[19] P.R.O. St. Ch. 1/2/58 and 2/17/131; M.W. Beresford, "The Lost Villages of Yorkshire", *Yorks. Arch. Journ.*, xxxviii (1953), 223-24 and 232.
[20] H.P.R. Finberg, *Gloucestershire, The History of the Landscape* (1955), 75.

Moulton, four miles north-east of Northampton, served as an adjunct to the castle in the county town. Yet the main burden of the maintenance of the park walls fell on the local villages and their names were cut inside the wall as a reminder. Although it was in decay soon after 1500 it appeared on Saxton's County map.[21] At Toddington (Beds.) Lord Henry Cheney built himself a new Elizabethan manor house on the opposite side of the parish from the medieval manor and park which the Peyvres had begun in 1251. In 1333 the park covered 120 acres, and in Agas' map of 1581 (Fig. 17, p. 181) the 481 acres of the "old park" are shown stocked with deer—

> inclosed with a Pale, runninge with a Redd Border [on the plan], furnished with 300 deere or thereaboute beside many great Beastes. . . .

But by 1645 the Pale was down, the park turned over to farm-land, and a smaller park (the present Toddington Park) enclosed from the extensive heathland near the Elizabethan house.[22]

Yet, despite these losses, the sixteenth century was on balance highly favourable to park-making, and as estate papers become more frequent in this period it is often possible to find the creation of a park recorded in successive surveys or even occasionally in an estate plan. Financial pressure was also forcing the Crown to review the royal estates, reassess their value and place some of them on the market. From these measures have resulted many maps and surveys which include park-land. Old castles, palaces and hunting lodges were examined to see whether they were worth the cost of repair, and the hopeless cases were assigned to the scrap merchant for the price of lead and stone. Along with the castles there sometimes was sold the park, and the plans of Sheriff Hutton (Fig. 25, p. 220) date from James I's sales. James' own fondness for hunting made him reluctant to see good parks lost, and when the first Commissions for the sale of Crown Lands were appointed in 1604 he specifically ordered[23] that no forest, chase or park was to be sold

[21] Studley: *V.C.H. Warws.*, ii, 183; Fulbrook: M. W. Beresford, "The Deserted Villages of Warws." *Trans. Birm. Arch. Soc.*, lxvi (1945-46), 90-91; in the early seventeenth century there was some reconversion to parkland: *V.C.H. Warws.*, iii, 91; Compton Wyniates: the park was licensed in 1520—*Cal. of Letters and Papers Henry VIII*, iii, pt. 1 (1867), grant No. 779, xii; the nucleus was made up of two areas depopulated in 1501 and 1512: Leadam, 418; Moulton: *V.C.H. Northants.*, iv, 94.

[22] 1333: P.R.O. C135/35/33; other details from 1581 plan, B.M. Add. MSS. 38065, Blundell and *V.C.H. Beds.*, iii, 438.

[23] SP14/4/15.

you are firmly and straightly to observe all these things, as you tender our favour and will avoid our displeasure.

When Charles I borrowed money from the City of London in the Great Contract of 1628 the lenders were allowed to take their pick of the royal manors which were to be put in pawn. Only two conditions[24] were made by the King: the City was not to take land where useful timber for the Navy was growing; and it was barred from

all forestes and Chastes and all Parkes nowe used and stored with deere.

There were also occasions when the Government turned an inquiring eye on private parks, quite apart from the Commissions which from time to time sought out emparking which had resulted in the eviction of villagers. Why should the Privy Council have been curious about the parks of provincial nobles and gentry? Partly, it is clear, in order to have the array of country gentry set down on paper, to keep an eye on the tax assessments and to note likely candidates for the less popular local offices. But there were other ways of compiling such a list, and the principal purpose of the parks inquiries was to know where the Government could look in time of war or threatened invasion when there was a sudden and urgent demand for horses. Gentlemen who kept parks had the duty of using them to breed horses.

The Government watched the woodlands to make sure that there was enough timber left for its Navy, and the parklands to make sure that there were horses at hand for the cavalry. The export of horses was only permitted under licence after 1563, and in 1562 a proclamation had revived the statute of 1558 whereby all having £1,000 a year in land were to keep six horses for demi-lances and ten for light horsemen. When, as in 1565, the man-power of the counties was mustered, the landed gentry were ordered to have these quotas of horses also at the ready for a census on July 31st. In 1569 another proclamation announced a separate muster of horses, and in 1580 the numbers at the last muster were declared to be still too small.[25]

VI

From 1579 however, we are no longer dependent on the chance survival of private or official records for knowing what English parks

[24] *Acts of the Privy Council, 1627-8*, 455-63; I am indebted to Dr. Robert Ashton for elucidating the negotiations with the City.

[25] Some returns of parks are in P.R.O. SP12/12, E163/13/10 and SP14/46.

were in existence, for Christopher Saxton's county atlas published in 1579 was the first to show parks by a separate symbol. Subsequent cartographers were unlikely to omit country houses and parks since the gentry were among the most likely purchasers of their wares; and the tradition began by Saxton's little park pales is continued in the distinctive dappled park-land of the Ordnance Survey maps.

Northamptonshire is a county of parks. Of the twenty parks shown by Saxton, eleven still survive, and there are a number of others which have been created since Saxton's day. In 1902 there were eighteen parks in the county with herds of fallow deer numbering from forty to three hundred, the largest being at the Knightley's park of Fawsley, visited in Chapter 4, where the medieval park had been extended in Elizabeth's time. The Dower House is now a ruin of ivy and Tudor bricks in this New Park.[26]

Some of Saxton's parks were old-established: one of them, Higham Ferrers, will be described in the next section of this chapter. Others were quite new. Richard Empson had obtained licence to impark 400 acres from the town fields of Easton Neston only in 1498, and John Spencer of Wormleighton had imparked Althorp in 1512, four years after his purchase of the manor.[27] The best documented of the Tudor parks in the county, however, is one which Saxton's map just missed. Within four years of Saxton's atlas Sir Christopher Hatton had begun to create Holdenby Park as a fitting setting for his new house of Holdenby.[28]

Elizabethan Northamptonshire was a prosperous county, its squires rearing sheep and cattle, selling wool and hides, moving into trade and marrying their daughters well. Sir Christopher's funds for his new House and park came not from these sources but from the estates, court offices and annuity with which the Queen had been rewarding her favourite[29] since 1564. In turn, it was the pleasure and duty of a gentleman to build a house worthy of a Queen and to surround it with an ornamental setting. As William Cecil wrote[30] to Hatton in 1579

[26] *V.C.H. Northants.*, i, 133; seven of the eleven parks shown in Saxton's map of Dorset are now disparked: Hutchins, i, lxxi.

[27] Spencer: *Calendar of Letters and Papers, Henry VIII.* i, pt. I, 684; Empson: C66/583, m. 4.

[28] Holdenby House: E. S. Hartshorne, *Memorials of Holdenby* (1868), plans 12-13; Park: p. 212 *infra* and plates 18-19.

[29] E. St. J. Brooks, *Sir Christopher Hatton* (1946), 153-66, with plan of 1587.

[30] Quoted E. S. Hartshorne, *op. cit.*, 20.

God send us both long to enjoy Her, for whom we both mean to exceed our purses in these buildings.

At that time Cecil was building and emparking at Burghley, near Stamford, and it was here that Norden addressed his patron when he dedicated his *Northamptonshire* in 1591. Hatton was by then Lord Chancellor, and Norden probably intended to add a second dedication to him. But the chances of publication faded, and when a second version of the text was prepared in 1610 Hatton and Burghley were dead, and the new dedicatory Preface was addressed to Sir William Hatton, the nephew of Sir Christopher. Norden left his description of Holdenby virtually unchanged, and his words will again serve for a bridge (as at Higham Ferrers and Sheriff Hutton) between the Elizabethan and the modern landscapes.[31]

> No shire within this Lande is so plentifully stored with Gentry, in regard whereof this Shire may seeme worthy to be termed the Herralds Garden.

The Elizabethan park was as much a demonstration of social rank as the pedigree and the coat of arms. If the College of Heralds did well out of Northamptonshire squires anxious for a pedigree and a coat of arms so did the builders, the painters, the plasterers, the joiners and the furnishers, for the new or refurbished manor house was a signal of rank and wealth, and a park was the approved setting for a house. In the oaks and grassland of the park there was space to course the deer, to hunt with the hawk and to ride at leisure, but there was also utility.

> Parkes, forests and chaces yealde often recreation to the Mynde, exercise to the Bodie and relief to the Table

wrote Norden,[32] and just as medieval parks had provided their owner with useful food, fuel and timber, so the Tudor parks were used for grazing sheep and fattening cattle, a sign that there was not always vigorous hunting in progress over the launds.

Holdenby had been inherited by a Hatton after the last de Holdenby had died childless in 1511. His *inquisition post mortem* says nothing of a park,[33] and the plan of 1580 (reproduced in Plate 19) shows the

---

[31] John Norden, *Speculum Britanniae Pars Altera or a Delineation of Northants.* (1720), 28.

[32] Norden, *op. cit.*, 31.

[33] *Calendar of Inquisitions Post Mortem, Henry VII*, ii, 152; G. Baker, *Northamptonshire* (1822), i, 194.

situation just before Sir Christopher Hatton began to make the park.

The country around Holdenby is gently rolling, with sufficient change of slope within short distances to provide privacy for a house and a vista from its windows. Norden began his description of Holdenby[34] in 1591 by praising Hatton's choice of site:

> the same House is very pleasantlie contrived, mountinge on an Hill environed with most ample and lardge Fields and goodly pastures, manie yonge Groves newly planted both pleasant and profitable

—here Beauty and Utility again jostle each other—

> fishe ponds well replenished, a Parke adjoyninge of Fallowe Deare with a large Warren of Conyes

—these will be seen on the map of 1587 in Plate 20—

and aboute the House are a good store of Hares.

The maps[35] of 1580 and 1587 both show that the House was separated from fields and park-land by gardens and woods. Norden was very impressed with these environs of the House:

> and above the rest is especially to be noted with what industrye and toyle of Man, the Garden hath bene raised, levelled and formed out of a most craggye and unsitable (sic) Grounde, now framed a most pleasante sweete and princely Place with divers Walks, manie ascendings and descendings, replenished also with manie delightful Trees of Fruite, artificially composed Arbors, and a Destiling House on the west end of the same Garden, over which is a Ponde of Water brought by Conduite Pypes out of the Feyld adjoyninge on the west $\frac{1}{4}$ of a myle from the same house.

To conclude, says Norden,

> the State of the same is such that it may well delight a Prince.

The Prince who came to Holdenby entered the parish from the east along the road from Northampton through Brampton. Even before the making of the park, a long straight drive led right up to the House, of which the main door faced east. To get to the village one followed a more winding lane on the north of the drive, along the edge of the North Field. The plan of 1580 shows fourteen houses

---

[34] All the following quotations are from Norden, *op. cit.*, 50-51.

[35] Lamport Hall, Northants. Record Office: Finch-Hatton MSS. 272 fo. 59 and 62; the survey of 1650 is printed in Hartshorne, *op. cit.*, viii-xxvii.

scattered around a village green: there had been twenty in 1511. To the north (the right of the map) was *The Spiney*, an enclosed wood which separated the Hall from *North Feelde* and the view of men at the plough. On the west there were ornamental gardens laid out in squares; on the south (or left of the plan) there were more gardens and terraces between the Hall and the church. Surrounding the church were trees more openly planted than the spinney on the north; they stretched down to a set of ornamental fishponds in the valley bottom. A hedge of trees began near the church and came eastwards around the orchard and the long *greene*.

The area described so far, the surrounds of the Hall, was probably considered as a small park, serving the old manor house of the Holdenbys which still had a few earthworks to point its site when the plan of 1580 was drawn. In 1591 Norden mentioned both the new and the old houses

> a very stately howse called Holdenby nere unto the scyte of the old mansion howse of the Holdenbys.

The ground between this older house, the church and the fishponds was all that comprised the medieval "park", for the map of 1580 shows the four open Fields occupying all the remaining ground. One of the four Fields, however, was named *Parke Feelde* from its proximity to this little park. There were three other Fields, two of which were soon to be radically transformed. *North Feelde*, the fourth and largest, was only destined for slight changes.

A second plan, drawn only seven years later in 1587, shows how the new owner of Holdenby created his Elizabethan deer-park (Plate 20). It is not quite so accurately drawn, but its scale and style are such that the plan of 1580 can easily be compared. There had been some alterations in the immediate surrounds of the Hall which can be briefly dismissed. The fourteen houses of the village were now only eight and had been rebuilt a little to the west of their old position; a new Spinney had been planted to match the older one to the west. There was a new inn. On the east the drive from Brampton still came straight to the Hall across the *Greene*, but a walled and gated courtyard had been built in front of the main entrance. The arches of this courtyard can still be seen as picturesque ruins, and the endpapers show an eighteenth-century sketch of them. More ornamental ponds had been dug in the enclosed ground near the church, and the formal garden on the north of the house had been planted as an orchard.

But these changes were small compared with the transformation of the southern half of the parish into a 600-acre park. The plan is almost self-explanatory: it pictures the five-mile circuit of the timber fence, tall and pointed to discourage the deer from escaping. The main drive from Brampton and the road from Harlston had to be admitted by a double gate. Within the park the cartographer shows the new inhabitants: there are two huntsmen, each with a hawk; deer are walking, leaping and feeding; rabbits sit up in alarm and run.

To create the park, *Fowlham Meadowe* has gone; *Parke Feelde* and *Longlande Feelde* have yielded up about a quarter of their area; and the whole of *Woode Feelde* is in the park. On the extreme left of the plan (south) the park pale does not reach as far as the stream and a narrow belt of meadow survives outside it.

Since *North Feelde* was untouched—and it was here that all the tenantry land lay in 1580—it would seem that Hatton had come to terms with the villagers, assigning them land in one sector of the parish in exchange for a free hand in the other. In 1587 a *sheep penne* appears in the *North Feelde* for the first time, while in *Parke Feelde* the trees have been cut down, so that the one may have gone down to grass while the other returned to the plough.

In addition to the enclosure of field-land and meadow the park-making involved some changes in the woodland. The 1587 plan shows that a new spinney has been planted at the corner of the old *Fowlham Meadowe*; a wood to the north-east of *Colpit Ashes* has been removed, but many single oaks have been planted near to where 55 acres of Chapel Brampton parish have been brought within the pale. The wood *Colpit Ashes* has been made more decorative and accessible by cutting four avenues through it.

In 1954 there were no longer five miles of oak paling around Holdenby Park, and no deer, no huntsmen, no rabbits. The whole line of the pale survived in field boundaries until wartime ploughing erased some of it on the Althorp side. On the east the Elizabethan boundary is well preserved, as Plate 21 shows. This view is taken from near the left-hand point of the compasses on the 1587 plan where the pale, which has been following the Holdenby-Brampton road, swings away in a southerly direction. The hedge and trees which have replaced the palings are growing on an artificial bank made by throwing up soil from an inner ditch, which was the deer-leap.[36]

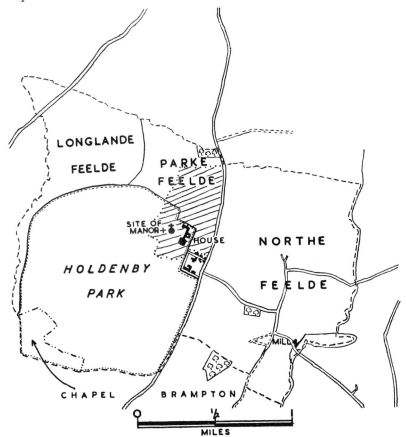

Fig. 23. Holdenby: key to the plans of 1580 and 1587 (Plates 19-20) showing Hatton's Park and the surviving parts of the three open Fields. Part of Chapel Brampton has been brought into the Park. The line-shading suggests the area of the medieval park of the Holdenbys.

VII

On the edge of the county, and some distance from his little sketch of Higham Ferrers church, Saxton showed the circuit of Higham

[36] Mrs. G. H. Lowther kindly showed me the House and grounds in the summer of 1954.

215

Park. Norden's account of Higham in 1591 made no mention of the park, probably because it was situated so far from the town and usually reckoned as part of Rushden. A description of the medieval park and its modern appearance was postponed from Chapter 6, because Higham is one of the earliest parks shown on Saxton's map and its history and dimensions are typical of many of the smaller post-Conquest private parks.

We have seen in Chapter 6 that the Northamptonshire town of Higham Ferrers had a castle standing only a stone's throw from the market place. Near the castle were a walled orchard, gardens, fishponds and a separate rabbit warren enclosed with walls and a gate. Yet, although there was a medieval park belonging to the lords of Higham, it did not adjoin the castle. The open-field maps show arable fields coming right up to the town on all sides. In this, Higham was very different from its Huntingdonshire neighbour, Kimbolton, where the Castle Park commenced at the end of the market-place.

There was no part of Higham park nearer than three miles from the castle, and the furthest part was four miles away. Intervening were the fields of Higham itself and the fields of Rushden (fig. 15). Because of its attachment to Higham the park ground was always reckoned as standing outside the normal parochial boundaries, and although the park has been broken up as farm-land the outline of the park pale is well preserved in the boundaries shown on the modern Ordnance Survey plans. The 600 acres of the park took the shape of a gigantic thumb-nail, the tip of the finger pointing south-east into Bedfordshire. Clearly, a piece has been taken out of Rushden parish, and another piece out of Newton Bromswold parish. These two tracts of land would have made an almost rectangular park with the county boundary on the long, straight south-eastern side. The curve of the thumb-nail is made by a third addition, a piece of Knotting parish, which brought 167 acres of Bedfordshire into the park and put them into Northamptonshire; the county boundary, which for some distance has been running straight along the old ridge road of "Forty Foot Lane", swings east in a curving arc around the park pale and then back to resume its old line.

A long belt of broken woodland stretches along the Bedfordshire-Northamptonshire border, surviving from the rough country, not particularly easy to crop, towards which the lords of Higham looked for their hunting. When did they acquire the park? John's charter of 1199 restoring the manor of Higham to the fifth earl of Derby speaks of

> the park of the same vill which heretofore we have had in our own hands

—that is, since the forfeiture of 1155, when there must already have been a park, since another document of 1199 speaks of an exchange

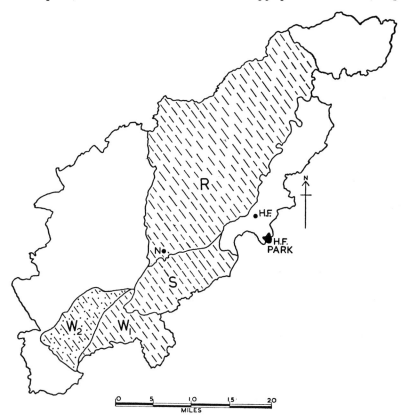

Fig. 24. Higham Ferrers Park, in relation to the thirteenth-century Forests of Rockingham (R), Salcey (S), and Whittlewood (W₁ and W₂).

of land "to enlarge the park in the time of the earl's great-grand-father" (1139-55); the woodland which went with the manor in 1086 may, indeed, have included a park. The exchange of lands to enlarge the park probably accounts for the curious intrusion into the next parish and county which has been noted earlier.

Henry III, who gave the Earl of Derby the borough charter of Higham, also made several grants of animals from the royal forests to re-stock Higham Park. In 1234 five bucks and twenty-five does were sent from Weybridge in Surrey, and in 1244 fifteen does and five bucks were sent from King's Cliffe, near Peterborough.[37] There was a herd of more than 300 in 1429, and despite the decay of the castle there were still deer in the park in 1624. The park provided hay for the deer and a surplus in some years for the castle horses. The fish-ponds and dove-cote of the park also yielded food for the castle. There was swine-grazing, and the park provided oaks for the repair of Higham mills, the castle and drawbridge, and for making market-stalls, while cart-loads of "crabbetre" went to repair the "kogges and runges" at the mill. Other timber was cut for the park lodges and the deer-houses, and from the mid-fifteenth century the park must have been largely cleared since the stewards' accounts then began to show heavy imports of timber from outside Higham.

Being distant from the castle, the park needed resident keepers who lived at a "Great Lodge" near the north-west corner of the pale. The moats of the Great Lodge are still well preserved near the farm-house known as Higham Park. In a fifteenth-century rental it was said to have within it a hall, a chapel, a chamber, a kitchen, a brew-house and a bakehouse. In the grounds were a dove-cote and two fishponds, one of which still contains water. There was a smaller lodge on the south side of the park which seems to have left no remains.

The park is now divided into twelve fields, and when it was visited in 1954 only a herd of frisky bullocks provided an element of the chase. The ground is heavy clay, and before field-drains it would have been unattractive to the plough; even now on the south it merges into Souldrop Wood. A few old oaks survive in the hedge-rows, but during the Civil War the timber was despoiled, the deer killed and some of the land put under the plough, and in 1669 it could only be referred to as "the late reputed park".[38]

On the south-west side of the park, where the Rushden boundary runs, the earthen bank, which formerly carried three and a half miles

[37] *Cal. Close*, ii, 468 and 534; v, 210 and 242.
[38] *V.C.H. Northants.*, iii, 280.

of "dead hedge" pale, is still well preserved for a short distance.[39]
The ditch on the outer side serves as a field-drain and is still a formidable obstacle to exploration. The crown of the bank has lost its
dead hedge but bears a fine crop of thistles (Plate 21). Elsewhere the
bank has been levelled and replaced by more conventional boundaries. When he saw the name on a map, a visitor would find it
difficult to imagine that this same ground had seen kings riding and
the liveried falconers of John of Gaunt coming from the moated
lodge.

VIII

We have now visited a new Elizabethan park and a number of
medieval parks. We have seen monastic parks sold off to speculators
and royal parks coming on to the land market under Elizabeth and
Charles I. The next park to be considered is Sheriff Hutton where a
fourteenth-century park, the appendage of a castle, became the
setting for a new Jacobean country residence for the financier and
monopolist, Sir Arthur Ingram. Sheriff Hutton also brings us into
contact again with John Norden at the end of his career. In the last
year of his life, 1624, he was in the North Riding executing a survey
of the manor of Sheriff Hutton, a small market-town nine miles
north of York. At the age of seventy-six he probably found it difficult
to make the perambulation of the bounds which the survey records,
but he had with him as partner his son, John Norden the younger,
who was also a well-known surveyor. The father's task may have
been to attend to the other part of the business, the evidences of the
tenants and the sworn statement of the thirteen jurymen. No plan
of the whole lordship was made, but the Park, with which we are
principally concerned, was "plotted". The plot is reproduced in
fig. 25.

The survey[40] was commissioned by Charles Prince of Wales, soon
to be king. He had just received the estate from his father and was
anxious to know its current value and its potentialities. There had
been a time when its royal and noble owners had prized Sheriff
Hutton as a residence: Henry VIII had established here the court
of his bastard son, the Duke of Richmond; Richard III imprisoned
his nephew and niece here. Charles I viewed the property more as a

[39] "Not walled but hedged": Norden, *op. cit.*, 30.
[40] B. M. Harleian MSS. 6288 and T. N. MSS. B417391.

source of income, and within three years had used it to reward a groom of the bedchamber on whom he bestowed the lease at a very nominal rent, about one-third of its real value. In 1628 he raised money by selling to the City of London the first option on the lease after its expiry, and the records of the ninety-eight tenants and their obligations which the Nordens had made was probably a useful

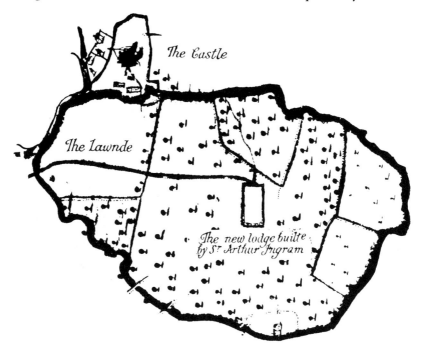

The Castle

The Lawnde

The new lodge builte by Sᵣ Arthur Jngram

Fig. 25. Sheriff Hutton, the Jacobean house in the fourteenth-century castle-park. From the survey by John Norden in 1624.

evidence to show the City aldermen, who had themselves employed the Nordens on other estates.[41]

The park was closely associated with the castle which, as the *plot* shows, adjoined the north-western corner, being separated only by what Norden described as

the formes of certayne decayed fishpondes,

[41] E.g. City of London Record Office, CRF 91: Norden's surveys of Kennington and Devon estates.

the small rectangles of the plan. The castle had been neglected since the Duke of Richmond's court left it in 1530, and Norden was moved to write of it as[42]

the case of a stately castle, the inward material transported, the walls ruined. . . . The bowells of this worthy pile and defensive house are rent and torne and the naked carkas lately by his Majestie alienated. . . .

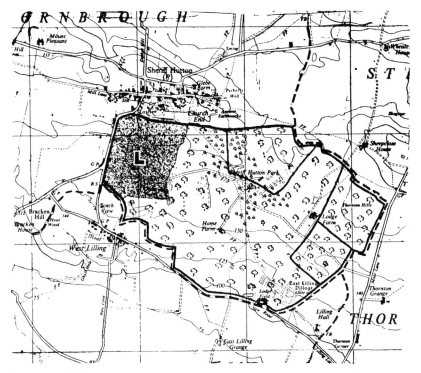

Fig. 26. Sheriff Hutton: the modern Ordnance Survey plan. Boundaries of 1624 have been added; the former *Lawnde* is shaded.

The park was actually older than the castle, which only dates from 1382 when John, Lord Nevill obtained the king's licence to enclose a plot of ground on his estate and to build a castle of "stone and lime"; but at the other end of the village, south of the church, are the earthworks of a castle of the motte-and-bailey type, probably built about 1140, and it was for this earlier castle that the park was

[42] B.M. Harleian MSS 6288.

221

designed. No park is mentioned in the surveys made at the deaths of the lords of Sheriff Hutton in 1281 and 1331, but the Ralph de Nevill who inherited the manor in 1331 obtained a licence for a free warren that same year, and four years later a licence for a park. At his *inquisition post mortem* there was "a park with deer".[43] It is easy to see why the king's permission was necessary before a Nevill built a castle, but why for a park? The licence itself explains: the woodland which Ralph proposed to empark lay within the bounds of the Forest of Galtres where the animals were preserved for royal use. Ralph proposed to build a deer-leap, a barrier against the escape of his animals and a barrier against other huntsmen, and the king's consent to this private park was therefore necessary. The vestiges of the old Forest of Galtres can still be seen to the south of Sheriff Hutton, in the heathland and stunted trees of Strensall Common which has been preserved against reclamation since the War Office took it a century ago as an artillery range. The Common was emparked[44] in 1214, but the green uniforms and arrows of the royal hunt have been replaced by the khaki uniforms of machine-gunners, and the place of the hunting lodge is taken by nissen huts. The modern keepers of the Queen's terrain can be seen listlessly painting the kerb-stones white.

In 1335 the land from which Sheriff Hutton park was to be made was described as "woodland". Was no arable land taken into the park, which approaches so near to the village houses? had the wood-land come right up to the edge of the gardens? and were the arable fields all in the other direction? The answers are uncertain, but on topographical grounds it is likely that some fields had been taken into the park whose terrain shows no change of slope nor a soil which would deter the plough. There were 1,600 acres of bad, ill-drained land in the township in 1624 but they lay on the north and south-east, in the extensive Carrs and Foss marshes. The well-marked ridge and furrow of a medieval type which is found all over the former *West Field* of the village also extends into the northern part of the park, especially in the corner nearest the castle, called the *Lawnde* in Norden's *plot*.

Yet there is no evidence of any objections from freeholders in 1335 when the park was proposed, and the reason may well be that the

[43] *Cal. Pat. 1334-8*, 79; P.R.O. C133/35/10 and C135/195/1.
[44] *V.C.H. Yorks., N.R.*, ii, 193.

demand for arable land was already on the decline, so that the 700 acres of open-fields on the north, east and west of the village were quite sufficient for current needs. In addition, there were 547 acres of common pasture and 280 acres of wet meadowland, besides the 1,600 acres of waste.[45]

If the village houses prevented the further extension of the parkland northwards, what of the other directions? On the east and south the park stretched as far as the boundary of the parish; on the west the York road formed the limit, and the park did not encroach beyond it into the West Field.

So long as the castle was occupied, the park served its owners for ornament, sport and venison. After the castle was abandoned the appointment of keepers continued, but they can have had little to do except preserve the herds for a master who never came near. In 1615 a "viewe of Game" reported "11 score and some odde deare of all sortes" in the park, and in 1624 Norden described it as

> well stored with fallow deere and sett with neere 4,000 decayed and decaying okes, the most of them headed.

Little oak-trees can be seen scattered over the parkland in his plan, Fig. 25, looking rather like the parkland in an air photograph: a very similar parkscape appears in Plate 22, which looks north-westwards towards Sheriff Hutton from a point to the west of where John Norden drew

> The new lodge builte by Sir Arthur Ingram.

James I had granted the park—then 596 acres—to Sir Arthur in 1621 at a time when the rest of the manor was retained in the king's hands. Then Ingram acquired the site of the castle, with a rabbit warren, fishponds and orchard adjoining, in return for paying the debts of Thomas Lumsden, who had got a lease from the king in 1618.

Since the castle had been extensively despoiled and could not be lived in, Lumsden had planned to build a new mansion within the park, but financial difficulties overcame him and it was Sir Arthur Ingram who in 1621 built the "New Lodge" which appears in Norden's plan. Sir Arthur does not seem to have valued the park for hunting: in 1625 he leased the park to a grazier who undertook to repair the fences and look after the deer and game. If Sir Arthur

[45] Areas from T.N. MSS. B417391.

needed a buck killing he was to pay this keeper 10s., and in 1628 he sub-let the whole park with its lodges and barns except the

New Buildinge of bricke lately builded and furnished.

When the City of London acquired the manor from Charles I Ingram took the opportunity to buy out the freehold from the king for £12,496. Apparently the terms of the bargain[46] struck between the City and the Privy Council had exempted all deer-parks

our said Park is at this present reasonably well repleynished with deere and therefore cannot passe to the said Lord Mayor and Aldermen.

Norden's plan shows the park already broken into several parts by hedges, but all except the *Lawnde* carried trees and can only have been used for grazing. The *Lawnde*, immediately below the castle, has no trees shown and may have had a grass crop. Between 1651 and 1670 the park was subdivided into closes. A survey (*c.* 1670) states[47]

The whole content of the land is 816 acres . . and is in law a parke, though att present devided into the severall closes.

and a rental shows that there were then twenty-seven separate fields.

In the 1670 survey of Sheriff Hutton one advantage of the park was said to be that:

there is noe high way through itt.

A gentleman could be safe from intruders. The House is now open to visitors on certain days, and the road along which they will come is that from the west across the bottom of the *Lawnde*. The modern park is smaller than that of 1624, and the first fields to be crossed have been farmed, but after a cattle-grid the old park is entered. Part of it still serves for its owners' recreation, but the sport has changed and the only pale to be seen is the wooden rail which forms the boundary of the cricket pitch. Outside the cricket enclosure the grassland is dotted with oaks, very much as in Norden's plan.

It is possible to come to the park by a footpath (shown by Norden) which has rather more atmosphere than the car-drive. It leaves the village near the castle ruins, passes the old fishponds and enters the

[46] T.N. MSS. A1/3.
[47] T.N. MSS.: "A particular of Sherrif Hutton park, 1670."

park at the north-west corner. There is also a second path, coming from the church past the earthworks of the earlier castle. There is also an interesting way out of the park for those who come on foot. It is a continuation of the two paths from the village and leaves the park at the south-east corner where the Old Lodge stood, joining Flaxton Lane near the house known as Lilling Hall. This path represents the old road from Sheriff Hutton to the village of East Lilling.

The village of East Lilling will be sought for in vain on the map. West Lilling can be found, and there is the name of the civil parish: Lillings Ambo (i.e. Lillings Both). The 1954 edition of the 2½-inch Ordnance Survey plan now shows the earthworks of the village streets and houses: previous editions show them as "Moats". Other documents apart, the identification rests with John Norden in 1624. When the perambulation of the bounds of Sheriff Hutton reached this point the jury declared:

> East Lilling it is called and retaineth the name of East Lilling township though at this day there do remain but only one house. But by tradition and by apparent ancient buildings and ways for horse and cart visibly discerned leading unto the place where the town stood, within Sheriff Hutton park, it hath been a place of some capacity, though now utterly demolished . . . how long since doth not appear.

Norden has led us from the landscape of the Stuarts to the landscape of the medieval villages whose desertion was described in Chapter 4. Norden's map shows that the site was within the park in 1624, for his park pale follows the same line as the modern parish boundary which brings the site of East Lilling inside Sheriff Hutton parish (figs. 25 and 26). It is not suggested, however, that East Lilling was depopulated when the park was made in 1335, for there were thirty-one taxpayers here in 1377 and at least seven houses in 1388. The date of destruction is not known,[48] but it was outside the memory of the oldest inhabitants in 1624.

IX

The isolation which Ingram sought for his new house at Sheriff Hutton did not have to be contrived at the expense of existing buildings; East Lilling is not an early Milton Abbas, the victim of

[48] 1624: B. M. Harleian MSS. 6288; other details from M. W. Beresford, "The Lost Villages of Yorkshire", *Yorks. Arch. Journ.* xxxviii (1954), 283, 302-3 and fig. iv.

the country house. For an interesting anticipation of Milton Abbas we must turn to Buckinghamshire, where the Aylesbury Museum has a manuscript map showing the old village of Wootton

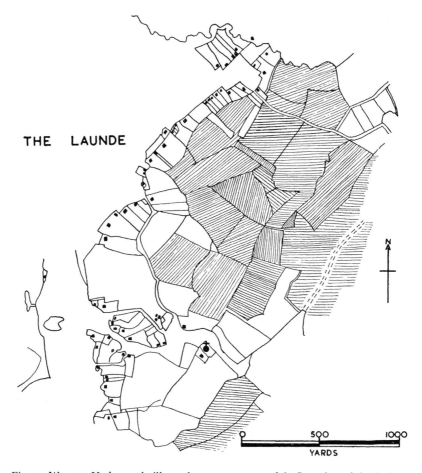

THE LAUNDE

Fig. 27. Wootton Underwood village, the open common of the Launde and the Furlongs of the open fields, drawn from the plan of 1649, before the making of the Grenville's park and the eclipse of the village and fields.

Underwood in 1649 before the rebuilding of the great House for the Grenvilles. Fig. 27 is a simplified version, showing the lay-out of the medieval village and the position of the open-field Furlongs. To-day the Ordnance Survey map shows the newer landscape of grass park-land and the long, double avenues of trees which patterned it.[49]

The park-land was given its present pattern by the Grenvilles who built the present house between 1704 and 1714. The western part of the park was previously a *Lawne* or *Launde*, a grassy clearing among woodland, but the eastern half was only achieved by removing the village and annexing most of the open fields. The plan of 1649 shows sixty-five houses, but there are now fewer than ten, all of them near the church, which has not been disturbed. A crude pictorial plan of the village was made sometime in the seventeenth century and is now in the Henry Huntington Library, California. This shows the *Launde* as open grassland with a few trees and a windmill.

The extensive woodland in which the old *Launde* lay has left a double mark on the village name: it is *wudotun* in a Saxon charter of 848, the wood-village; by the thirteenth century it had acquired the suffix of "Underwood" like its neighbour Grendon, while there is also "wood" in the names of its other neighbours, Kingswood and Woodham, where to-day there are still large blocks of woodland.[50]

The shape of the old village also bears the strong imprint of its origin in a woodland clearing. Only near the church is there any suggestion of a street, and at that a straggling one. The *Green* opens out into the *Launde*, which in 1580 was a common, and the houses straggle along an indented frontage of more than 2,000 yards. These houses have every appearance of being set along the edge of a forest, an ever-lengthening line of squatters set at the frontier of the two worlds on which the villagers drew for their sustenance: on the west the wooded park-land and on the east the fields. As the need for more land developed, the medieval fields extended eastwards to the edge of the parish, giving the pattern of furlongs shown on the 1649 plan. Westwards, the *Launde* blocked reclamation, and in the early eighteenth century the field-land was almost all swallowed up by the extension of the park. In the last twenty years the process has begun to move in the opposite direction again.

Wootton Underwood is a pleasant place to visit despite the fallen fortunes of the House. Substantial parts of the avenues still stand, but

[49] Plan by George Sargeint: Aylesbury Museum; re-drawn, in part, over modern O.S. 6″ plan in *Geog. Journ.*, cxii (1951), fig. 7; see also P.R.O. E134/22-3 Eliz., Bucks. No. 16.

[50] *P.N. Bucks.*, 113; G. Lipscomb, *History of Bucks.* (1831), i, 586.

the visitor will see very little signs of where the old village lay. The work of the landscape engineers was very thorough, although the keen eye will discern irregularities in the paddocks near the church and some others at the north end of the park. Having been under grass a mere 250 years the former open fields have suffered less obliteration, and there are several blocks of ridge and furrow which correspond with the Furlongs of the 1649 plan.

And so, all over England, the enlarging and creating of parks continued. When the second Earl of Nottingham built his new house at Burley on the Hill between 1694 and 1702 he found the existing park insufficient. What had satisfied a Duke of Buckingham now seemed too small and further farm-land was cast into the park. The Earl lost £600 a year in farm rents as the price of his satisfied eye, looking from Burley across the rolling Rutland grass.[51] With opulence, the scale of house and park increased in step. At Badminton, made by the first Duke of Beaufort in the last decades of the seventeenth century, the Worcester Lodge was two and a quarter miles from the House and there was a two and a half mile avenue of trees.[52] In many parts of England one may pass by the fossilized remnants of these great avenues pointing like a compass needle to the great country house of their creator. But the same economic pressure which has emptied so many country houses of their old families has also made it difficult for a park-owner to keep all his acres under grass, and many of these avenues now have their feet in plough-land. Some stretches have fallen to the timber contractor, leaving isolated pairs of elms or oaks still loyally pointing the way, inviting the eye to go where the carriage can no longer pass.

The park of Castle Howard, Yorkshire, made out of the fields of the depopulated village of Hinderskelfe, has surpassed Badminton by having a main avenue of four miles crossing the park. This vista can be enjoyed by anyone, for the road is public. Any motorist who fancies a four-mile straight will be disconcerted by the narrows of the southern gate-house and the turns at the roundabout by the obelisk. This particular avenue is very restrained; its focus is not the Great House, which lies half a mile off to the east, but the obelisk of 1714, commemorating the victories of the Duke of Marlborough. On one face of the monument a plaque also records the victories of the

[51] H. J. Habakkuk in J. H. Plumb, ed., *Studies in Social History* (1955), 164.
[52] S. Rudder, *Gloucestershire* (1779), 253.

park-maker—the completion of the house and park in 1731, bringing nearly all the 1,500 acres of the township into the park.[53]

Across the Pennines, the park-makers of the eighteenth century found more employment in Cheshire than in Lancashire and the counties further north. Lancashire has relatively few great parks from any period. The plain lacked the smooth undulations which gave the landscape gardeners of the south their opportunity, and the Pennines were too bleak and too remote to attract the gentry from London. From the middle of the eighteenth century industrial development must also have been a deterrent. The Victorian cotton manufacturer, as Disraeli's Coningsby found, liked to build a villa within sight of his mills, and was not often tempted to sink his savings into the purchase of a large and remote country house, but merchants, ship-owners, bankers and East Indiamen had less need to keep within earshot of industry, and few members of this class wished to be reminded of their daily bread by the sight of smoking chimneys over the plantations.

Some of the old county families of Lancashire, however, prospered sufficiently to be able to develop the ground around their ancestral manor. The modern park of Knowsley, the seat of Lord Derby, was a century ago the largest in the north of England. It occupied 2,000 acres of the township of Knowsley and had another 500 acres in neighbouring townships. The village name "Knowsley" itself originally meant "the clearing made by Cenwulf", and in 1292 the first reference to Knowsley park is a "wood called a park"; the woodland was still largely uncleared. By 1325 the park had "herbage", that is open, cleared ground for grazing, and in the middle years of the fourteenth century the park was taking in other land; it was a good time for park-making, with so much semi-derelict land after the plagues. In the mid-sixteenth century the park was further enlarged by the Stanleys, now not by taking in abandoned land or uncleared woodland but by encroaching upon the cornlands. A rental of that period says

> the demesne lands which were wont to be sown yearly are now enclosed within the park of Knowlsey, and there lie in pasture,

[53] *V.C.H. Yorks. N.R.*, ii, 110-11; M. W. Beresford, *art. cit.*, 284-86 and fig. 5; other plans in Laurence Whistler, *The Imagination of Vanbrugh and his Fellow Artists* (1954). I am indebted to the Hon. Geoffrey Howard for access to these plans in the Castle Howard estate office.

but there were curious scars on the landscape. In several places potters were said to be digging clay. In the next two centuries the park grew until it eventually stretched over two-thirds of the township, the House becoming the principal residence of the Stanleys after Lathom was destroyed in the Civil War.[54]

In these eighteenth-century parks, some of them new, some of them enlargements of medieval parks, the art of the landscape gardener found its widest expression. The first of the three great practitioners, William Kent, aimed to "chasten or polish the living landscape" of Nature, and he would have approved the avenues and circular clumps of trees which an unknown landscape gardener added to the 1649 plan of Wootton Underwood at some later date. An unpolished, "natural" Nature came into fashion later in the century with Lancelot (Capability) Brown and Humphrey Repton. Repton's professional card shows a surveyor with his tripod, an assistant with a measuring pole, a lake in a hollow, and a tree-covered slope crowned by a ruined tower (probably a sham). By the side of the lake are five workmen with picks, shovels and barrows carrying away earth under the direction of another landscape gardener. The blemishes of Nature are being removed in the interests of Art.[55]

The expense of maintaining parks and large country houses in the last thirty years has been such that a number of the finest parks are now in the care of the National Trust or of various public authorities. It is no longer true that the Parks Department of municipal authorities are concerned only with Victorian recreation-grounds with bowling greens, flower beds and football pitches. More than one parks superintendent has on his hands the grounds of a medieval castle or of an abbey or of a former ducal mansion.

x

The final visit which we shall make to an English park takes us to a municipal park which is neither Victorian nor the appendage of a decayed country house. It is older than any surviving English country house and it owes very little to the improving hand of man.

[54] *V.C.H. Lancs.*, iii, 157.
[55] This card is reproduced by H. C. Darby, "The Changing English Landscape", *Geog. Journ.*, cxvii (1951), 388.

It has large stretches of unimproved woodland and heath which have survived from the medieval chase. Indeed, the chase may have been used by Saxon kings: for the customs of the manor,[56] declared in 1309, were believed to originate in a grant from King Athelstan, who died in 939.

Sutton Park, five miles north of Birmingham, is oval in shape with a diameter of two and a half miles from north to south and two and a quarter miles from east to west. The town of Sutton Coldfield lies outside the east gate of the park, which has been the property of the Corporation since its first charter in 1528. The settlement of Sutton (=the south-town) probably originated as a hunting lodge at the southern end of the great chase of Sutton which used to extend over the border from Warwickshire into Staffordshire until it touched Cannock Chase.[57]

Most of Sutton Chase has been subdued and tamed, first by medieval agriculture and latterly by industry and suburbia, so that the surviving open space is doubly prized both as a historical relic and as an open space preserved against the encroachment of building. Its 3,500 acres provide a natural recreation ground for Birmingham, Walsall and their suburbs and in 1957 were chosen for the Jubilee Scout World Jamboree.

At its fullest extent the Chase included part of Staffordshire and also other parishes in Warwickshire outside Sutton. Here, on the border of the two counties and at the watershed between Tame and Trent, was a broad belt of poor quality land nicknamed the Cold-field. Seven thousand acres of Sutton parish, outside the park, remained as open heath until the Enclosure Act of 1824. So little was this land prized for agriculture that there was an old custom which permitted liberal use of the heathland by any townsman who cared to plough out a portion of it; and each year "lot acres" were assigned and balloted for, and the next year left to revert to waste and recover their heart after cropping.[58] Further east and north the Chase had been diminished by assarting and by the creation of small enclosed parks. About 1200 Drayton Bassett Park was made "within Cold-field Forest"; a park was made at Weeford in 1289 and at Little Barr

[56] Dugdale, 911.

[57] *P.N. Warws.*, 49; *V.C.H. Warws.*, iv, 230 *sqq.*; this account suffers from its authoress's curious failure to consult the Corporation's archives.

[58] M. W. Beresford, "Lot Acres", *Ec. Hist. Rev.*, xiii (1943), 74-79.

in 1297; Sutton Park itself, as an enclosure from the open Chase, is first mentioned in 1315 as

enclosed and fenced, with a fishpond and outwoods;

but it was probably older.

In 1150 the king had given the southern part of the two royal chases of Sutton and Cannock to the Earl of Warwick, keeping Cannock Chase for himself. But in 1289 it was conceded that the earls had always had the additional right of pursuing into Cannock any deer started in Sutton. Customs accepted as authentic in 1309 show that whenever the earl came to hunt, the villeins used to drive the wild beasts for him; between his visits they maintained his fences, prepared traps and cut trackways; they were allowed to pasture their animals in the Chase and to take all dead wood for their fires. The other villein services which they rendered at the plough and in the fields at harvest were correspondingly very light.

This community was in a depressed state in the early sixteenth century. The king had confiscated the earl's manors but no longer came himself to hunt. The weaving industry, which at that time still survived in the villages of north Warwickshire, was in decay, for cloth was being made cheaper and better in other parts of England. The five pools which the earl had built in the park about 1420 (probably for fulling-mills) were neglected and allowed to drain dry. The town's fortunes were revived by the grant of incorporation which Henry VIII gave in 1528 at the suit of a native of Sutton, John Vesey, Dean of the Chapel Royal at Windsor and Bishop of Exeter. Vesey also persuaded the king to endow the new Corporation with the park, and himself founded a grammar school.

Although local tradition ascribes everything in the subsequent development of Sutton Coldfield to Vesey's work, the district also prospered by the development of the metal trades in the near-by Black Country. In 1577 one of the neglected dams (still known to-day by the name of its fifteenth-century tenant, Bracebridge) was reconstructed as a 35-acre pool serving a mill where sword-blades were made. The park must have been a curious setting for industry, rather like the valleys of Wyre Forest and the Weald in its scatter of mills among woodland. In Greenwood's map of 1821 two of the pools were still giving power for forges. One drove a button-mill, and they continued until steam conquered all the Midland industries.

Blackroot, a 15-acre pool shown in Plate 22, was made as late as 1757. A hundred years ago the park was only just beginning to be used for recreation by the people of Birmingham, but the building of the two railways (one of which has a station named Sutton Park) made it easier of access. The ratepayers of Sutton still maintain a toll of admission for "foreigners" from outside the Borough in the best traditions of the petty market-towns of 1528.

But these tolls are a small price to pay for the preservation of the park still so largely in a natural state, with only a few planted coppices. It is said that part of the park was ploughed during Cromwell's Protectorate, but this may be one of the many folk-myths which blacken Cromwell's name. But those who decried Cromwell's vandalism saw part of the grassland in the south-west of the park broken for cropping during the Second World War, and within sight of the tractors another part of these wastes was turned into a prisoner-of-war camp which straddled the Roman road and— not inappropriately—housed Italian prisoners.

As the irregular shape of the park-bounds on the north-east show, several bites have been taken out of the park since 1528, and there is a curious island of private land which faces the visitor almost as soon as he has entered the main (Town) gate. As early as 1581 there were complaints that members of the Corporation had taken 600 acres from the park as their private property by making favourable exchanges. In 1675 judgment was given against the Corporation in a Chancery case, the court declaring that the enclosure of the park was not at the Corporation's choice, but needed the freeholders' consent.[59] Four Oaks Park, a gentleman's residence of the eighteenth century, has obviously (from its relation to the sweeping curve of the park pale) been once part of Sutton Park. (Fig. 28.)

In 1756 an Act of Parliament was obtained to authorize the sale by the Corporation of 48 acres of park to Simon Luttrell (later Baron Irnham), the Act declaring that the Corporation and majority of those entitled to common rights in the park were satisfied with a compensatory annual rent of twelve pounds, eight of which were to go to relieve the poor rate. The preamble to the Bill[60] had an air of

[59] *20th Report of the Charity Commissioners*, Parly. Papers, 1829, vii (19), 1060; decree of 1617: P.R.O. E178/4684.

[60] "Bill to grant part of a Common called Sutton Coldfield": Birm. Ref. Acts, Local and Personal, 28 Geo. III.

patrician assurance when it described Luttrell's purchase of the old Manor House of Four Oaks and his intention to improve it:

> he proposes to erect and build instead thereof a new and substantial house . . . and in order to render the same more commodious and convenient he is willing and desirous to enclose and take in a Piece of Ground, part of the same Park containing about 48 acres adjoining to the said House, in order that the same shall be planted, improved and disposed of in Conveniencies and Ornaments to his Intended Seat.

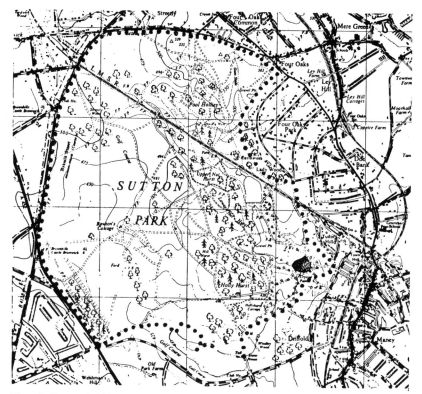

Fig. 28. Sutton Coldfield, showing the modern bounds of the Park (black dots). The small private enclosure near the Town Gate is shaded. Note also the sweeping encroachment of 1756 to make Four Oaks Park in the N.E. corner.

Obviously neither Vesey nor Henry VIII had intended to provide a park which the Corporation could from time to time sell off in pieces to local squires, but in a Parliament of squires there was no opposition to the Bill. Perhaps the coolest effrontery was the recital of the clause in the charter of 1528 designed to encourage the settlement and cultivation of the extensive waste lands in Sutton by allowing enclosure of up to 60 acres around a new house in return for 2d. an acre per annum to the Corporation chest. This clause, designed to encourage the settlement and cultivation of the waste lands by poor people, was twisted to support Luttrell's ambition to have a private park at the expense of the public.

It is significant that in 1778 a bill to promote a full enclosure of the wastes, both in and outside Sutton Park, failed, the Corporation voting seventeen to three against it; and it was fifty years before the outer wastes were finally enclosed under an Act of 1824, leaving the Park itself intact. The final alteration of its bounds came in 1826 when Sir Edmund Hartopp obtained another 63 acres of the park to add to his estate; but in return he gave up 97 acres of pasture, some of it the meadow near the present Main Gate. He also laid out the first road from the town to this Gate, for the old entrance had been from near the Manor House by Driffold (fig. 28, p. 234), well south of the town.[61]

Four Oaks Park has since surrendered to the builder of middle-class villas, but Sutton Park has only slightly altered to meet its new role. A golf-course has partly civilized one stretch of heath; the pools, long lost to industry, have their refreshment rooms, thatched shelters and notices warning one against the dangers of cycling across the dam. Just outside the park pale, alongside one of the fifteenth-pools, is a private amusement park of a twentieth-century kind where more sophisticated tastes may ride on the switchback railways, throw for coconuts and be carried through the darkness of the Cave of Love.

But in the slades of Hollyhurst and Darnel Hurst the music of the roundabouts is soon lost, and one can walk for two and a half miles in a straight line before encountering suburbia again at the Staffordshire gate. There is room for a boy to learn how to cross a bog; how to remember footpaths through dense woods; how to cross streams without getting wet; how to climb trees; and how to be home nevertheless in time for supper and bed.

If affection is generously spread in these closing pages it is because good fortune led me to be born just 100 yards inside the boundaries

[61] *V.C.H. Warws.*, iv, 230.

of this borough, and gave me the freedom of Vesey's park and Vesey's Grammar School. Once a year the pleasure of the former and the rigours of the latter were brought into contact, and the squirrels, who did not expect so many visitors so early in the season, were startled by an inrush of cross-country runners, some in white, some in blue and some in red. Among the latter, redder than the shirt with effort, was the author.

A boy is lucky who can have the advantages of living in a town and yet be within walking distance of a piece of natural countryside hardly scarred by agriculture. It is a good place to receive an early education in the geography and history of the open air.

Appendix

THE MATERIAL FOR THE SIX JOURNEYS

*Instead of a few photographed
village maps there will be many . . .*

F. W. MAITLAND *Domesday Book and Beyond* (1895)

Appendix

THE MATERIAL FOR THE SIX JOURNEYS

I

Six groups of journeys have now been described, and the effort will have been vain if it has not provoked some readers to take down again a local map or to consider a well-known piece of countryside near their home in the light of these six inquiries. If, indeed, curiosity has been stimulated there is a certain duty to suggest where the gear may be acquired for similar journeys into other local landscapes. There is no point in disguising that some of the equipment is hard to come by, not because it is expensive of money but because of the effort needed. It is not likely that this will daunt a serious inquirer, and the place-by-place accumulation of experience is itself a major part of any field-worker's equipment.

Except for those born with a strong taste for the solitary, field-work is an activity which gains by companionship. Four eyes see more than two, and the scepticism of a second tongue is a useful corrective to an over-ambitious interpretation of some new find. Some people have found their enthusiasm for local history kindled in larger groups: perhaps in a W.E.A. or extra-mural class or in the Local History group of one of those Archaeological Societies which have not degenerated into afternoon tea-lectures for the over-sixties. Indeed, some techniques of inquiry, particularly the deciphering of handwritings, are discouragingly difficult to acquire without the assistance of a tutor or a more experienced friend.

There are some teachers of history who deplore letting amateurs loose on documents before they have mastered all the printed sources. I do not share this view, for experience with adult classes and summer schools suggests that properly selected documents and maps have a compelling fascination likely to carry the student through a hard winter of work before spring makes field-work again possible. Properly selected documents offer the student the exhilaration of discovery within a small field. They beget confidence and the

239

appetite to master the more technical aspects of handwriting and documentary forms.[1]

I have therefore put documents and maps on the same footing as printed books in the short commentary on my source-materials which follows. I know also that those who are the custodians of English archives are always willing to give time to assist a serious student in the early stages of inquiry, and I have no diffidence in recommending anyone seeking to pursue my topics in his own locality to knock loudly, first on the door of his local library for the printed books, pamphlets and journals: and then on the door of the local Record Office where documents of parish, estate and county will be waiting.

It is no part of my intention to go beyond the more accessible sources for the limited range of historical inquiries which have occupied the preceding six chapters. There are perfectly good bibliographies of local history in general and of some towns and counties in particular, and local libraries will direct inquirers to these.[2] Most English counties have their local Archaeological or Historical Society, often with a long tradition of lectures, a *Journal* and the publication of the text of documents in a *Record Series*. There is also a Standing Conference for Local History whose secretariat[3] will put inquirers in touch with local experts. For many counties there are county *Histories* (usually of the eighteenth or nineteenth century) which vary in quality but usually offer the basic history of manors and sometimes of the major topographical features. A few counties are assisted further by a completed *Victoria County History* with a parish-by-parish account. Northumberland has its own excellent substitute.[4]

---

[1] Many amateurs have found their way among old handwriting made smoother by the Essex Record Office's booklets, *Some Examples of English Handwriting* and *Some Further Examples of English Handwriting*, now (1956) re-issued as one. The most substantial collection of plates and transcripts is C. Johnson and H. Jenkinson, *English Court Hand*, 2 vols. (1915), and H. Jenkinson, *The Later Court Hand in England*, 2 vols. (1927).

[2] E.g. *English Local History Handlist* (Historical Association Pamphlet No. S2, 2nd ed. 1952); *Field Archaeology: some Notes for Beginners* (Ordnance Survey, 1951); F. G. Emmison and I. Gray, *County Records* (Hist. Asscn. Pamphlet No. S3, 1948); Royal Commission on Historical Monuments, *Reports* are in course of publication, county by county. For a model county bibliography see Robert Douch, *A Handbook of Local History, Dorset* (1952).

[3] c/o National Council of Social Service, Bedford Square, London, W.C.1.

[4] *Northumberland County History*, various editors (1893-1940), 15 vols. For progress of *V.C.H.* inquire General Editor, Institute of Historical Research, Senate House, London, W.C.1.

II

The study of boundaries begins with the earliest written perambulations in the Anglo-Saxon charters. These will be found (in Anglo-Saxon and Latin) in the great collections of Birch and Kemble.[5] Of greater accessibility are the brief notes on those charters which appear in the footnotes of the parish-by-parish sections of the English Place-Name Society's county volumes.[6] The Domesday Book description of a particular place can most easily be read in translation in the *Victoria County History*, and should the particular county have progressed as far as the parish histories, the footnotes of the *V.C.H.* will provide a fairly complete indication of the documentary and printed sources available for later centuries. Since many *V.C.H.* volumes were written before the opening of local Record Offices and the revival of interest in parish records, it is always wise to inquire further from the local lord of the manor, from the incumbent and churchwardens, the custodians of the parish documents and from local archives.

The descriptions of boundaries in manorial or estate records are more likely to be hit upon in the course of a general scrutiny of local material than by deliberate search, for they occur as part of other documents (such as court rolls and terriers) which are unlikely to be indexed except by place and date. The late Dr. G. B. Grundy projected an edition of all boundary charters, but only seven counties were published.[7] In the interpretation of boundary charters, as in all topographical inquiry, the Ordnance Survey maps are indispensible companions. The current maps on the larger scales—especially the 1:25,000 and the six-inch sheets—are the record of modern boundaries of county, parish and field; while the older editions—particularly the first editions of the one-inch and six-inch maps—take us back into an age when industrial and population

[5] W. de G. Birch, *Cartularium Saxonicum* (3 vols., 1885-93); J. M. Kemble, *Codex Diplomaticus Aevi Saxonici* (6 vols., 1839-48).

[6] *The Place-names of . . . shire*, various editors, 24 vols. to date (1956). For progress inquire Hon. Secretary, English Place-name Society, University College, Gower Street, London, W.C.1.

[7] *Proc. Dorset Natural History and Archaeological Society*, lv-lxi (1933-39); *Saxon Charters of Gloucestershire* (2 parts, 1935-36); Trans. Birmingham Archaeological Society, lii-iii (1931), for Worcestershire; *Saxon Oxfordshire* (Oxon. Record Society, xv, 1933); *The Saxon Charters and Field-names of Somerset* (1935).

growth had still had only a limited effect on the older features of the landscape.

Moving back from the Ordnance Survey maps, many English countries were mapped on scales of from one to three miles to an inch[8] in the period 1750-1820, the age of turnpikes, coaching and canals. Before 1750 the county maps are usually on too small a scale to do more than show the principal roads, the outer limits of urban areas and the position of country seats and parks. This type of map is the direct successor of the Elizabethan county atlases of Saxton and Norden described and illustrated above.

For early plans of villages and their fields or for single estates within them it is necessary to pass from printed maps to manuscript plans. Until fairly recently both private owners and public custodians had tended to neglect the maps in their possession in favour of documents, and if an old estate plan has survived it is often not because anyone prized it as an historical evidence but because it made a pleasant wall-decoration or was of some practical use in the estate office. As to the location of these old plans, outside the libraries and Record Offices no more general guide can be given than that they may lurk anywhere from a parish chest to the attics of a country solicitor's office.[9]

Two important sets of maps showing boundaries have a better chance of preservation. The Enclosure Award maps are described in the next section of this Appendix, but the maps which accompany the Tithe Awards are on an equally large scale and have the advantage of showing the field-names and land-use just before the middle of the last century. More than one copy of each map was made, and one should be found in each parish chest, one with the Diocesan Registrar (or in a Diocesan or County Record Office) and one with the Tithe Redemption Commission in London.

There is no printed list which indicates all the maps and plans available in the great national collections at the British Museum

[8] There is a convenient list of these cartographical aids to historical research in R. V. Tooley, *Maps and Mapmakers* (1949); see also Audrey M. Lambert, "Early Maps and Local Studies", *Geography*, xli (1956), 167-77.

[9] In addition to Mowat's book mentioned in Chapter 3, open-field maps have been published in quarto by the Bedfordshire Historical Record Society; examples of other early plans will be found in F. G. Emmison, ed., *The Art of the Map-maker in Essex* (1947).

and the Public Record Office.[10] The Manuscripts Room of the former keeps a pasted-slip index of maps and surveys arranged both by county and chronologically; the Map Room of the Museum is mainly concerned with printed maps, but it has some manuscript plans and a growing collection of photostat copies of early plans in private ownership. It also has copies of early drafts of the first one-inch Ordnance Survey sheets. The Public Record Office has on the shelves of the Round Room a typescript index of maps and plans earlier than 1600, which is being continuously augmented, and other maps will be found in the old *Rentals and Surveys* List.

The same maps and documents which describe boundaries may well also particularize the field-systems, tenure and land-use of the open field village, and the student of these matters will search as widely as the student of boundaries. Should a village have been enclosed by Act of Parliament, the Enclosure Award and map will be of particular interest. Mr. Tate's county lists are now nearly all in print, but many County Record Offices will have some later accessions.[11] If the open fields disappeared before the period of Parliamentary enclosure (i.e. before *c.* 1720) the inquiry widens and becomes more complicated. If there was an enrolled agreement it may be with the County records; if it is enrolled in Chancery it may appear in the place index to the Chancery Decrees at the P.R.O. If the enclosure took place in the more turbulent days of the sixteenth century it may have left its mark in a Star Chamber dispute or in one of the Government inquiries into illegal enclosure.

The surveys, that is the written valuations of manors made for their lord or the Exchequer before the days of maps, may also yield evidence of field systems. The largest single collection of manorial valuations is that of the feudal inquiries, the *inquisitions post mortem* which followed the death of a tenant in whom the Exchequer had a financial interest. So long as lords of manors were actively engaged in working their demesnes—in general until about 1400—the *extents*

---

[10] See T. C. Skeat, *The Catalogues of the Manuscript Collections (in the) British Museum* (1951); M. S. Guiseppi, *Guide to the Public Record Office*, 2 vols. (1923-24). A new *Guide* is in progress, but the *Introductory* part (1949) is still a little distant from the subject. The Calendars and Indexes which have appeared in print are conveniently listed in H.M. Stationery Office, *Government Publications, Sectional List No. 24* (1949).

[11] Twenty-seven county lists have been issued to date (1956), e.g. *A Hand List of Lancashire Enclosure Acts and Awards* published by Lancashire County Council, 1946.

which accompany the inquisitions are full of topographical information.

There are very few documents early enough to record the foundation of a village and the first decades of life within it.[12] In general, the centuries before Domesday Book are silent—and in the extreme north even Domesday is lacking—so that the evidence of parish shapes, village patterns and place-names must be used as an unsatisfactory substitute if the silence is to be broken. For a belt of country in East Anglia and the Midlands there survive the records of the great inquiry of 1279 (the "Hundred Rolls"). Although primarily a feudal inquiry, these records offer useful evidence of the relative size of villages.[13]

The records of manorial administration, where they have survived, are indispensible in indicating the type of farming on the lord's demesne and the relationships of lords and tenant. In doing so, they also provide much incidental evidence on the fields, roads and buildings among which the life of the manor was conducted. The location of these manorial records is always a matter of local inquiry, and—like other private muniments—they may well remain not with the present lord of a manor but with a previous owner's family or with the local archive collection where they have gone for safer keeping. The dissolution of the monasteries brought a great deal of medieval documents into the Augmentation Office and the Exchequer, and the P.R.O. is also the heir to a mass of documents acquired when estates were forfeit to the Crown or spent a period in royal guardianship.

In recent years there has been a renewed interest in the records of taxation as an indication of the size of villages and towns, the wealth of their better-off inhabitants and their occupational structure. This type of evidence has been printed for a few areas and the examples will show what awaits inquirers elsewhere.[14]

[12] For a fuller discussion of sources, R. H. Hilton, "The Content and Sources of Agrarian History before 1500", *Ag. Hist. Rev.*, iii (1955), 3-19; for buildings, the county *Reports* of the Royal Commission on Historical Monuments (in progress).

[13] Printed by the Record Commission, 1812-18; the unpublished Warwickshire Section is being edited for the Dugdale Society by Dr. R. H. Hilton.

[14] E.g. the selection in J. Tait, ed., *Taxation in Salford Hundred 1524-1802* (Chetham Society, lxxxiii, 1924); F. H. Dickinson, ed., *Kirby's Quest for Somerset etc.* (Somerset Record Soc., iii, 1889); W. F. Carter, ed., *The Lay Subsidy Roll for 1332* (Dugdale Society, vi, 1926).

From the early seventeenth century onwards the estate records of larger properties begin to be available in greater numbers.[15] These papers are the records not of manors but of working estates and of rent-receiving landlords, and they must serve as a bridge between the old unenclosed villages and the enclosed fields of the first Ordnance maps whenever there are no formal records of enclosure. Local farming practice in the eighteenth century is a subject due for a revival of interest, and the various reports to the Board of Agriculture and the handbooks of the farming journalists are good companions with which to pass to the county plans of the same period.[16]

III

I have surveyed the source material for the study of depopulated villages in Chapter 9 of my *Lost Villages of England*,[17] but local estate papers and newly acquired documents in local archives are always likely to afford additional information about the sites which I listed and to add others to that list. A county-by-county list of depopulated villages is being maintained for the Deserted Medieval Villages Research Group by Mr. J. G. Hurst, and he will always be pleased to have more news from the field.[18] Air photographs and local correspondents are continually augmenting the original lists, particularly in Lincolnshire, Northumberland and Durham.

The availability of copies of air photographs is too complex a subject to treat here, for questions both of security and copyright are involved in the R.A.F. cover, which comprises the most extensive geographical range of any British collection. The R.A.F. photographs were not, however, taken for historical purposes, and the available cover for any particular place will sometimes be disappointing in quality.[19] The Cambridge Committee for Aerial Photography is rapidly building up a magnificent repertoire of Dr.

[15] For a fuller discussion of sources, Joan Thirsk, "The Content and Sources of Agrarian History after 1500", *Ag. Hist. Rev.*, iii (1955), 66-79.

[16] For an introduction to these, H. C. Darby, "Some Early Ideas on the Agricultural Regions of England", *Ag. Hist. Rev.*, ii (1954), 30-47.

[17] Lutterworth Press, 1954.

[18] Deserted Medieval Village Research Group, c/o Council for British Archaeology, Bolton Gardens, London, S.W.5.

[19] Inquiries: Under-Secretary of State for Air, Dept. S4(d), Air Ministry, London, S.W.1.

St. Joseph's photographs.[20] These are mainly "obliques", that is taken over the side of the plane, in contrast with the R.A.F. collection, which are mainly "verticals". There are other, commercial firms specializing in air photographs; their coverage is likely to be more selective, but they will undertake special work on commission.

IV

The sources for the history of the new towns described in Chapter 5 are necessarily local and peculiar to the towns in question. In other parts of England it would be necessary to turn to other sources: the estate documents of the bishop or feudal lord on whose land the new town was set; the records of the royal demesne for towns founded by the king; the municipality's own records. Unluckily, the period of foundation is often earlier than the oldest surviving Chancery and Exchequer enrolments. The absence of a town from Domesday Book is not conclusive—if it were, London and Winchester would be classed as "new towns"—but the silence should arouse suspicion. Published local histories sometimes show awareness of the late arrival of a town on the scene, often by an apology for there being no early remains and no early mention in documents. The shape of streets, the alinement of parish boundaries, the absence of fields are clues which are best sought in the first edition of the Ordnance Survey map or, in the case of the boroughs, in the plans which accompany the report of the Royal Commission on Municipal Corporations.[21] I hope to be able to produce in the next few years a list of these English New Towns and an estimate of their significance in economic development.

V

Anyone who wishes to discover for himself the flavour of life in his own town in the Elizabethan period stands just within the threshold of ample documentation. Good paper, leather-bound minute books, strong deed-boxes and authoritarian town clerks have conspired together to preserve a fair quantity of Elizabethan documents in

[20] Inquiries: Dr. J. K. St. Joseph, Committee for Aerial Photography, Sidgwick Avenue, Cambridge.

[21] *Reports of the Royal Commission on Muncipal Corporations.* Parliamentary Papers, 1835, xxiii-vi; 1837, xxvi-viii.

many towns and cities. Some fortunate cities, such as Alderman Hill's Lincoln,[22] already possess informed Histories based solidly on documents; the less fortunate may profit by the example and gain an appetite for more. But the survival of interesting documents is by no means the prerogative of the great city. Many small provincial towns have municipal collections bulky enough to keep many students busy many years. Some, but by no means all of these collections were briefly described in the *Reports* of the Historical Manuscripts Commission,[23] but many cupboards have been turned out since then, and in every case the first inquiry should be to the Town Clerk or archivist.[24]

Those beginning the study of urban history will neglect Gross' bibliography at their peril,[25] for there is no point in doing again what has already been done. The selected extracts from records published by some towns and cities are also useful guides to suggest what one is likely to encounter elsewhere: but—as in all archives—it will always be the unexpected and the unusual which, stumbled over, bring the greatest interest and profit.

The early plans of towns are less likely to lie fugitive than village and estate plans, and librarians will guide the inquirer to published town plans, which begin to appear in the late sixteenth century, and to the various county atlases which had inset plans of the more important urban centres. From the eighteenth century, local topographers have produced a stream of town plans for engraving and sale. There should be no mystery about the topography of any large English town after the mid-eighteenth century.

VI

There is no single modern work where one can find the extent of English park-land at any given period, but the local development of parks is becoming a popular subject with historical geographers, and

[22] J. W. F. Hill, *Medieval Lincoln* (1948); *Tudor and Stuart Lincoln* (1956).

[23] Summary guide in H.M. Stationery Office, *Government Publications, Sectional List No. 17* (1947); see also "Index to all Collections reported on . . . up to 1942" in *22nd Report* of the Commission, 66-103.

[24] The Secretary of the National Register of Archives, c/o The Public Record Office, Chancery Lane, London, W.C.1., will give information about documents which are still in private hands but upon which reports have been made to the Register.

[25] C. Gross, *A Bibliography of British Municipal History* (1897).

an atlas of park-land may not be many years away. In Elizabethan England the county plans of Saxton and Norden indicate the distribution of the main parks, but the scale of their plans is small and not all the minor parks were noted. The larger county plans of the eighteenth century and, of course, the early Ordnance Survey plans, were more accurate recorders of park pales.

The local estate office is a likely source for early plans and surveys of estates which had park-land, and the royal parks are well represented in those classes of P.R.O. documents which derive from the administration of forests and Crown land. The Map and Manuscripts Rooms of the British Museum should also be consulted. The Crown was also interested in the licensing of parks, and other documents derive from its concern about naval timber, about the supply of horses for the cavalry and about any enclosures of village lands which might accompany a new park. These different occasions brought the local commissions of inquiry, and where there were commissions there may always be documents.

In many instances the *V.C.H.* will give the outline history of a park; useful pictorial illustrations from the seventeenth to the nineteenth centuries will be found in the plates of the older works on local history and topography. Their authors depended largely on the owners of parks for patronage, and a full-page engraving of a country house in its park setting was almost as necessary as a branching family tree. For parks of the same period a visit to an art gallery will show how the landscape of parks appeared to those artists who used park-land as a background to a family portrait or as the setting for a picture of the country house.[26]

VII

Finally, for the man who walks through a landscape with an inquiring historical eye, there are always the works of those who walked the same way before him. Since Elizabethan times the English reader has enjoyed perambulating England by proxy, and there is no better winter sport, when the weather drives the traveller from the field, than to turn again to the English travellers and topographers of earlier ages.

[26] See also J. R. Abbey, *Scenery of Great Britain and Ireland in Aquatint and Lithography, 1770-1860* (1952).

Interspersed with much that is tedious—and even historically dubious—there will be found unexpected paragraphs which suddenly clarify what maps and documents have left ambiguous or unsaid. The great tradition runs through John Leland, William Camden, Celia Fiennes, Daniel Defoe, Arthur Young and William Cobbett before becoming submerged in the guide-books of the Railway Age and the glossy topographies of the Petrol Age. There are, however, some signs of a modern revival in topographical writing among authors whose equipment passes beyond a pair of scissors, a jar of paste and the taste for elegizing in country churchyards.[27] The minimum equipment is an affection for the landscape of town and field; a good pair of boots; and the firm determination that study of documents and exploration of the landscape shall be conducted side by side, and that neither branch of the inquiry shall be self-sufficient. Only this deserves the name of History on the Ground.

[27] Three landmarks in the renaissance were H. C. Darby, *An Historical Geography of England* (1936), A. L. Rowse, *Tudor Cornwall* (1938), and W. G. Hoskins, *Midland England* (1949); the same trend may be observed by comparing the pre- and post-war volumes of the *V.C.H.*, or the *Reports and Inventories* of the Royal Commission on Historical Monuments.

INDEX

AGAS, Ralph
  Tangham sheep walk plan, 47
  Toddington plan, 89, 153, 154, 155, 179, 180, 181, 182, 183, 208
  Oxford plan, 180
  Preparative, 180
Air photographs, 84, 96, 245, 246
Airmyn, 132, 133
Allesley, 108
Alnmouth, 132
Althorp (Northants.), 110, 210
Ampthill, 183
Andrewes family (Northants.), 111
Arable, 76, 78, 83
  conversion to pasture, 66, 88, 99, 101, 102, 107, 108, 174-5
Arundel, Thomas Howard, *2nd Earl of*, 107
Ashby St. Ledgers, 38
Assarting, 31, 44-5, 77-8, 191
Aumale (Albemarle), William de Fortibus, *Earl of*, 136, 142, 147
Auvergne, Rogationtide processions, 28, 29
Axholme, Isle of, 52

BADBY, 39, 49
Badminton (Glos.), 228
Baggrave, 115
Bainbridge, T., Higham Ferrers plan, 166n
Baldock, 131, 138
Barby, 38, 42
Barnard Gate, 99
Beaufort, Henry Somerset, *1st Duke of*, 228
Bedfordshire, 87, 92, 216
Bellassis, *Sir* William, 54-5, 58, 60
Bere (Merioneth), 130
Berwick-upon-Tweed, 132
Beverley, 131, 139
Bishops Cannings (Wilts.), 32
Black Death, 96, 97, 131
Blagrave, John, Feckenham Forest plan, 47
Blandford, 199
Bletchingdon, 194
Boltby, 34, 57, 58
Bolton, Little (Yorks.), 193, 195
Boston (Lincs.), 131, 132, 138
Boundaries, 25-62
  Anglo-Saxon charters, 26, 32, 40n, 42, 241
  oral traditions, 27, 50
  perambulation, 27, 28-30
  diocesan, 34-5
  features, 39-42

  disputes, 47-49, 53-60, 120-1
Braunston (Northants.), 27, 37-8, 40-44
  boundaries, 37-8, 40-42
  Domesday Book, 43
  population, 1891...43
Braunstonberry (Northants.), 41n
Breckland (Norf.), 100, 113
Brington, Great, Spencer tombs, 110
Bristol, 127, 154
Bromley (Staffs.), 194
Brown, Lancelot ("Capability"), 111, 113, 199, 230
Buckingham, Henry Stafford, *2nd Duke of*, 207
Buckingham, 85
Buckinghamshire, 70, 84, 87
Buntingford, 131, 138
Burghley, William Cecil, *Baron*, 154, 155, 157, 207, 210
Burley on the Hill (Rutland), 228
Byland, Old, 34, 39, 52-62
  field system, 52-3, 56
  Byland Abbey, 53-4, 57, 61
  boundaries, 53, 56-60, 62
  Wetherlays dispute, 54-60
  Saxton's plan, 55-7, 58, 59, 60-2
  Domesday Book, 61
  church, 61
Byland Abbey, 53-4, 57, 61

CAMBRIDGE, 147, 154
Cannock Chase, 232
Castle Donington, 195
Castle Howard (Yorks.), 198, 228
Catesby, 39
Cattle, 53, 90, 175, 178
Cause (Salop.), 130
Cawthorne, 187
Cecil, William, *Baron Burghley*, 154, 155, 157, 207, 210
Census, 27, 43, 98, 113, 122
Chalford, Upper and Lower (Oxon.), 103-5, 108
Chancery, 108, 233, 243
Chapel Ascote, 107, 115
Charles I, 219-20, 224
Charters, Anglo-Saxon boundary-, 26, 32, 40n, 42, 241
Charwelton, 40, 111
Chastleton Camp, 39
Chelveston, 33, 34, 51
Chernock, *Sir* Villiers ("Sir Villers"), 90-1

Chertsey Abbey, plan, 26
Cheyney, *Lord* Henry, 154, 180, 190, 208
Chichele, Henry, *Abp.* of Canterbury, 117, 159, 167, 176
Chipping Norton, 103
Churches
  foundation, 35-6
  amalgamation of benefices, 100
  fairs and markets in churchyards, 144, 165
Churchill, John, *1st Duke of Marlborough*, 228
Cistercians, 61, 134, 197
Clerke, Thomas, Whatborough plan, 50, 117-120, 123
Cold Kirkby, 60, 61
Compton Verney, 113
Compton Wyniates, 207
Cope, William, 108, 109
Cornwall, Duchy of, 51
Cromwell, Henry, *Baron Cromwell*, 117, 120
Cromwell, Oliver, *the Protector*, 233
Crop-marks, 84
Crown lands, sale of, 208

DALE Town, 34, 54n, 60
Damer, Joseph, *Earl of Dorchester*, 198, 201
Darby, *Prof.* H. C., 31, 45
Daylesford, 39
Dean (Oxon.), 103, 105
De Montfort, Simon, 182, 207
Depopulated villages, 34, 41n, 50, 54, 60, 95-123, 206n, 207, 225-8, 245
Derby, *Earls of, see* Ferrers *and* Stanley
Deserted Medieval Villages Research Group, 245
De Valence, William, 204
Devizes, 32
Devereux, Robert, *2nd Earl of Essex*, 116, 120, 121
Dewsbury, 52
Domesday Book, 31, 43, 45, 61, 70, 72, 87, 88, 97, 131, 160, 171, 191, 192, 241, 244
Dorchester, Joseph Damer, *Earl of*, 198, 201
Drayton Bassett Park, 231
Drewsteignton, 194
Dunsmore Heath (Warws.), 34, 40n.
Dunsthorpe (Lincs.), 100
Dunwich, 127

EAGLE (Lincs.), 130-1
Earthworks, 39, 95-6, 103, 105, 107, 122-3, 137, 187-8, 207, 225
Easton Neston Park, 210
Eastwell (Kent), 194

Eccleshall, 194
Edmund, *Earl of Lancaster*, 142, 168, 171
Edward I, 130, 134, 143
Elford (Staffs.), 26, 48, 49, 203
Elkington (Northants.), 97
Ely Abbey, 195
Empson, Richard, 210
Enclosure
  Awards, 27, 81, 90, 243
  Commissions, 101, 105, 108, 117
  by agreement, 90
Essex, Robert Devereux, *Earl of*, 116, 120, 121
Essex, 34
Evesham Abbey, 49
Exchequer, 55, 60, 97, 99, 108, 115, 117, 120, 135, 137, 142, 193, 243, 244
Eynsham, 99

FAIRS, 128, 134, 136, 137, 142, 144, 147, 159, 163, 172, 174
Falcliff (Northants.), 41n
Fallow, 76
Farrar, Clifford, 21, 138
Fawsley, 110-13, 210
  church, 110, 111, 112, 113
  Knightley family, 110-13
  market, 111
  taxation, 111
  depopulation, 111
  census, 113
  park, 113, 210
Feckenham Forest (Worcs.), 47
Ferrers, Robert, *Earl of Derby*, 162, 169, 179
Ferrers, William, *5th Earl of Derby*, 163, 218
Feudal services, 193, 194
Field names, 46
Fields, open, 44, 45, 67, 68-70, 82-4, 86, 89, 243
Fiennes, Celia, 249
Finch, Daniel, *2nd Earl of Nottingham*, 228
Fineshead Priory, cartulary, 26
Folkingham, William, *Feudigraphia*, 67, 82, 83
Forcett, 188
Forest
  royal, 191-3, 208, 209, 218
  statutes, 191, 192
  Forest Proceedings, 192
Forest clearance, 31, 44-5, 77-8, 191
Fountains Abbey, 195-6, 198
Fulbrook Park (Warws.), 207
Furlongs, 44-5, 74-5, 78

GALTRES, Forest of, 222
Gascoigne, *Sir* William, 205 ·

Gidding, Great (Hunts.), 47, 65
Gidding, Little (Hunts.), 115
Glebe terriers, 79
Gloucester, 27
Goblet, *Dr. Y. M.*, 155
Goldsmith, Oliver, *The Deserted Village*, 102, 201
Grafton (Wilts.), 194
Grass, *see* Pasture
Great Contract, 1628...209
Greenwood, C., Warws. plan, 232
Grenville family, 227
Grimsby, 131, 136
Grundy, *Dr. G. B.*, 241

HALSTEAD (Leics.), 118, 119, 122
Hameringham, 100
Hartlepool, 132
Hartopp, *Sir* Edmund, 235
Hatfield (Herts.), 195, 204
Hatton, *Sir* Christopher, 155, 210, 211, 212
Hatton, *Sir* William, 211
Heawood, E., 155
Hedon, 132, 134-5, 137, 138, 139-49, 173, 174
   fairs, 134, 142, 144, 147, 174
   site, 135, 139
   borough charters, 135, 142-3
   taxation, 139, 145
   tolls, 141, 142
   market and market-place, 142, 144, 164, 173
   boundaries, 143, 144, 145
   churches, 143, 147-8
   area, 144
   population, 145
   hospitals, 147
   harbours, 148
Heneage, *Sir* Thomas, 157
Hesketh Dyke (Yorks.), 59, 62
Heyford, Upper (Oxon.), 86
Higham Ferrers, 20, 27, 29, 33, 50-1, 153-4, 157-79, 180, 181, 215-19
   boundaries, 50-51, 164
   Norden's plan, 153, 154, 157-9, 165-8, 170, 176-7, 178, 180, 181
   castles, 158, 159, 160, 163, 167-8
   markets and market-place, 159, 162-3, 165-7, 171-4
   fairs, 159, 163, 165, 174
   borough charters, 159, 163, 164, 168-9
   Domesday Book, 160, 171
   site, 162
   Ferrers family, 162-3, 217-18
   burgages, 164
   rents, 164
   Bainbridge's plan, 166-8, 177
   Archbishop Chichele, 167, 176

   manorial customs, 169-70
   Moot-hall, 170
   products and industries, 174-6
   enclosure, 177
   Twyniho's terrier, 177-8
   population, 178-9
   Park, 216-19
   Worthe's terrier, 157, 164, 177, 178, 180
Hinderskelfe (Yorks.), 228
Hodnell (Warws.), 107, 108, 109, 110, 115
Hodnet, 193
Holdenby (Northants.), 203, 210, 211-15
   Norden's *Speculum*, 211, 212, 213
   Park, 210, 212, 213, 214
   plans, 211, 212-14
Hole (Devon), 194
Holmby *see* Holdenby
Horses, legal duty to keep, 209
Hospitallers, 130
Hovenden, *Dr.* Robert, 68, 71, 92, 95, 117, 121
Hovenden House, Fleet, 187
Howard, Thomas, *2nd Earl of Arundel*, 107
Hull, *see* Kingston-upon-Hull
Hundred Rolls, 97, 136, 244
Hundson Park (Herts.), 193
Hurst, J. G., 245

INGRAM, *Sir* Arthur, 219, 223, 224, 225
Inquisitions *ad quod damnum*, 193
   post mortem, 193, 194, 222, 243
Irchester, 162
Irnham, Simon Luttrell, *Baron*, 233

JAMES I, 208
Jeffreys, Stephen, Chalford plan, 103
Jervaulx Abbey, 197, 198

KENT, William, 230
Kerr, *Rev.* W. J. B., 167
Kimbolton Castle, 160, 168, 216
Kings Cliffe Park, 207
King's Lynn, 132
Kingston-upon-Hull, 132, 133, 134, 139
   Edward I's acquisition of Wyke, 134
   fair, 134
   borough charter, 134
Kirkstall Abbey, 197-8
Kirkstead Abbey, *Psalter*, 26
Knightley family, 110-12, 113, 115, 117
Knights Templar, 138
Knotting (Beds.), 216
Knowsley (Lancs.), 229

LANCASHIRE, 149, 229
Lancaster, Duchy of, 55, 157, 166, 168, 169, 170, 177
Lancaster, Edmund, *Earl of*, 142, 168, 171

Langdon, Thomas, 117
  Maids Moreton plan, 68, 71, 72-8, 79, 80, 81, 82, 84, 85
  Salford plan, 68, 87, 88, 89, 90-2
  Whitehill plan, 86
  Upper Heyford plan, 86
Langford, John, 88
Launde Priory, 117, 118, 120, 121
Leather tanning, 175-6
Leeds (Yorks.), 189, 198
Leicestershire, 39, 122
Leland, John, 148, 157, 160, 207, 249
Lichfield, *Bp. of*, 49, 194
Lidstone (Oxon.), 103
Lilling, East (Yorks.), 50, 120, 225
Lincoln, 247
Lincoln Heights, 32
Lincolnshire, 26, 30, 35, 100, 113
Little Barr Park, 231
Liverpool, 131
London, 127, 147, 154, 180
  City of London, 220, 224
Luddenden (Yorks.), 52
Ludford Magna, 100
Luttrell, Simon, *Baron Irnham*, 233

Magna Carta, 191
Maids Moreton, 49, 66, 70-86
  Langdon's plan, 68, 71, 72-8, 79, 80, 81, 82, 84, 85
  Domesday Book, 70, 72-3
  furlong names, 74-5
  field names, 76
  Peyvre family, 77
  glebe terrier, 79
  Enclosure Award, 81-2
  mills, 82
Manchester, 52, 149
Manor
  records, 46, 243-4
  villein services, 129, 169, 232
  privileges, 164, 169-71
  feudal services, 193, 194
Maps, 25-8, 32, 46-7, 51-2, 65-8, 69-70, 114, 153-4, 158, 241-3, 247-8
Marefield, 115
Market Deeping, 138
Markets and market places, 128, 134, 136, 137, 142, 144, 159, 162-3, 165-7, 170-4, 182-3, 202
Marlborough, John Churchill, *1st Duke of*, 228
Marshal, William, *1st Earl of Pembroke*, 181
Marston Moor, 205, 206
Mead, *Dr.* W. R., 74, 84
Meadow customs, 79, 89-90
Meaux Abbey, 134, 135, 136, 137, 146
Milton, Joseph Damer, *Baron*, 198, 201

Milton Abbas, 198-203
  plans, 198-9, 202, 203
  removal of old town, 198-201
  market and market place, 199, 202
Minting (Lincs.), 32
Monasteries, 49, 53, 57, 61, 76, 97, 99, 111, 117, 118, 120, 121, 134, 135, 136, 137, 146, 195-8
Moreton *see* Maids Moreton
Moulton Park (Northants.), 208
Mountfort, *Sir* Simon, 108
Municipal Corporations, Royal Commission on, 246
Murton (Yorks.), 34, 53, 54, 55, 59, 60

Nevill, John de, *5th Baron Nevill*, 221
Nevill, Ralph de, *4th Baron Nevill*, 222
Newbold (Leics.), 115
Newcastle-upon-Tyne, 127, 178
Newnham (Northants.), 49
Newton (Isle of Purbeck), 130
Newton Bromswold (Northants.), 216
Nicholson, Robert, 157
Nidderdale, 35
Norden, John, *the elder*, 50, 55, 101, 102, 113, 120, 157, 242
  Surveiors Dialogue, 48
  Higham Ferrers plan, 50, 51, 153, 154, 157-9, 165, 167-8, 170, 176, 177, 178, 180, 181
  Peterborough plan, 154, 155
  Speculum Britanniae, 154-7, 158, 180, 211
  Preparative, 156
  Holdenby, 211, 212, 213
  Sheriff Hutton plan, 219-21, 222, 223-4
Norden, John, *the younger*, 219, 220
Northampton, 174, 179
Northamptonshire, 37-9, 43, 154, 175, 179, 210, 216
Norwich, 154, 178
Nottingham, Daniel Finch, *2nd Earl of*, 228
Notton (Yorks.), 52
Nuneham Courtenay, 198

Ordnance Survey, 20, 27, 28, 32, 36, 42, 43, 49, 53, 58, 59, 62, 82, 98, 120, 180, 190, 195, 210, 216, 225, 227, 241, 243, 246, 248
Oseney Abbey, 76
Owston (Leics.), 115, 122
Owston Abbey, 121
Oxford, 154, 180
Oxford. All Souls College, 47, 49, 51, 66, 68, 72, 73, 76, 79, 81, 82, 85, 86, 87, 88, 90, 92, 95, 117, 120, 121, 176
Oxford. Corpus Christi College, 86

Oxford. Oriel College, 103, 105

Paris, Matthew, 182, 204, 205
Paris. Bibliothèque Nationale, 155
Parish boundaries, 26, 27-8, 29-34, 36
  civil, 32, 36
  patterns, 32-4, 44
  ecclesiastical, 36
Parks
  definition, 192
  monastic, 195-7, 198
  royal, 192, 193, 195, 208, 209
  municipal, 188-9, 198, 230-5
  disparking, 207-8
Pasture
  conversion from arable, 66, 88, 99, 100,
    101-2, 107-8, 115, 174-5
  pasture rights, 58-9, 178
Paull Fleet, 148
Pembroke, William Marshal, 1st Earl of,
  181
Peterborough, 154, 179
Peverel, William, 162
Peyvre (Pever) family, 77, 182, 208
Pipewell Abbey, 97
Plague, 96, 97, 99-100, 129, 131, 145
Plans, 25-8, 46-7, 51-2, 65-8, 69-70, 114,
  153-4, 158, 241-3, 247-8
Population
  migration, 34-5, 37-9, 145-6
  data, 43, 61, 73, 88, 97-8, 103, 108, 122,
    145, 178-9, 225
Ports, 131-7, 139, 142-3, 148
Portsmouth (Hants.), 131
Privy Council, 120, 181, 209, 224

Radbourn (Warws.), 107, 115
Radway, 35
Rathborne, Aaron, The Surveyor, 68
Raunds, 33, 179
Ravenserod (Yorks.), 135-7, 139, 146
  site, 135-6
  market and fair, 136, 137
  Hundred Rolls, 136
  borough charter, 137
  destruction by sea, 137, 146
Ridge and furrow, 83-5, 118-9, 207, 222,
  228
Rievaulx Abbey, 54n, 56, 61, 198
Roads, 80, 193
Rogationtide processions, 26-30
  origin, 28
  order of service, 28-9
  significance, 30
  local variations, 30
Romney Marsh, 47, 100
Roundhay Park, Leeds, 189

Royston (Herts.), 131
Ruddy, Rev. H. E., 43
Rushden (Northants.), 51, 216
Ryknild Street, 188

St. Ives (Hunts.), 138
St. John of Jerusalem, Order of the Knights
  of, 130
St. Joseph, Dr. J. K., 22, 246
St. Mary's Abbey, York, 133
Salford (Beds.), 74, 87-92
  Langdon's plan, 68, 87-92
  Domesday Book, 87, 88
  Manor, 88
  meadow customs, 89-90
  flocks and herds, 90
  Enclosure Act, 90, 91
Saxton, Christopher, 20, 27, 51, 56, 242
  Old Byland plan, 52, 55-7, 58, 59, 60, 61,
    62
  County atlas, 203, 210
  Higham Ferrers Park, 215
Senior, William, Jervaulx Abbey plans,
  197n
Sheep, 47, 90, 101-2, 103, 111, 178
  Byland Abbey flocks, 53, 58-9
  Salford flocks, 90
Sheriff Hutton, 208, 219-225
  Norden's plan, 219, 220, 221, 222, 223,
    224, 225
  royal ownership, 219-20, 223
  castles, 220-1, 223
  park, 219, 220, 221-25
Sherwood Forest, 26
Shields, North and South, 132
Snorscomb, 115
Somerset, Henry, 1st Duke of Beaufort, 228
Speed, John, 155
Spencer, Albert Edward John, 7th Earl
  Spencer, 106
Spencer, Sir John, 108-10, 210
Spencer, Robert, 1st Baron Spencer, 107
Spencer, Thomas, 110
Spencer, Sir William, 110, 111
Stafford, Henry, 2nd Duke of Buckingham,
  207
Stanley family, 229-30
Stanwick St. John (Yorks.), 188
Star Chamber, 205, 243
Statutes
  re enclosure, 91, 231, 234-5
  against depopulation, 101, 108
  re markets and fairs, 165, 172
  re forests, 191, 192
  re emparking, 194
  re horses, 209
Staverton (Northants.), 38, 40
Stonar, 127

Stoneton, 107, 115
Stow, John, 178
Stowe (Bucks.), 71, 198
Strensall Common, 222
Strips, 73-4, 82-4, 177-8
  origin, 78
  consolidation, 91, 95
Studley (Warws.), 207
Survey, courts of, 48, 50
Surveyors, *see* Agas, Bainbridge, Blagrave, Clerke, Folkingham, Greenwood, Jeffreys, Langdon, Norden, Rathborne, Saxton, Senior, Speed, Twyniho, Worthe, Wyatt
Sutton Coldfield, 231-6
  Sutton Chase, 231-2
  Sutton Park, 231-5
  villein services, 232
  incorporation, 232, 235
  industries, 232
  Enclosure Bills, 234-5

TANGHAM (Suffolk), 47
Tate, W. E., 243
Taxation, 97, 99, 108, 122, 134, 137, 139, 244
  1334...99, 108, 121, 139
  poll tax, 1377...111, 145, 179
Templars, Knights Templar, 138
Terriers, 47, 66, 73, 79, 157, 177
Thanet, Isle of, 26
Thornbury (Glos.), 207
Thoroton, Robert, 66
Thorpe (Notts.), church, 100
Thorpe-in-the-Glebe, church, 67
Tilgarsley (Oxon.), 99, 108
Tithes, 27, 36-7, 242
Toddington (Beds.), 89, 153, 154, 155, 179-83, 208
  Agas's plan, 153, 154, 155, 179, 180, 182, 183, 208
  site, 180
  area, 181
  manor houses, 182
  market and market-place, 182-3
  Park, 190, 208
Tolls, 141, 169, 171, 233
Tusmore, 95, 96, 97-8, 108
  plague, 96, 98
  Domesday Book, 97
  population, 97, 98
  Park, 97, 193
Twyniho, Edmund, Higham Ferrers terrier, 177-8, 180

VESEY, John, *Bp. of Exeter*, 232, 236
Victoria County Histories, 240, 241, 248

Villein services, 129, 169, 232
Villers, *Sir* (Sir Villiers Chernock), 90-1

WALSINGHAM, *Sir* Francis, 155-6
Warenmouth (Northum.), 130
Warrington (Lancs.), 149
Warwickshire, 34, 37, 38, 39, 232
Watergall, 107, 115
Watling Street, 37, 39
Weald, The, 34
Wearmouth (Co. Durham), 130
Weeford Park, 231
Welton (Northants.), 38, 42
Weobley, 192
Whatborough, 50, 86, 95, 105, 115-23
  site, 122
    Clerke's plan, 117-19, 123
    ridge and furrow, 118, 119
    Carter v. Cromwell, 117, 120-1
    enclosure, 121
    taxation, 121, 122
    population, 121, 122
Wheeler, *Sir* Mortimer, 188
Whichford, 193
Whitehill (Oxon.), 86
Whittlewood Forest, 71
Wight, Isle of, 101
Willoughby (Warws.), 37, 38, 42
Wilstrop, 205-7
Wilstrop family, 205
Winchelsea, 143
Windmills, 82
Windsor Park, 195, 198
Withcote, 115, 122
Witton, East, 197
Woburn Park, 203
Wolfhampcote, 37, 41n
Wolsey, Thomas, *Cardinal*, 101, 105, 108
Woodchester, 26
Woodhouse Moor, Leeds, 189
Woodstock Park (Oxon), 192, 198
Wool, 102, 111, 134
Wool-growers, 111
Wootton Underwood (Bucks.), 226-8
Works, Ministry of, 176, 198
Wormleighton, 105-10
  site, 105
  plans, 106, 107, 108
  Spencer family, 107, 108-9
  population, 108
  taxation, 108
  conversion to grass, 108
  Enclosure Commission, 108
  manor houses, 109
  church, 110
Worthe, John, Higham Ferrers terrier, 157, 164, 177, 178, 180

Wotton, *Sir* Edward, 54, 55, 58
Wyatt, James, 199
Wyke (afterwards Kingston-upon-Hull), 133-4
  site, 133
  Holy Trinity Chapel, 133

market and fair, 134
  acquisition by Edward I, 134
Wykeham, East and West (Lincs.), 100

YORK, 154, 178
Yorkshire, 43, 120